Computer-Supported Collaborative Learning Series

Series Editor

Christopher Hoadley

Associate Editors

Jan van Aalst
Isa Jahnke

More information about this series at http://www.springer.com/series/5814

Yael Kali • Ayelet Baram-Tsabari
Amit M. Schejter

Editors

Learning In a Networked Society

Spontaneous and Designed Technology
Enhanced Learning Communities

 Springer

Editors
Yael Kali
Department of Learning, Instruction,
and Teacher Education
University of Haifa
Mount Carmel, Haifa, Israel

Ayelet Baram-Tsabari
Faculty of Education in Science
and Technology
Technion – Israel Institute of Technology
Haifa, Haifa, Israel

Amit M. Schejter
Department of Communication Studies
Ben-Gurion University of the Negev
Beer Sheva, Israel

Donald P. Bellisario College
of Communications
The Pennsylvania State University
State College, PA, USA

Computer-Supported Collaborative Learning Series
ISBN 978-3-030-14609-2   ISBN 978-3-030-14610-8   (eBook)
https://doi.org/10.1007/978-3-030-14610-8

This Springer imprint is published by the registered company Springer Nature Switzerland AG
The registered company address is: Gewerbestrasse 11, 6330 Cham, Switzerland

Preface

As I write this at the end of 2018, strong winds of change are blowing. Technological change and, in particular, the advent of global information networks like the World Wide Web have begun less and less to appear to be utopian tools and more to be dystopian ones. Many of the battles to be fought for the future of human society are starting to appear less in the realm of individual technologies or individual social choices (whether cultural, legal, or organizational) and more to be related to the global complex system of people, information, and technology.

As scholars and the public attempt to understand the major shifts happening in our increasingly global, increasingly networked society, we have many tools at hand from social science to philosophy to systems science. Many scholars and pundits write from these perspectives on how information networks are changing democracy, civil society, journalism, social interactions, and even education.

Education has historically held a critical role in past transformations of society. In many ways, the formal structures society uses to inculcate the young serve as a bellwether: they reflect the hopes and fears of today's society; they presage the society to come. Moreover, major shifts in society have in turn produced major shifts in the assumptions, modalities, and structures of how we educate people. The Renaissance helped produce the university, and the university helped sustain the Renaissance. The Enlightenment helped produce many institutions that blended knowledge building with knowledge dissemination, from research universities to forms of public discourse. But beyond this relationship between broad change and educational institutions, we now have a new perspective: educational research.

It is only in the last hundred years or so that we have developed a scientific literature on education and on its overlooked, but more powerful, older sibling: learning. On the one hand, this field grew from the very limited and practical problem of architecting schools and formal educational settings. On the other hand, learning—one of the central phenomena of the field of education research—is not limited to such settings. In its broadest definition, learning is the process by which individual humans change their thinking and actions, whether to be more well-adapted to stable circumstances or to adapt to changes in their environment. Many in the academy believe that if they are not working with children in schools, they need not concern themselves with what the field of education research has found. This is a deeply unfortunate, and incorrect, assumption. The study of education and, more essentially, the study of learning have profound insights to offer those who want to understand how we replicate the society of the past and how we transform into the society of the future.

The team that has put this book together has profited mightily from understanding this opportunity to connect research on technology, people, and information to research on learning. Learning scientists, people who study not only how learning happens but how to orchestrate it in all settings, have partnered with scholars from information sciences, sociology, law, and communications to ask the big question: how is learning changing in our increasingly networked society? The partnership also includes technologists—computer scientists, designers, and experts in human-computer interaction—who are best poised to understand the technical underpinnings and the possibilities associated with technological change. Together, they inquired over a multi-year and inter- and transdisciplinary research project on learning in a networked society. This book represents not only a culmination of efforts from an intellectually diverse team in one research center but also a dialogue of the ideas from that center with scholars from around the world who help connect the work to the broader themes, such as how we handle fake news, how an increasingly global information landscape is accommodated by religious groups who may mistrust dominant global perspectives, how the law shapes the way we learn from the information we have access to, and so on.

The field of CSCL and the book series in which this volume appears could easily be misunderstood to be limited to some simpler, narrower topic about kids doing classroom exercises online together. Instead, the field and this book series hew more to this more profound combination of trying to study the science and the design of information, people, technology, and, most of all, learning. The level of comfort CSCL has, with not only describing and explaining the technological winds of change and their impacts but also proactively designing the experiences people go through in response to these changes, is an asset that can be used to help address many of the intimidating challenges posed by today's technology-rich global environment. If learning is adaptation and growth, what better stance to take in the face of a rapidly evolving sociotechnical environment? Other fields do take an interventionist, agential stance with technology. Advertising and marketing attempt to manipulate consumer behavior. Videogame design attempts to produce fun and engagement. Management information systems attempts to produce corporate efficiency. But education attempts to produce individual growth, development, and fulfillment. As such, it represents a powerful perspective for influencing, understanding, and, ultimately, inventing the technology-rich future we will inhabit. If these issues and perspectives appeal to you, I recommend this volume and indeed the other volumes in the CSCL book series.

New York University   Christopher Hoadley

Acknowledgments

LINKS (Learning In a Networked Society) was born in the spring of 2013. A team of researchers from four academic institutions specializing in more than half a dozen scholarly disciplines and supported by a substantial grant as part of Israel's national effort to create centers of research excellence set foot to explore the vast terrain of learning in the information society.

Six years, hundreds of papers, scores of meetings, and half a dozen annual gatherings later, we are proud to present LINKS' own synergetic offspring—an edited book comprised of chapters that demonstrate what a joint interdisciplinary effort can bring about. Extending the biological metaphor allows us to acknowledge how the genealogy of academic work is expressed in this cooperative effort. Indeed, it involves parents (academic supervisors), children (graduate students), and grandchildren (their respective students), and it brings together academic marital relationships, creates new families, discovers relatives near and far (disciplinary contacts), and eventually brings about a village to grow an edited book.

In the case of this book, it took the cooperation of researchers in education, communication, sociology, information and knowledge sciences, law, health and welfare, and human-computer interaction (HCI) from the University of Haifa, Ben-Gurion University of the Negev, the Technion – Israel Institute of Technology, and the Interdisciplinary Center, Herzliya, to create the Learning In a Networked Society (LINKS) community. As editors of this book, we would like to express our deepest gratitude to all who have made contributions to this work.

First, indeed, are our fellow researchers and the institutions that supported their work: from the University of Haifa, Dror Angel, Keren Aridor, Osnat Atias, Sarit Barzilai, Hava Ben-Horin, Maya Benichou, Dani Ben-Zvi, Niva Elkin-Koren, Yoni Har-Carmel, Dorit Geifman, Oren Golan, Yotam Hod, Carmel Kent, Adi Kidron, Hana Manor, Nakhi Mishol-Shauli, Shai Olsher, Carmit Pion, Daphne Raban, Sheizaf Rafaeli, Amit Rechavi, Ornit Sagy, Tamar Weiss, and Michal Yerushalmy; from the Ben-Gurion University of the Negev, Nelly Elias, Malka Shacham, Iris Tabak, and Noam Tirosh; from the Technion – Israel Institute of Technology, Yaela Golumbic; and from the Interdisciplinary Center at Herzliya, Oren Zuckerman.

We were very fortunate to enjoy the support and contributions of collaborators from all over the world, who agreed to contribute overarching insights to our collaborative work and enrich this book: Clark Chinn from Rutgers University, Ulrike Cress from Knowledge Media Research Center and the University of Tuebingen, Christopher Hoadley from New York University, and Lynn Schofield-Clark from the University of Denver. Within this international group, we are especially thankful to Christopher Hoadley—the editor of the Computer-Supported Collaborative Learning (CSCL) book series—who helped conceptualize this book and provided invaluable comments on early versions of the chapters. His interdisciplinary and historical perspective on learning in a networked society, and CSCL as a field, as expressed in the first chapter of this book served as a cornerstone in framing our arguments. We also greatly appreciate the preface he wrote.

The LINKS community was home to dozens of graduate students and postdoctoral fellows, without which it simply would not have been able to exist. We thus owe gratitude to each and every one of them for the enlightening discussions, thoughtful comments, and hard work they contributed to the joint effort.

This project and this book would of course not have been possible were it not for the generous support of the Israeli Centers of Research Excellence (I-CORE) Program of the Planning and Budgeting Committee and the Israel Science Foundation (project number 1716/12) and the invaluable assistance and devotion of Ella Fire and Liat Maoz.

Our work in the past 6 years has been nurtured with professional support from multiple figures in our institutions' research authorities. We are especially thankful to the University of Haifa's research authority and particularly to the devoted work of Sharon Link, Director; Arie Marko, Co-Director; and Nir Adelsberg, Management, who were not only committed to provide help on an everyday basis but also resourceful in finding creative solutions to administrative challenges that our multi-institutional interdisciplinary endeavor required.

We extend special thanks to the tremendous help and devotion of our project manager, Debbie Huck, the midwife of this book and the heart and soul of the LINKS community. LINKS could not have happened without her thoughtful coordination, and this book would not have come about without her organizational skills, attention to detail, total commitment, and true dedication to LINKS and its intellectual heritage.

LINKS is a dream come true. Our sincere gratitude goes to all of the fellow dreamers and travelers on this journey who made it happen.

Yael Kali (University of Haifa)

Ayelet Baram-Tsabari (Technion – Israel Institute of Technology)

Amit Schejter (Ben-Gurion University of the Negev)

Contents

Part III   From Designed to Spontaneous TEL Communities

Part IV   Commentary and Future Directions

Chapter 1
Five Waves of Conceptualizing Knowledge and Learning for Our Future in a Networked Society

Christopher Hoadley and Yael Kali

Abstract This chapter describes five waves of learning mediated by information-communication technologies. Each wave is identified with particular pedagogies and technologies, and – critically – particular social conceptions of education that those pedagogies and technologies helped bring into being: Wave 1 – information dissemination and consumption; Wave 2 – constructivism and mind tools; Wave 3 – collaborative and social learning; Wave 4 – distributed Intelligence; and Wave 5 – eudaemonic learning. We argue that Wave 5-inspired research requires an epistemological shift, taking into account the mix of intentional and unintentional, engineered vs. accidental, and emergent vs. designed aspects of learning. We demonstrate how the research presented in this book moves toward a vision of research and design of eudaemonic learning. That is – the learning in a networked society research looks at learning as a component of how individuals and society mutually develop each other, while studying how technology helps create the conditions for such learning.

Keywords Knowledge · Knowing · Learning · Eudaemonic learning · Mutualism · Social transformation · Networked society · Information-communication technologies (ICTs)

Since ancient times, notions of knowledge, knowing, and learning and their relation to society have inspired human thought. Throughout history, attempts to answer various questions had led to the development of various conceptions of learning and ideologies for education: What is the nature of knowledge? How do we come to

C. Hoadley
NYU, Department of Administration, Leadership and Technology, New York, NY, USA
e-mail: tophe@nyu.edu

Y. Kali (✉)
Department of Learning, Instruction, and Teacher Education, University of Haifa,
Haifa, Israel
e-mail: yael.kali@edtech.haifa.ac.il

© Springer Nature Switzerland AG 2019
Y. Kali et al. (eds.), *Learning In a Networked Society*, Computer-Supported
Collaborative Learning Series 17, https://doi.org/10.1007/978-3-030-14610-8_1

know? What is the role of education in serving society? What is its role for serving individuals? And what is the role of culture in learning and education? The unprecedented advancements in information and communication technologies (ICTs) in the past decades, and their tremendous effects on every aspect of our lives, have stimulated contemporary conceptualizations on learning and education that seek to meet new challenges and opportunities evoked by these changes in modern society.

Research on learning and on information technology have both contributed much to the development of such conceptualizations. Both these research areas use, as a touchstone, an important, kaleidoscopic concept: that of *knowledge*. While commonsense definitions such as those that view knowledge as information that is ingested, comprehended, and recalled are still quite useful, the notion of a networked society helps us expand this concept in useful ways. Throughout this book, we see that by exploring learning in a networked knowledge society we can expand the definition of knowledge following advances in various disciplines, including learning sciences, information sciences, sociology, communication, psychology, and others. One historical distinction between "learning" theorists (educational researchers, psychologists, etc.) and "technology" theorists (computer scientists, information scientists, etc.) was that the first focused on knowledge as a property of people, something in their heads, while the others focused on knowledge in the use of representations and symbol systems, whether human or artificial. But as John Seely Brown and Paul Duguid highlight in their book *The Social Life of Information* (Brown & Duguid, 2017), knowledge is hard to pin down to either brains or symbols. Knowledge is as knowledge does, and information retrieval alone does not explain the myriad ways in which knowing does or doesn't influence actions in the world, whether by people, organizations, or even computers. Knowledge has become increasingly understood to be a property of distributed systems in which knowledge may be applied, rather than a property of a person, a database, or an organization.

As life has become more networked and more technologically embedded, the role of knowledge has shifted. Increasingly, we see sociotechnical systems that exhibit knowledge that may rest in no one place (Hutchins, 1995). Conceptions of knowledge have expanded to concern themselves with *who* is knowing, what their roles are, and what power structures allow or inhibit access to knowledge creation, dissemination, and application. We see learning as linked with identity formation and identity linked with the practices that demonstrate knowing, such that we may think of learning a body of knowledge as a shift in role and in identity, to become a person who participates in the practices of that knowledge. Epistemically, there has been an explosion in the ways that people construct knowledge for themselves and share it with others, taking us far beyond the scientific revolution of the enlightenment and into a world of postmodernism, "fake news," and contested truths (see Barzilai & Chinn, Chap. 4). And throughout, we see tensions between deliberate and accidental ways of knowing. These shifts have powerful implications for what it means to learn or to foster learning.

In the sections ahead, we describe five waves of learning mediated by information technologies and link these to the interdisciplinary and transdisciplinary approach that we believe represents the future of research on learning in a networked knowledge society. First, we examine the five waves in turn. Next, we look at how the theoretical and interdisciplinary nature of the Learning In a NetworKed Society (LINKS) endeavor relates to Wave 5 learning and provide examples of research that aims toward a different conceptualization of knowledge. Finally, we make some suggestions about the implications this perspective has on the future of research on knowledge and learning.

Five Waves of Technology-Mediated Changes in Learning

The shifting nature of knowledge and its role in society help surface and reframe one of the key issues that arises in considering learning in a networked society: the tensions between studying learning as it emerges naturally and the implications for designing learning environments specifically to support learning, or as we have elsewhere described it, the continuum from spontaneous to designed learning environments (see Chap. 2). Certainly, the systemic view of knowledge, and therefore learning, brings us to a deeper set of questions than the knowledge generated when students encounter information presented by a teacher. How knowledge in the form of identities, practices, norms, laws, and connectivities arises in the networked world brings complexity to both spontaneous and designed learning. In this section we explore these issues more directly from a design lens. How can learning designs take account of the complexity of learning in a networked society?

Following Hoadley (2016), we look at five waves of learning and technology that emerged in the past. These waves are less of an attempt to divide history into particular time periods, but more of a developmental trend that appears to align well with the emergence of how we use knowledge in the networked society. These five waves of learning with technology are Wave 1, information dissemination and consumption; Wave 2, constructivism and mind tools; Wave 3, collaborative and social learning; Wave 4, distributed intelligence; and Wave 5, eudaemonic learning. Each of these waves might be identified with particular pedagogies, particular technologies or artifacts that supported those pedagogies, and – critically – particular social conceptions of education that those pedagogies and technologies helped bring into being. Each wave has involved some upheaval of not only educational structures but, more generally, practices and social structures that underpin society's relationship to knowledge and learning. Yet, even in upheaval, each wave builds on, and to some extent incorporates, the prior waves. We summarize the five waves in Table 1.1, and then discuss each one in detail.

Table 1.1 Five waves of knowledge and learning

Wave	Characterization of learning	Conception of knowledge	Sample tools or paradigms
Wave 1: information dissemination and consumption	Learning is ingesting and recalling correct information in efficient ways	Knowledge as accretive, authoritative, strongly identified with vetted information	Teaching machines, authoritative texts or mass media, behavioral conditioning
Wave 2: constructivism and mind tools	Learning is construction of understanding using tools to manipulate information to aid in thinking and comprehension. Agency plays an important role	Knowledge as the inner cognitive configurations that align with valued expert conceptions	Hypertext authoring systems, scaffolded constructivist learning environments, microworlds
Wave 3: collaborative and social learning	Learning is an enculturation, discursive, and shared meaning-making process	Knowledge as common ground or culturally embedded shared discourses, texts, practices, values, and norms	Online discussions, shared editing tools, tools for social negotiation, and for learning as a community
Wave 4: distributed intelligence	Learning is a reconfiguration of systems of people and tools so that individuals, organizations, assemblages, or ensembles can function intelligently	Knowledge as a property of systems of people and tools (especially semiotic representations) and the contexts in which they operate	Organizational learning, knowledge management tools, crowdsourcing (e.g., Wikipedia, Foldit)
Wave 5: eudaemonic learning	Learning is a process of mutual transformation between an individual and society toward individual and collective development	Knowledge as a property of a journey of transformation in which the identity, positionality, and social role of people (individually and collectively) evolves toward greater harmony and social fulfillment	Transformative education, decolonizing pedagogies, e.g., the MECS approach (Sagy et al., Chap. 6), and some eTextbook endeavors (Har-Carmel et al., Chap. 10) described below

Wave 1: Information Dissemination and Consumption

The first wave, information dissemination and consumption, can be thought of as covering the shifts in knowledge and learning that took place from the invention of the printing press until the early twentieth century. Prior to the printing press, access to information itself was sharply limited, bards might travel with lengthy sagas, and priests and scholars might hand-produce scrolls and books, but, generally, learning involved becoming enmeshed in knowledge available very locally and circumscribed by position in social hierarchy. The invention of the printing press eventually led to an explosion not only in books but in literacy and in the ability of people to share information across time and space, both within rigid hierarchies and against them. The invention of the Taylorist production model of schooling took advantage of these information artifacts, and to a first approximation, the provision of information was synonymous with teaching. The long tail of this trend can be seen carrying into the twenty-first century. Instructional media – books, but also radio and television – would become the subject of the field of instructional design. Developing "correct" information, presented in "optimal sequencing," connected to well-described goals (whether recalling information or performing certain skills and behaviors) was central to the emerging field of instructional design. The famous behaviorist B.F. Skinner proposed "teaching machines" (Skinner, 1968), in which technology would provide information, quiz the learner, and provide immediate feedback in terms of positive or negative reinforcement. In Skinner's proposal, we see many hidden assumptions about the nature of knowledge: that it is standardized, that it is to be transmitted from experts to novices, that it manifests through behaviors (such as correct multiple-choice answers or correctly performing tasks), and that the act of teaching is really about providing stimuli (information) and feedback.

Wave 2: Constructivism and Mind Tools

The second wave, constructivism and mind tools, might be associated with early to late twentieth-century teaching. Piaget's conception of constructivism, that the act of learning requires the work of constructing knowledge on the part of the learner, shifts the focus from providing information to engaging thought. In this model the role of a teacher is not to transmit information to the learner and ensure correct transmission through feedback but, instead, to foster activities by the learner that lead to engagement with information, permitting the learner to either assimilate it into their existing knowledge (akin to simple transmission) or to accommodate it by restructuring their current understandings.

By the time personal computing became available in the 1980s, powerful tools were becoming available to support the work of learners as they constructed their understandings. For instance, Papert advocated using programming languages as "things to think with" in his constructionist educational philosophy (Papert, 1980); Jonassen (Jonassen, 1996; Jonassen & Marra, 1994) called technologies that assisted learners in manipulating and constructing information (like dynamic hypertext systems) and their own knowledge "mindtools." Specialized software was created to allow learners to explore, inquire, and construct understanding, like simulations and microworlds for science, learner-friendly word processing and editing tools, and so on. In this wave, we see an increasing move toward learner agency and autonomy. Much of the learning research from this era focuses on ways teachers and carefully designed curricula and learning environments support the cognition of individual learners. The presumptions about knowledge remain relatively friendly to a notion of expertise and providing "correct" information but problematize the ways in which that information is taken up by the learner. A somewhat radical development at this time is that while people might have constructed equally valid understandings of a particular topic, they might have done so by different routes and that their conceptualizations are not directly transmissible through information dissemination, although they might be indirectly transmissible through information and structured learning environments (diSessa, 2014).

Wave 3: Collaborative and Social Learning

The third wave, collaborative and social learning, would be associated with the late twentieth century and particularly with the advent of the Internet. In the 1970s, researchers like Johnson and Johnson began describing the possibilities of collaborative learning, and in the 1970s and 1980s, theorists like Cole and Scribner helped describe the social construction of learning. Early applications like mainframe-based online learning (Dear, 2017; Hiltz & Turoff, 1978) and, then later, web-based collaborative environments helped make messaging and collaboration the "killer apps" for computer networking (e.g., email, texting, or social networking). The technologies for collaboration have had important impacts on the design of learning environments. First of all, collaboration technologies allowed people to transcend the school walls and collaborate across space and time and additionally across learning contexts. Secondly, collaborative technologies allow designers to mold the communication by shaping the medium used to communicate, leading to the rise of computer-supported collaborative learning. The tools could be used to scaffold particular forms of collaboration, to permit people to present themselves with identities similar or dissimilar to those they exhibit in face-to-face venues, and to form communities of interest or communities of practice (Gee & Hayes, 2012; Lave & Wenger, 1991) that wouldn't otherwise be possible without technologies. Quickly, the infrastructures of connectivity have multiplied, stretching from the first introduction of public-facing Internet Service Providers for dialup connectivity in the mid-1990s to the present day, in which half the human race has Internet access (often via wireless smartphones). The net effect of these developments is that society as a whole has become more able to allow communication, and this has permeated learning contexts. Though not all pedagogies worldwide have evolved to incorporate collaboration and computer-mediated communication, the trend seems to be inexorable toward including collaborative learning in education and to use technologies to support that collaboration.

Wave 4: Distributed Intelligence

In Wave 4, we see the convergence of waves one through three in learning and intelligence that are distributed across sociotechnical systems. This wave presumes access to technology allows for emergence of complex forms of knowing and learning that would not have been possible before. Within educational contexts, knowledge-building communities became one paradigm for supporting intentional, learner-driven pedagogy through collaboration; in a knowledge-building community, there is explicit acknowledgment of a dual goal of helping individuals learn and of helping the community as a whole create networked representations of knowledge. In knowledge-building communities, individuals may not know as much as the whole group "knows," and learners rely on others and on shared databases to advance inquiry, much like the division of labor in scholarly research communities.

Theories like distributed cognition (Hutchins, 1995) and distributed intelligence (Pea, 1993) help explain how learning in this model is a systemic property of people-plus-tools, as much as it is of individuals who use tools. Within education, technologies for crowdsourcing help illustrate what Wave 4 learning looks like. For example, Wikipedia is the world's largest encyclopedia, which is constantly updated and continuously authored by people worldwide. Because of the lack of traditional editorial vetting, Wikipedia does not maintain "accuracy" in traditional ways, yet in many cases, it represents a responsive, distributed way to synthesize information and make it usable by large numbers of people. Learning takes place when individual contributors amass primary citations and synthesize them into encyclopedia article form, when users read the articles to give themselves an introductory understanding of a topic, and when users read or participate in the "talk pages" of an article, thereby examining the processes and potentially conflicts in creation and maintenance of these knowledge representations.

Furthermore, one can argue that knowledge in society generally advances through the creation of this artifact, which can be downloaded and remixed for many purposes and which is updated far more contemporaneously than traditional encyclopedias. A second example would be the Foldit project in which people across the Internet play a game to help predict how protein molecules fold in three-dimensional space (the way these molecules fold is an important but not fully solved scientific problem). By gamifying problems in biochemistry, an amazing thing happened; thousands of people with no prior interest in biochemistry became experts at protein folding; humans without biochemistry training began to exceed the accuracy of both the best algorithms science could produce and the best experts could do at predicting folds; and through game-related communities, collective participants began to advance science. It's important to note that the knowledge being learned might not be extractable by interviewing individual participants; rather the collective group of players and their social and technical infrastructure, plus the Foldit team, "know" how proteins fold in a way that individuals don't. This has led to the remarkable outcome of a peer-reviewed journal article on protein folding being published in the journal *Nature* with more than 50,000 co-authors. Learning for distributed intelligence includes learning ways to be smart in tandem with other people and represents a shift from traditional individualistic learning goals.

Wave 5: Eudaemonic Learning

Where learning for distributed intelligence differentiates learning-as-individual from learning-as-individual-part-of-systems, the learning goals are still fairly recognizable as things we might traditionally find in textbooks: how a protein folds, the basic information about an encyclopedia topic, etc.; eudaemonic learning looks at learning as a component of how individuals and society mutually develop each other. In the *Nichomachean Ethics*, Aristotle (350 B.C.E./ 2000) describes *eudaemonia*, variously translated as "happiness" or "flourishing," as a state in which individuals grow in their capacities and actions but do so in dialogue with the society they live in. The *Nichomachean Ethics* therefore rejects happiness as solely fulfilling "duty" (in which society's needs are met irrespective of whether individuals' needs are met). It also rejects happiness as some sort of individual bliss that is amorally disconnected from society. Instead, the *Ethics* characterizes happiness as eudaemonia – the flourishing that happens when individuals reach their potential through finding their place in society and improving it.

If we look at how technology changes the relationship between individuals, learning, and society, we see that technologies are creating the space for a fifth wave of technology mediated learning. Technology is loosening the ties between fixed learning goals and formal, institutionalized educational pathways. For example, the concept that universities must train students for jobs which haven't been invented yet reframes what it means to prepare students for careers. Technologies also allow people to fluidly pursue goals related to their role in society without institutional support or formal training (young YouTube stars come to mind).

Like the fourth wave, this wave sees the learner as part of a larger societal system. Unlike the fourth wave, the emphasis is less on supporting individuals as they become parts of larger sociotechnical systems that know (or more cynically, as they become cogs in larger sociotechnical systems that act intelligently for goals set by others) and more on a mutually reinforcing sense of personal and societal progress and development. In eudaemonic learning, we open the possibility of learning that helps a person create new ways of knowing in society that allow her or him to fulfill roles that haven't yet been created, of a mutualism between knowledge-in-action at the social and at the individual level.

For example, take the life's arc of Aaron Swartz (Knappenberger, Knappenberger, Braff, Fink, & Annenberg Weingarten, 2014; Swartz, 2015), who as an adolescent invented the RSS technology for newsfeeds, creating a novel way for people to publish and read websites; later in life he helped create the website Reddit, which was not only a new technology for collaboration but which represented a relatively novel form of community in which people on the Internet could share information at a scale difficult to achieve in other more traditional communication structures. The influence between individual and society was bidirectional. For instance, Swartz learned about and became frustrated with old forms of copyright law and created changes by working as an activist for copyright reform and helping to build code for the Creative Commons project. What helps mark this example as eudae-monic learning is that the learning of the individual and the learning of society are yoked and that technology helps create the conditions for novel relations between individual-as-learner and the organizational learning taking place in larger commu-nities. Sometimes people learn so they can fit into a relatively unchanging commu-nity – this is the model of learning that inspires our form of institutionalized education as something for the young or for newcomers to particular communities. But, as many educational philosophers have pointed out through history, society grows and changes too, and the type of learning made by society can be much more directly driven by individual learners through technologies that empower construc-tion of novel forms of knowledge-sharing and knowledge-building. In both cases the learning is a type of "becoming" that is based on the link between individual and society. Eudaemonic learning suggests that studying education and studying social change overlook an important link between the two that appears when both are considered as processes of transformation based on mutually constituted processes of what it means to "know."

Moving Toward Eudaemonic Learning Research

We argue that the research presented in this book moves toward a vision of research and design of eudaemonic learning. By studying and supporting learning in a net-worked knowledge society, the scholarship presented here has tapped into recipro-cal relationships that develop between individual learners, groups, communities, and society, as their transformations interact with each other. For example, below we discuss how Sagy et al. (Chap. 6) propose the concept of Mutualistic Ecology of Citizen Science (MECS) to set an agenda for citizen science not only as a way in which the scientific agenda of a few is supported by the learning and contributions of many "helpers" but as mutualistic ecologies in which the aspirations and knowl-edge agendas of the individuals and the group influence each other bidirectionally. Another example we examine in detail below is Har-Carmel et al.'s analysis of the role that eTextbooks play (Chap. 10) in revolutionizing educational ecosystems and – at the same time – the roles that individuals play within these ecosystems, as students and teachers become co-authors of their own textbooks. Through these examples we hope to show how research and design with a eudaemonic learning framing is not like research and design on learning as an individualistic, cognitive phenomenon, but rather can be seen as embedded in a much richer definition of learning and knowledge.

Transdisciplinary Research on What, Who, and How People Learn in a Networked Society

The application of the Wave 5 eudaemonic learning lens for exploring and supporting learning in a networked society, as conveyed in the chapters of this book, is a direct consequence of the process in which they were conceived. Raban and Geiffman, who retrospectively studied this process (Chap. 3), describe three main research themes that were identified at early stages by the multidisciplinary team of researchers who have developed this book as part of the LINKS center. The three themes which emerged in a dialogical process between the LINKS researchers have to do with questions regarding *what* is being learned, including the knowledge perspective, both human and machine (the knowledge and understanding theme); *who* learns, including issues of diversity, as well as interactions between individual and group learning (the diversity theme); and *how* people learn, including participation in practices and norms within knowledge communities (the practices and norms theme).

Inspired by the multivocality within the learning sciences (e.g., Suthers, Lund, Rosé, Teplovs, & Law, 2013), one of the first cornerstones in the dialogical process of LINKS researchers was the realization that the notion of LINKS cannot be understood without a synergistic interdisciplinary perspective. The next step was to negotiate terminology and develop shared language between the researchers, who represent various fields: education and the learning sciences, instructional design, communication, information sciences, knowledge management, law, social welfare, and human-computer interface. Words such as "learning" or "community" (among many others) required considerable unpacking before they were accepted as common denominators for conceptualizing the notion of LINKS. In fact, although most researchers used the term "community" in various ways, some of the researchers did not consider their work as related to "learning" prior to the establishment of the LINKS center. The negotiation of terminology enabled the development of a multifaceted perspective of such terms. It also enabled the identification of the three research themes described above (knowledge and understanding, diversity, and practices and norms in learning, or more compactly, the what, who, and how of learning) and the realization that innovation resides within the intersections of the themes.

Another pivotal notion, which was recognized at early stages of the LINKS work, was that the three themes were typically studied either with naturalistic lenses, exploring spontaneous learning within society, or with interventionist lenses, exploring how designed environments shape learning. As the LINKS center progressed, additional research questions were identified and enriched the lessons learned especially where all three themes meet, acknowledging a continuum between spontaneous to designed learning (see Tabak, Ben-Zvi, & Kali, Chap. 2). As we illustrate in the next sections, the LINKS book chapters, which have been written during the culminating stage of the LINKS work as a center, represent (a) the inter and transdisciplinarity nature of the research, (b) the intersection of the three themes, and (c) the whole spectrum of the spontaneous-designed continuum.

This book also helps illustrate, through synthesis and commentary of international researchers outside the LINKS center, how these three traits inform the larger issues encountered in the CSCL field, as well as the notions of learning and knowledge, more broadly.

Ingredients of Wave 5 Eudaemonic Learning Research

This section lays out some of the research questions that have guided individual LINKS researchers prior to or at beginning stages of the LINKS collaboratory, which served as ingredients for the Wave 5 studies described in this book. We cluster these questions by fields of study to illustrate how the work in each of the fields tended to focus on specific aspects of the above traits and how the synergistic work enabled the development of the eudaemonic learning research, which more fully address all three of them (transdisciplinarity; intersection between the *what, who,* and *how* people learn themes; and the spontaneous-designed continuum). Figure 1.1 visually illustrates this point, which we elaborate below.

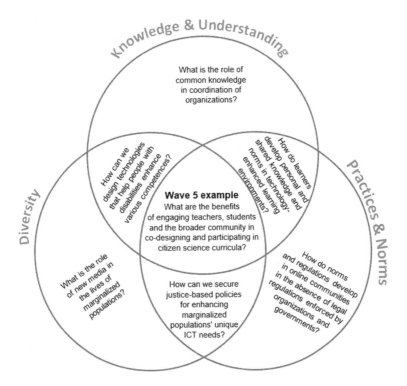

Fig. 1.1 Example pre-LINKS research questions within each of the individual themes and at the intersections between each two themes. The research question at the intersection of the three themes represents Wave 5 studies that have emerged from the synergistic collaboration in LINKS

For instance, LINKS researchers from the education and learning sciences field, asked questions such as: How do learners develop personal and shared knowledge and norms in technology-enhanced learning environments? (Hod & Ben-Zvi, 2015); What is the role of context in such environments? (Tabak, 2004); How can mobile technologies be designed to support inquiry processes in education? (Yerushalmy & Botzer, 2011); How can we support teachers in designing coherent technology-enhanced learning environments? (Kali, Linn, & Roseman, 2008; Kali, Mckenney, & Sagy, 2015); How do we foster learners' epistemic thinking in ways that can advance meaningful online knowledge construction? (Barzilai & Zohar, 2012). That is, typically, education and learning scientists were concerned with questions dealing with two of the themes: knowledge and understanding and practices and norms, or the intersection between the two. They usually explored these themes within the designed arena of the spontaneous-designed continuum.

When we look at the questions that guided the work of the knowledge and information science researchers, we find examples such as: What is the role of common knowledge in coordination of organizations (Nov & Rafaeli, 2009)? What are the relations between knowledge-seeking and social relationship networks (Rechavi & Rafaeli, 2012)? What are incentives for original knowledge creation in the social networked environment (Raban & Rafaeli, 2007)? Similar to the learning scientists, the information researchers were interested in issues at the intersection between the knowledge and understanding theme and the practices and norms theme. However, if we use the distinction described above regarding the conceptualization of knowledge, it can be seen that while the learning researchers typically used the "knowledge as a property of people" conceptualization, the information researchers focused on the "knowledge in the use of representations and symbol systems." Another difference between the information and the learning researchers was the tendency of the former to focus on exploring spontaneous phenomena in the networked society, and the latter to focus on technology-enhanced environments designed specifically for educational purposes.

The sociologists and communication researchers, at the beginning stages of LINKS, studied questions such as: What is the role of new media in the lives of marginalized or bounded populations? (Campbell & Golan, 2011; Elias & Lemish, 2009); How can we secure a justice-based rather than a utility-based theoretical framework for enhancing their unique ICT needs? (Schejter & Tirosh, 2016). They also studied questions regarding other types of populations or the public in general, for instance, with regard to science communication: How can web-based tools be used to identify public interest in science (Baram-Tsabari & Segev, 2011)? How can public communication of science be enhanced and potentially serve as a bridge between school and everyday science (Baram-Tsabari & Osborne, 2015)? As indicated from the questions that have guided their research before joining LINKS, these researchers usually dealt with issues related to the diversity theme, the practices and norms theme, or the intersection between the two. The study of these issues mainly dealt with the spontaneous arena of the spontaneous-designed continuum, while conclusions were aimed at informing policy.

The Law scholars in LINKS too studied the intersection between the diversity and the practices and norms themes (with a stronger focus on the latter) and the emphasis on implications of spontaneous phenomena in the networked society. They explored research questions such as: Does law matter in an information environment? What can we learn from the experience of applying a particular legal regime to the online environment (Birnhack & Elkin-Koren, 2010)? What are the new challenges regulators face to secure user rights and shape online behavior? How do norms and regulations that enable online collaboration develop in the absence of legal regulations enforced by organizations and governments?

Finally, another research perspective of the LINKS collaboratory came from social welfare and Human Computer Interaction (HCI) researchers. These researchers referred to questions such as: How do we design technologies that help people with disabilities to enhance various competences (Gal et al., 2009)? How can tangible user interfaces be designed to promote behavior change among disadvantaged and disabled populations (e.g., youth diagnosed with ADHD) (Zuckerman, Gal-Oz, Tamir, & Kopelman-Rubin, 2015)? These questions indicate a clear interest in the diversity theme, which interacts with either the knowledge and understanding or the practices and norms themes, and a strong focus on the designed area.

The above examples illustrate that taken as a whole, LINKS researchers had covered the three themes and various intersections between them, as well as addressed issues spanning the whole spontaneous-designed spectrum, but that each of the individual research trajectories had dealt with a partial aspect of this whole picture. In contrast, research projects such as the MECS and the eTextbooks endeavors, which had developed from the synergistic work in the LINKS center and stemmed from these ingredients, represent a more integrated Wave 5 approach to explore eudaemonic learning in the networked society, as we elaborate in the next section.

An Integrated Wave 5 Approach to Explore Eudaemonic Learning in the Networked Society

The question found at the intersection of the three themes in Fig. 1.1 – What are the benefits of engaging students, teachers, school leaders, and scientists in co-designing and participating in citizen science curricula? – is one of the questions that currently guides the research in a newly established center that has developed from the LINKS work and, specifically, from the notion of MECS, described by Sagy et al. (Chap. 6). We view the research in the "Taking Citizen Science to School: Breaking Boundaries between School and Society" center, as an example of the Wave 5, eudaemonic learning, since it integrates the traits of (a) interdisciplinarity (integrating ideas from science communication, science education, mathematics education, technology-enhanced learning, and the learning sciences); (b) intersection between the three themes of what, who, and how of learning; and (c) covering a wide spectrum of the spontaneous-designed continuum. The integration of the three traits is illustrated in the following excerpt from Kali et al. (2017):

> Taking Citizen Science to School brings together three pillars which, together, create a robust theoretical and practical foundation for meaningful STEM learning in the 21st century.... The first pillar, Vision II of scientific literacy, articulates the goal of our initiative: To cultivate a scientifically knowledgeable citizenry to take part in democratic decision-making processes of social significance (Aikenhead, 2005; Bybee & DeBoer, 1994; Roberts & Bybee, 2014). The second pillar, Science and Data Literacies, articulates the key competencies necessary for STEM learning (NGSS Lead States, 2013; NRC, 2012; Wild, Utts, & Horton, 2018). Lastly, the Connected Communities of Learners pillar draws on state-of-the-art conceptions of learning that have practical implications on how to design and foster innovative learning environments in the networked society (Cole & Packer, 2016; Hod, Ben-Zvi, & Bielaczyc, 2016; Sawyer, 2014). To bring these theoretical ideas to the field, we have developed an implementation strategy inspired by the notion of change laboratory (Sannino, Engeström, & Lemos, 2016). We seek to build the capacity of existing local school ecologies in the northern geographical and/or social periphery of Israel to engender sustainable change and innovation. Doing this involves identifying and realizing a shared vision between researchers (scientists who use a citizen science approach, science communication and education researchers) and practitioners (teachers, school staff, managers, and leaders) who co-create knowledge, which is at the heart of the research-practice partnerships and teachers as designers' movements (Coburn & Penuel, 2016; Kali et al., 2015). (Kali et al., pp. 3–4)

Another example of a Wave 5 eudaemonic learning research that has developed from the LINKS work is the eTextbook trajectory described in Chap. 10. In their study, combining frameworks from law and education, Har-Carmel et al. explore questions that arise when ICT components are embedded into textbooks. They illustrate how such embedding reduces the authoritative presence of the textbook but also increases the autonomy of both teachers and learners to control teaching and learning processes. They ask, for instance, questions regarding managing the rights of different contributors (e.g., students, teachers, and policy-makers) to eTextbooks, such as: Who has the right to edit and transform a work created by many? How should the output of collaborative production be managed and subsequently governed? Acknowledging that eTextbooks are becoming the key vehicle for facilitating students' access to knowledge, as well as for revolutionizing traditional pedagogical practices, and classroom culture, they argue that the law is lagging behind the rapid rate of the societal change.

This argument illustrates the three traits of Wave 5 eudaemonic learning research: first, learning is explored in transdisciplinary ways (integrating law and education); second, it concerns the three dimensions of learning in a networked society, dealing with ways in which *various sectors of society* negotiate authoritative issues regarding *what* and *how* knowledge is taught and learned in schools; and third, it combines the study of spontaneous processes that have emerged in recent years in the society, as well as the examination of designing policies and practices to meet the emerging needs that such processes bring about. These three traits have spurred a eudaemonic mindset for exploring learning, which examines how new agendas for societal development are recognized as a consequence of emergent practices such as co-authoring of eTextbooks among various stakeholders. But this chapter also shows that the reciprocal changes characterizing Wave 5, before reaching a "eudaemonic equilibrium," are often disruptive. eTextbooks may offer new possibilities for students and teachers to pursue new goals, but, as Har-Carmel et al. illustrate, these new opportunities shake the ground beneath existing practices and policies.

The Future of Research on Learning

In the sections above, we have demonstrated that the technologies which have led to the networked knowledge society have implications for how we foster and study learning. In this section, we attempt to outline what some of those implications are for designers and for researchers.

Knowledge as a Property of Systems, Not People

Taking seriously the idea that knowledge is systemic and distributed has a number of implications for the design and study of learning. One major implication is the need to examine knowledge-in-representation, i.e., the information involved in learning, in conjunction with knowledge-in-practice, i.e., the practices, norms, and social structures in which the learning is embedded. While traditionally learning scholars have acknowledged the context of learning, the cultures of learning, and the practices of expertise as important components in teaching and learning, the systemic view demands a more rigorous construal of "knowing" as a process, rather than an outcome. This is a stark contrast from putting knowledge-in-the-head at the center of research and design, e.g., by relying on pre- and posttest measures in studies or classroom assessments. From a design perspective, this may suggest an extension of the notion of "backward design" (Wiggins & McTighe, 1998). Where backward design attempts to design instruction by working "backward" from the assessments that would indicate individual proficiency in the knowledge goals, a more systemic view would work backward from indicators of societal shift or proficiencies in the knowledge goals. For instance, a knowledge-in-people perspective might debate the relative advantages or disadvantages of providing calculators in school math programs on the individual cognition of learners as they perform mathematical tasks. But a knowledge-in-systems perspective would instead question the degree to which calculators in school are preparatory for the use of calculators in society more generally and would treat as a positive outcome any configuration in which people writ large can do their necessary math.

One powerful example of using a systemic view of knowledge to research learning is the work done in the tradition of cultural historical activity theory (Engeström, 1999, 2002). As a theoretical framework for research, cultural historical activity theory helps unpack and explain the systems of knowledge and practice that take place, e.g., analyzing systems of activity in a hospital healthcare setting and how practices, roles, divisions of labor, and ways of knowing emerge from the activities in the system. From a design standpoint, cultural historical activity theory helps designers consider not only what knowledge we want people in the system to use but the shifts in the interlocking systems of activity, divisions of labor, artifacts, etc. that would be required to bring about such knowledge (or more accurately, bring about knowing and acting in the desired way). Activity theory thus helps identify some of the many parts of the overall system in which knowledge and knowing happens that can be targeted by the designer to try to increase learning and knowledge.

Reciprocity Between Individual and Societal Learning

The nature of eudaemonic learning emphasizes the need to consider the reciprocities between individuals and society that lead to flourishing. This suggests a view of education not as an engine for replicating society as it is to new generations, but as an engine of social transformation. Sadly, most transformational views of education simply wish to bring "what works" in a few settings to more people, without considering the structural inequalities that underlie why education works for some and not others. To be truly transformational of society, we need to not just scale some isolated educational interventions, but to rethink how systems (of which educational institutions are just one part) could be more just and more supportive of human flourishing. For example, a narrow reading of education might emphasize teaching job skills that currently provide economic benefit to an elite, such as the currently trending example of teaching computer science, since computer science jobs are relatively plentiful and well-paid. A eudaemonic view would question: Will having more computer scientists allow more people to flourish? Will a broader or more diverse cadre of computer scientists challenge or transform economic disparities or ethnic and racial injustices that currently lead to only a small subset of learners studying computer science? If we train everyone to do computer science, how will society transform and will that lead to greater human flourishing? (See Chap. 7, Kidron et al., for a discussion of how technology might be supportive of a more democratic view of education.)

Flyvbjerg (2001) has examined this issue through the lens of Aristotle's types of knowledge: episteme, techne, and phronesis (roughly, logico-deductive knowledge like science, craft or practical knowledge like hands-on skills, and value-oriented or moral knowledge like ethics or humanities). Flyvbjerg points out the need to understand that research in all social sciences fails if it ignores the need to unpack and establish values. This is perhaps nowhere more evident than in educational research and design. A learning sciences or psychological or engineering approach to learning will fail if we cannot grapple with questions of what education is for and what values or aims it strives toward.

While scholars who study or invent systems of education for transforming society are nothing new (Freire, 1985, 2011), historically, such researchers have been pigeonholed into roles related to transforming the lives of particular disadvantaged groups (e.g., developing countries, illiterate learners, etc.). Although such work does explicitly make claims about transforming society as a whole, researchers and designers studying knowledge often do not take such a broad or holistic view. People looking to do social transformation (e.g., economic development), technological transformation (e.g., new platforms for knowledge management), or individual learning (even with learners who appear to be well-served by current social or economic systems) would do well to consider the knowing-in-systems approach and to put learning at the center as a process by which both individuals and society are transformed (Jackson, 2008). New design methodologies can consider the value-setting, and social-individual duality of educational designs by embodying more democratic processes of research and design (Bang, Medin, & Atran, 2007; Bevan & Penuel, 2018; Design-Based Research Collective, 2003; DiSalvo, Yip, Bonsignore, & DiSalvo, 2017; Whyte, Greenwood, & Lazes, 1989).

Designed and Spontaneous Learning and the Increasingly Distributed Nature of Learning Design

If we accept the two prior claims that learning is a property of systems and not just of individual people and that there is a bidirectional influence between societal and individual learning, a corollary is that not all learning will be the result of designed learning environments or systems, and most learning will take place in contexts that mix designed and naturally occurring features. For designers, this suggests a shift away from design-as-control to design-as-influence. Within the instructional design community, we see this shift as designers grapple with emergent learning environments like constructivist learning or collaborative learning environments (Hannafin, Hannafin, Land, & Oliver, 1997; Jonassen, 1990; Jonassen & Rohrer-Murphy, 1999; Kirschner, Strijbos, Kreijns, & Jelle Beers, 2004). In this way, a designer might move from a self-conception as a detached engineer creating optimized instructional materials or lesson plans and more as a change agent participating in a messy social system that might include, but is never limited to, formal educational contexts.

Within the larger technology design community, this has been reflected in a shift from the design of technology tools qua tools instead to the design of sociotechnical systems (Baxter & Sommerville, 2011; Carayon, 2006; Clegg, 2000) in which the technological artifacts are considered not in isolation but as embedded in networks of people, organizational structures, resources, etc. In the sphere of research, different groups of researchers are familiar with studying learning-as-designed vs. learning-as-emergent or accidental learning. However, most researchers are hesitant to blend these stances because most research paradigms used (psychology, educational measurement, anthropological or ethnographic research, action research) take a strong stance on whether research methods can or should be interventionist and how researchers relate to any intervention in context. Herbert Simon explores some of these tensions in his book *The Sciences of the Artificial*. He states:

> The contingency of artificial phenomena has always created doubts as to whether they fall properly within the compass of science. Sometimes these doubts are directed at the teleo-logical character of artificial systems and the consequent difficulty of disentangling pre-scription from description. This seems to me not to be the real difficulty. The genuine problem is to show how empirical propositions can be made at all about systems that, given different circumstances, might be quite other than they are.
>
> ...
>
> Finally, I thought I began to see in the problem of artificiality an explanation of the diffi-culty that has been experienced in filling engineering and other professions with empirical and theoretical substance distinct from the substance of their supporting sciences. Engineering, medicine, business, architecture, and painting are concerned not with the nec-essary but with the contingent--not with how things are but with how they might be--in short, with design. The possibility of creating a science or sciences of design is exactly as great as the possibility of creating any science of the artificial. The two possibilities stand or fall together. (Simon, 1969, p. x-xi)

Within our context of eudaemonic learning, we thus envision a shift in the epis-temology of learning research. The researcher must take into account the mix of intentional and unintentional, the engineered vs. accidental, and the ambient and emergent vs. the designed aspects of a system, and this must necessarily cause reflection on the role of the research to describe, explain, or predict any aspect of contingent systems, i.e., systems of people and society learning in relation to one another. This suggests that neither a purely experimental nor a purely descriptive/ interpretivist framing is adequate by itself but that these framings need to be joined when interpreting findings about, as Simon quips, systems that "might be quite other than they are." Current innovations in research methodologies attempt to grap-ple with these issues, for instance, drawing upon ideas from improvement science (Bryk, Gomez, Grunow, & LeMahieu, 2015; Penuel, Allen, Farrell, & Coburn, 2015), systems change (Banathy, 1996) and change laboratories (Sannino et al., 2016), or design-based research methodologies (Design-Based Research Collective, 2003; Kali & Hoadley, in press; Tabak, 2004). The key insight Simon had in 1969, which remains unresolved, is exactly how "sciences of design" and "sciences of the artificial" (which in our case includes an ever more technologically networked soci-ety) can, indeed, stand together.

Bibliography

Aikenhead, G. S. (2005). *Science education for everyday life: Evidence-based practice*. New York: Teachers College.

Aristotle. (350 B. C. E./2000). *Nichomachean ethics* (W. D. Ross, Trans. Electronic edition ed.). Cambridge, MA: MIT.

Banathy, B. H. (1996). *Designing social systems in a changing world*. New York: Springer.

Bang, M., Medin, D. L., & Atran, S. (2007). Cultural mosaics and mental models of nature. *Proceedings of the National Academy of Sciences of the United States of America, 104*(35), 13868–13874. https://doi.org/10.1073/pnas.0706627104

Baram-Tsabari, A., & Osborne, J. (2015). Bridging science education and science communication research. *Journal of Research in Science Teaching, 52*(2), 135–144.

Baram-Tsabari, A., & Segev, E. (2011). Exploring new web-based tools to identify public interest in science. *Public Understanding of Science, 20*(1), 130–143.

Barzilai, S., & Zohar, A. (2012). Epistemic thinking in action: Evaluating and integrating online sources. *Cognition and Instruction, 30*(1), 39–85.

Baxter, G., & Sommerville, I. (2011). Socio-technical systems: From design methods to systems engineering. *Interacting with Computers, 23*(1), 4–17.

Bevan, B., & Penuel, W. R. (Eds.). (2018). *Connecting research and practice for educational improvement: Ethical and equitable approaches.* New York: Routledge.

Birnhack, M., & Elkin-Koren, N. (2010). Does law matter online-empirical evidence on privacy law compliance. *Michigan Telecommunications and Technology Law Review, 17*, 337.

Brown, J. S., & Duguid, P. (2017). *The social life of information: Updated, with a new preface.* Brighton, MA: Harvard Business Review Press.

Bryk, A. S., Gomez, L. M., Grunow, A., & LeMahieu, P. G. (2015). *Learning to improve: How America's Schools can get better at getting better.* Cambridge, MA: Harvard Education Press.

Bybee, R. W., & DeBoer, G. E. (1994). Research on goals for the science curriculum. In D. L. Gabel (Ed.), *Handbook of research on science teaching and learning* (pp. 357–387). New York: Simon & Schuster Macmillan.

Campbell, H. A., & Golan, O. (2011). Creating digital enclaves: Negotiation of the internet among bounded religious communities. *Media, Culture & Society, 33*(5), 709–724.

Carayon, P. (2006). Human factors of complex sociotechnical systems. *Applied Ergonomics, 37*(4), 525–535.

Clegg, C. W. (2000). Sociotechnical principles for system design. *Applied Ergonomics, 31*(5), 463–477.

Coburn, C. E., & Penuel, W. R. (2016). Research-practice partnerships in education: Outcomes, dynamics, and open questions. *Educational Researcher, 45*(1), 48.

Cole, M., & Packer, M. (2016). Design-based intervention research as the science of the doubly artificial. *Journal of the Learning Sciences, 25*(4), 503–530.

Dear, B. (2017). *The friendly orange glow: The untold story of the PLATO System and the Dawn of Cyberculture* (First ed.). New York: Pantheon Books.

Design-Based Research Collective. (2003). Design-based research: An emerging paradigm for educational inquiry. *Educational Researcher, 32*(1), 5–8, 35–37.

DiSalvo, B., Yip, J., Bonsignore, E., & DiSalvo, C. (Eds.). (2017). *Participatory design for learning.* New York: Routledge.

diSessa, A. (2014). A history of conceptual change research: Threads and fault lines. In R. K. Sawyer (Ed.), *Cambridge handbook of the learning sciences* (2nd. ed., pp. 88–108). Cambridge, UK: Cambridge University Press.

Elias, N., & Lemish, D. (2009). Spinning the web of identity: The roles of the internet in the lives of immigrant adolescents. *New Media & Society, 11*(4), 533–551.

Engeström, Y. (1999). Innovative learning in work teams: Analyzing cycles of knowledge creation in practice. In Y. Engeström, R. Miettinen, & R.-L. Punamäki (Eds.), *Perspectives on activity theory* (pp. 377–404). Cambridge: Cambridge University Press.

Engeström, Y. (2002). New forms of expansive learning at work: The landscape of co-configuration. In G. Stahl (Ed.), *Computer support for collaborative learning 2002* (pp. 22–23). Boulder, CO: International Society of the Learning Sciences.

Flyvbjerg, B. (2001). *Making social science matter: Why social inquiry fails and how it can succeed again.* (S. Sampson, Trans.). New York: Cambridge University Press.

Freire, P. (1985). The politics of education: Culture, power, and liberation. South Hadley. In *Mass.: Bergin & Garvey.*

Freire, P. (2011). *Pedagogy of the oppressed.* (M. B. Ramos, Trans. 30th Anniversary Edition ed.). New York: Continuum International Publishing Group.

Gal, E., Bauminger, N., Goren-Bar, D., Pianesi, F., Stock, O., Zancanaro, M., et al. (2009). Enhancing social communication of children with high-functioning autism through a co-located interface. *AI & SOCIETY, 24*(1), 75.

Gee, J. P., & Hayes, E. (2012). Nurturing affinity spaces and game-based learning. In *Games, learning, and society: Learning and meaning in the digital age* (Vol. 123, pp. 1–40).

Hannafin, M. J., Hannafin, K. M., Land, S. M., & Oliver, K. (1997). Grounded practice and the design of constructivist learning environments. *Educational Technology Research and Development, 45*(3), 101–117.

Hiltz, S. R., & Turoff, M. (1978). *The network nation : Human communication via computer*. Reading, MA: Addison-Wesley Pub. Co.

Hoadley, C. (2016, May 11). *Cyberlearning and educational technology: Current R&D, future trends, and how educational institutions will need to change*, Invited talk presented at Provost's Commission on Creating the Next in Education Talk Series, Georgia Tech, Atlanta. Retrieved 1 February 2018 from http://www.provost.gatech.edu/commission-creating-next-education-speaker-series

Hod, Y., & Ben-Zvi, D. (2015). Students negotiating and designing their collaborative learning norms: A group developmental perspective in learning communities. *Interactive Learning Environments, 23*(5), 578–594.

Hod, Y., Ben-Zvi, D., & Bielaczyc, K. (2016). Revisiting learning communities: Innovations in theory and practice. In C. K. Looi, J. L. Polman, U. Cress, & P. Reimann (Eds.), *Transforming learning, empowering learners: The international conference of the learning sciences (ICLS)* (Vol. 2, pp. 1335–1337). Singapore: International Society of the Learning Sciences.

Hutchins, E. (1995). *Cognition in the wild*. Cambridge, MA: MIT Press.

Jackson, M. G. (2008). *Transformative learning for a new worldview: Learning to think differently*. London: Palgrave Macmillan.

Jonassen, D. H. (1990). Thinking technology: Toward a constructivist view of instructional design. *Educational Technology, 30*(9), 32–34.

Jonassen, D. H. (1996). *Computers in the classroom: Mindtools for critical thinking*. Eaglewoods, NJ: Merill/Prentice Hall.

Jonassen, D. H., & Marra, R. M. (1994). Concept mapping and other formalisms as mindtools for representing knowledge. *ALT-J, 2*(1), 50–56.

Jonassen, D. H., & Rohrer-Murphy, L. (1999). Activity theory as a framework for designing constructivist learning environments. *Educational Technology Research and Development, 47*(1), 61–79.

Kali, & Hoadley. (in press). Five waves of conceptualizing knowledge and learning for our future in a networked society. In U. Cress, C. Rosé, A. Wise, & J. Oshima (Eds.), *International handbook of computer-supported collaborative learning*. New York: Springer.

Kali, Y., Baram-Tsabari, A., Ben-Zvi, D., Hod, Y., Sagy, O., & Tal, T. (2017). Taking citizen science to school: Breaking the boundaries between school and society. Unpublished proposal accepted by the Israeli Science Foundation as a Fostering Meaningful Learning in Schools research center.

Kali, Y., Linn, M., & Roseman, J. E. (2008). Designing Coherent Science Education: Implications for curriculum, instruction, and policy. In *Technology*. New York: Teachers College Press.

Kali, Y., McKenney, S., & Sagy, O. (Eds.). (2015). Teachers as designers of technology-enhanced learning. [Special issue]. *Instructional Science, 43*(2), 173.

Kirschner, P., Strijbos, J.-W., Kreijns, K., & Jelle Beers, P. (2004). Designing electronic collaborative learning environments. *Educational Technology Research and Development, 52*(3), 47–66.

Knappenberger, B. (Writer), Knappenberger, B., Braff, Z., Fink, M., Annenberg Weingarten, C. (Producers). (2014). *The Internet's own boy* [Feature Film]. Participant Media. http://www.takepart.com/internets-own-boy/index.html

Lave, J., & Wenger, E. (1991). *Situated learning: Legitimate peripheral participation*. New York: Cambridge University Press.

National Research Council [NRC]. (2012). *A Framework For K-12 science education: Practices, crosscutting concepts, and core ideas*. Washington DC: National Academies Press.

National Research Council [NRC]. (2013). *Next generation science standards: For states, by states*. Washington DC: National Academies Press.

Nov, O., & Rafaeli, S. (2009). Measuring the premium on common knowledge in computer-mediated coordination problems. *Computers in Human Behavior, 25*(1), 171–174.

Papert, S. (1980). *Mindstorms*. New York: Basic Books.

Pea, R. (1993). Practices of distributed intelligence and designs for education. In G. Salomon (Ed.), *Distributed cognitions: Psychological and educational considerations* (pp. 47–87). New York: Cambridge University Press.

Penuel, W. R., Allen, A.-R., Farrell, C., & Coburn, C. E. (2015). Conceptualizing research-practice partnerships as joint work at boundaries. *Journal for Education of Students at Risk (JESPAR), 20*(1–2), 182–197.

Raban, D. R., & Rafaeli, S. (2007). Investigating ownership and the willingness to share information online. *Computers in Human Behavior, 23*(5), 2367–2382.

Rechavi, A., & Rafaeli, S. (2012, January). Knowledge and social networks in Yahoo! Answers. In *System Science (HICSS), 2012 45th Hawaii international conference on* (pp. 781–789). IEEE.

Roberts, D. A., & Bybee, R. W. (2014). Scientific literacy, science literacy, and science education. In N. Lederman & S. K. Abell (Eds.), *Handbook of research on science education* (Vol. II, pp. 545–558). Abingdon: Routledge.

Sannino, A., Engeström, Y., & Lemos, M. (2016). Formative interventions for expansive learning and transformative agency. *Journal of the Learning Sciences, 25*(4), 599–633.

Sawyer, R. K. (2014). The future of learning: Grounding educational innovation in the learning sciences. In R. K. Sawyer (Ed.), *The Cambridge handbook of the learning sciences* (2nd ed., pp. 726–746). New York: Cambridge University Press.

Schejter, A. M., & Tirosh, N. (2016). *A justice-based approach for new media policy: In the paths of righteousness*. New York: Springer.

Simon, H. A. (1969). *The sciences of the artificial*. Cambridge, MA: MIT Press.

Skinner, B. F. (1968). *The technology of teaching*. Englewood Cliffs, NJ: Prentice-Hall.

Suthers, D. D., Lund, K., Rosé, C. P., Teplovs, C., & Law, N. (Eds.). (2013). *Productive multivocality in the analysis of group interactions*. New York: Springer.

Swartz, A. (2015). *The boy who could change the world: The writings of Aaron Swartz*. New York: New Press.

Tabak, I. (2004). Reconstructing context: Negotiating the tension between exogenous and endogenous educational design. *Educational Psychologist, 39*(4), 225–233.

Whyte, W. F., Greenwood, D. J., & Lazes, P. (1989). Participatory action research: Through practice to science in social research. *American Behavioral Scientist, 32*(5), 513–551.

Wiggins, G., & McTighe, J. (1998). Chapter 1: What is backward design? In G. Wiggins & J. McTighe (Eds.), *Understanding by design*. Alexandria, VA: Association for Supervision and Curriculum Development.

Wild, C. J., Utts, J. M., & Horton, N. J. (2018). What is statistics? In D. Ben-Zvi, J. Garfield, & K. Makar (Eds.), *The first handbook of research on statistics teaching and learning* (pp. 5–36). New York: Springer.

Yerushalmy, M., & Botzer, G. (2011). Guiding mathematical inquiry in mobile settings. In *Constructing knowledge for teaching secondary mathematics* (pp. 191–207). New York: Springer.

Zuckerman, O., Gal-Oz, A., Tamir, N., & Kopelman-Rubin, D. (2015). Initial validation of an assistive technology to enhance executive functioning among children with ADHD. In *Proceedings of the 14th international conference on interaction design and children* (pp. 299–302). New York: ACM Press.

Part I
Learning in a Networked Society

Chapter 2
Technology-Enhanced Learning Communities on a Continuum Between Spontaneous and Designed Environments

Iris Tabak, Dani Ben-Zvi, and Yael Kali

Abstract Our approach to learning in a networked society is grounded in the assumption that "schooling" and "society" cannot be considered separate entities. Consequently, research in this area should draw on both educational and social sciences. Bringing together the theoretical and practical tools of both domains allows us to examine the types of interaction, knowledge construction, social organization, and power structures that: (a) occur spontaneously in technology-enhanced learning communities or (b) can be created by design. In this chapter, we present issues that characterize learning in a networked society, such as school-society digital disconnect, digital divides, and the purposeful or invasive permeation of ideas between communities. We discuss the complementary roles that educational and social sciences can play in studying these issues. We conclude with an overview of each of the chapters in this book, highlighting the ways in which they integrate or juxtapose disciplinary lenses to investigate different aspects of learning in a networked society.

Keywords Spontaneous and designed learning environments · Learning communities · Technology-enhanced learning · School-society digital disconnect · Digital divides · Networked society · Contemporary education · Co-creation of knowledge · Inter-disciplinary research

Access to massive information "at your fingertips" is said to hold promise for an egalitarian global society. Yet, even a cursory examination reveals that mere physical access to technological infrastructure does not necessarily enable people to use these resources to achieve their goals nor does it enable different groups of people

I. Tabak (✉)
Ben-Gurion University of the Negev, Department of Education, Beer Sheva, Israel
e-mail: itabak@bgu.ac.il

D. Ben-Zvi · Y. Kali
University of Haifa, Faculty of Education, Haifa, Israel
e-mail: dbenzvi@univ.haifa.ac.il; yael.kali@edtech.haifa.ac.il

© Springer Nature Switzerland AG 2019
Y. Kali et al. (eds.), *Learning In a Networked Society*, Computer-Supported Collaborative Learning Series 17, https://doi.org/10.1007/978-3-030-14610-8_2

to employ these resources to the same extent (Tsetsi & Rains, 2017; van Deursen & van Dijk, 2013; Warschauer & Matuchniak, 2010; see also Chaps. 5 and 7 of this volume). Thus, a central challenge for contemporary education is to identify the knowledge, competencies, and dispositions that go beyond "mere access" and create novel educational settings to develop them. This Introduction begins by laying out a conceptual framework that serves as the backbone for the entire book. The theoretical constructs that underlie this framework are then explained, followed by an overview of the entire book.

Spontaneous and Designed Learning Environments

While daily interactions are increasingly engulfed in mobile and networked information and communication technologies (ICTs), in-school learning interactions are, by comparison, technologically impoverished (Selwyn, 2006, 2014). As a result, students mostly view schools and schooling as irrelevant to their current and future lives, remaining largely unreceptive to the curriculum (Kolikant, 2009). This phenomenon has been referred to as the *school-society digital disconnect* (Selwyn, 2006; Weninger, 2018) that constitutes both a curricular and a technological disparity. The traditional school curriculum emphasizes factual acquisition and the precise application of predefined procedures, but the workforce of the future will need to be proactive and innovative, with the ability to solve ill-structured problems that cannot be addressed with algorithmic solutions (Collins & Halverson, 2009; Levy & Murnane, 2006). Current curricula are not designed for these needs nor for preparing the future workforce to operate in loose hierarchies and distributed collaborations (Collins, 2017; Malone, 2004). Even if students were to embrace the current curriculum more intensely, it would fall short of providing requisite knowledge and skills, because these have not been clearly identified in relation to the power and availability of ICT.

We may thus no longer consider "schooling" and "society" as separate entities but rather bring together the theoretical and practical tools of scientists in both the social and educational sciences to examine what types of interaction, knowledge construction, social organization, and power structures (a) occur spontaneously in technology-enhanced learning (TEL) communities or (b) can be created by design. We refer to these, respectively, as the study of *spontaneous*, naturally occurring environments, and of *designed* environments. In both cases, we strive for analytic insights into the implications of these interactions for transformation of knowledge, power, and well-being.

Learning in a Networked Society (LINKS) is thus presented in this book via seven interdisciplinary research projects (Chaps. 5, 6, 7, 9, 10, 11, and 12) that explain learning on a continuum between the spontaneous and the designed environments (Fig. 2.1). These chapters represent lessons learned from synergistic projects among researchers from the fields of education, educational psychology,

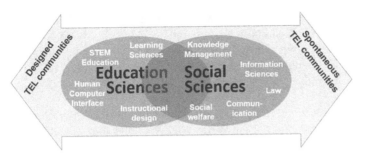

Fig. 2.1 The LINKS continuum between designed and spontaneous TEL communities

learning sciences, science education, science communication, communication, social welfare, knowledge management, information sciences, law, human computer interface, and instructional design, as part of the LINKS Israeli Center of Research Excellence (I-CORE). The book also features introductions and commentaries of world leaders in education, learning sciences, and communication who frame their studies within the context of the networked society (Chaps. 1, 4, 8, and 13).

The Shift to Community and Communication in Education and Technology

One highly significant development in contemporary education is the shift of research and practice away from focus on the individual learner to the view that knowing and understanding are anchored in cultural practices within communities (Bransford, Brown, & Cocking, 2000; Farnsworth, Kleanthous, & Wenger-Trayner, 2016). Several sociocultural theoretical frameworks have been developed to describe learning as active participation in a community. Communities of practice (Wenger, 1998), communities of learners (Rogoff, 1994), and knowledge-building communities (Scardamalia & Bereiter, 1994) are three such constructs that have exerted considerable influence on educational research and practice. Although they may have some nuanced distinctions, they share three fundamental tenets: activity, participation, and enculturation. The active nature of learning is embodied in students' participation in negotiating meanings, developing understanding, and evaluating and orchestrating their own learning in collaborative environments (Brown & Campione, 1994). These forms of participation are, in turn, viewed as processes of enculturation: students assume increasingly central roles in the community and immerse themselves within a culture of learning through which they acquire competence in language, social practices, rituals, and values (Berry, 2007). For the community to function effectively, the participants must negotiate and agree on standard values and norms that guide and constrain social behavior (Basil-Shachar, Ben-Zvi, & Hod, 2014; Cialdini & Trost, 1998). Participation in a community yields not only valued—and mostly shared—products but contributes to the ongoing development of all members, as they take up and build on each other's knowledge and actions (Hod & Ben-Zvi, 2014, forthcoming; Rogoff, Bartlett, & Turkanis, 2001; see also Chap. 7 of this volume).

Interestingly, this shift in education coincides with technological advancements, such as the introduction of the World Wide Web and subsequently Web 2.0 technologies, which reoriented end-user computer interaction from individual work to communication, contribution, and collaboration. Thus, there appear to be concomitant and complementary changes in pedagogy and technology (Tabak, 2009). Several technological innovations have been designed to enhance learning processes in communities, streamline particular activities, and encourage people to function as partners in thinking and as agents of enculturation (Roschelle, Grover, & Bakia, 2016). For example, dynamic visualization tools (Kali & Linn, 2007; Yerushalmy & Botzer, 2011) provide participants with a shared focal point for the explicit external visual display of information, enabling them to visually inspect, comment on, and modify each other's ideas vis-à-vis these representations (see, e.g., Biehler, Ben-Zvi, Bakker, & Makar, 2013). Furthermore, some of these tools reflect the ways in which experts conceptualize, visualize, and represent knowledge in their respective disciplines. These specialized tools can guide learners' interactions in accordance with the norms of the discipline (Tabak & Reiser, 2008) and serve as agents of enculturation.

The benefits of collaborative visualization and modeling of disciplinary norms and expertise are especially strong when these interactions occur not just between individuals or groups of individuals and technological tools but when the tools are inherent components of the technology-enhanced communities in which the learners are immersed. Such interactions can also lead to important insights regarding what it means to learn in a networked society. For example, location-based augmented reality games (Oleksy & Wnuk, 2017), such as Mad City Mystery (Squire & Jan, 2007), in which students of various ages used hand-held computers for authentic scientific inquiry in an outdoor environment, spurred them to develop scientific argumentation skills. Multiuser virtual environments (MUVEs), such as Quest Atlantis (Barab et al., 2010), in which elementary school students used their avatars to collaboratively solve socio-scientific problems, supported complex learning, thinking, and social practices. Participatory simulations, designed, for example, with NetLogo (Levy & Wilensky, 2008), in which students take an active part in a simulation (e.g., play the role of predator or prey), helped students develop complex systems conceptual understanding.

Blurring School-Society Boundaries to Overcome Disconnects and Divides

Despite the strong educational potential and the increasing presence of ICT in formal and non-formal educational environments, there is little evidence of an overall positive effect of the use of ICT on the quality of learning (Kulik, 2003), primarily because state-of-the-art technologies in education are not used predominantly to challenge but rather to sustain traditional pedagogical approaches (Nachmias, Miodusar, Forkosh-Baruch, & Tubin, 2003; Salomon & Ben-Zvi, 2006). Several methods have been adopted to address this limitation, including studies devoted to scaling-up of educational innovations (Cobb & Jackson, 2011; Goodyear & Dimitriadis, 2013; Gutiérrez & Penuel, 2014; Roschelle, Tatar, & Kaput, 2008), engaging in participatory design with schools (Asher et al., 2010; Cobb et al., 2010; Penuel, Roschelle, & Shechtman, 2007), and forming research-practice partnerships (Coburn & Penuel, 2016; Kali, Eylon, McKenney, & Kidron, forthcoming; Kali, Linn, & Roseman, 2008; McKenney, 2016). At the risk of oversimplification, we suggest that these approaches share focus on *disseminating* learning environments that were *designed* from a school-centered approach.

This book proposes a novel approach—partnership between *social and educational scientists* to generate productive synergy between the study of *spontaneous* and *designed* technology-enhanced communities. As reviewed above, educational science has much to offer regarding the manner in which representations and participant structures can advance specific learning goals effectively. This understanding, however, applies primarily to existing school frameworks with rather rigid, hierarchical definitions of student and teacher roles.

By contrast, social scientists currently devote considerable attention to understanding the ways in which people adopt these technologies in their daily lives. Their position is primarily analytic in nature, studying—without any explicit intervention—the numerous virtual communities that interact using social networking platforms (e.g., Facebook, Twitter) or Web 2.0 platforms (e.g., Wikis, Blogs) without any overt educational intention (see, e.g., Chap. 11 of this volume that illustrates use of new media in religious communities). Social scientists may thus provide significant insights into the ways in which "crowds" can self-organize in pursuit of shared information-based goals, building on ideas such as Schelling's (1978) classical notion that individual micromotives create macrobehaviors in society. Network analysis techniques enable characterization of the structure of communities in technology-enhanced endeavors such as Wikipedia or YouTube (Kumar et al., 2010; Xu, Park, & Park, 2017), as well as explanation and prediction of individual behaviors in these communities (Lu & Hampton, 2017; Wasko, Teigland, & Faraj, 2009). Understanding these broader, spontaneous contexts of technology-infused learning is especially important in light of findings suggesting that breadth rather than intensity of ICT use plays the greater role in developing literate, mathematical, and scientific proficiency (Biagi & Loi, 2013; Comi, Argentin, Gui, Origo, & Pagani, 2017).

Social science analysis can also explain how societal power and authority take on new meaning in an information-based digital network, providing and denying access to groups of individuals in ways that differ from traditional economic or demographic barriers (Castells, 2007). Other advances in the study of social networks have uncovered how these entities are characterized by power law distributions (Barabási & Albert, 1999; Kim & Hastak, 2018), rather than the more familiar normal distributions. This, in turn, raises questions about the nature of expertise, access, and equality, as well as inquiring whether there is room for more intervention to address these new sources of potential inequity. Studies of online communities in the social sciences can also help us understand the inherent motivation to engage in social media and its impact on identity and social well-being (Elias & Lemish, 2009; Lam & Smirnov, 2017).

The understanding that social scientists glean from the study of *spontaneous* technology-enhanced communities is a powerful force in directing our attention to learning that may occur incidentally within online communities (Fiesler, Morrison, Shapiro, & Bruckman, 2017; Matthews, 2016; Steinkuehler & Williams, 2009; Ziegler, Paulus, & Woodside, 2013), offering new interpretations of learner interactions and inspiring new ways to conceive of *designed* learning environments. At the same time, educational research offers important new directions for social science research. In particular, it provides theoretical frameworks and methodological approaches for fine-grained analysis of the development of specific knowledge structures. In addition, social scientists may be motivated to adopt a more interventionist stand, thereby enhancing the study of equality and digital divides.

Despite the powerful potential for cross-fostering of ideas between the educational and social sciences, one key question arising inquires whether educational scientists—who focus on the interventionist, design-based study of learning—and social scientists, who concentrate on analytic study of spontaneous social interaction and knowledge construction, can engage in a productive collaboration. This book seeks to answer this question by adopting an interdisciplinary lens, through which these perspectives have been integrated, or at least juxtaposed, to develop new insights regarding what it means to learn in an information-based networked society.

Co-Creation of Knowledge: Bridging School and Society and Educational and Social Sciences

The LINKS investigative lens focuses on the *co-creation of knowledge* (Lewis, Pea, & Rosen, 2010), reconceptualizing learning from a school-based, individual acquisition of knowledge and skills to an ongoing process of production of knowledge through joint activity. It also repositions the study of ICT from a dichotomy of "educational" versus "generic" tools, to a streamlined study of the role of technology, or *new media*, in the co-creation of knowledge across the various contexts that comprise an information-based networked society. Similar constructs, such as "co-construction through interaction," have been studied by both educational and social scientists (e.g., Bell, Tzou, Bricker, & Baines, 2012; Denis & Kalekin-Fishman, 2009; Gee & Green, 1998). But the term and conceptualization of *co-creation of knowledge* as used by LINKS applies more specifically to processes in ICT which greatly extend the range of interaction typically studied in the past.

In adopting *co-creation of knowledge* as our focus, rather than the conventional view of learning as an activity accomplished in schools (and other intentional, circumscribed environments), we view it as an endeavor that occurs all day long throughout life; people continually engage in collaborative activities within different communities for a variety of purposes. In some cases, knowledge goals may be more clearly specified and directed, and in other cases they may be more loosely defined and emergent. For example, in a secondary mathematics classroom, students and teachers annotating a digital textbook may have the specific, institutionally specified goal of achieving a basic understanding of the nature of mathematical functions; but these same youths, later in the day, while communicating with other youths and adults throughout the world about methods for determining the top-achieving players on a massively multiplayer online role-playing game (MMORPG), may derive shared insights concerning statistical analysis techniques, without having this as a pre-specified, intentional educational goal.

Adopting the same lens to understand the processes in both educational and social sciences highlights the research prospects that lie beyond the artificial pitfalls and blind spots that may have constrained past studies of *spontaneous* and *designed* learning environments. More importantly, it diminishes the boundaries between schooling and society, opening the door for interdisciplinary conceptual frameworks that can help minimize the school-society digital divide and better equip citizens for lifelong learning in an information-based networked society (Kali, Tabak, Ben-Zvi, Kidron, et al., 2015).

What's in the Book?

To convey the notion of the LINKS continuum (Fig. 2.1) and highlight the lessons that can be learned from the integration of the various perspectives it affords, this book is divided into four parts: Part I sets the stage for an inter- and transdisciplinary stance on learning in a networked society. First, Hoadley and Kali (Chap. 1) describe five waves of learning mediated by information technologies and link the interdisciplinary and transdisciplinary nature of the LINKS project to the current, fifth wave (Wave 5), of this progression. The current introduction (Chap. 2) then follows by framing the argument (Chap. 2). Then, Raban and Geifman introduce the LINKS Center by examining the changes in its members' research topics during the first 3 years of interdisciplinary synergistic work (Chap. 3). Using topic modeling techniques, they show how research innovation can be achieved by bridging among scientists from various disciplinary perspectives. In the case of LINKS, these topics cover multifaceted research about learning, including normative, behavioral, cognitive, practical, and social aspects.

Part II examines the LINKS continuum with a focus on lessons that can be learned from the spontaneous to the designed arena. The section offers a societal lens for exploring spontaneous learning within TEL communities in the networked society, to inform the design of future policies, practices, and environments for learning. As an introduction to this section, Barzilai and Chinn (Chap. 4) describe current post-truth challenges and explain how designing epistemic education can address such challenges. Their conceptualization offers a lens to view each of the other chapters in Part II as ways in which new opportunities and challenges for learning in the networked society can stimulate and inspire innovations in designed TEL environments. Then, Schejter and Baram-Tsabari introduce a provocative claim in Chap. 5, warning us that despite their great promise for learners in the networked society, new media can serve as a double-edged sword. Using the case of public spontaneous engagement in science, this chapter illustrates that some ICT affordances can also bring about new challenges for non-expert audiences, which need to be considered in educating for life with ICTs. Another case illustrating the trajectory from the spontaneous to the designed is presented by Sagy and colleagues in Chap. 6. The authors examine a genre of research called citizen science that has rapidly developed in the past decade, afforded by the abundance of ICTs. Juxtaposing theoretical frameworks from science communication, science education, data science education, and learning communities, this chapter sheds light on the learning of non-scientist TEL communities and informs design for citizen science endeavors. Part II ends with Chap. 7—Democracy, Communication, and Education in the Twenty-First Century (Kidron, Tirosh, Kali, and Schejter). Inspired by Dewey's seminal book *Education and Democracy* (1916), this chapter reexamines the relations among democracy, communication, and education 100 years later, in the context of the networked society. The authors analyze a case study that exemplifies new possibilities for spontaneous learning, created by contemporary technological capabilities when implementing democratic values, norms, and practices in a TEL environment for higher education.

Part III examines the LINKS continuum from the opposite, complementary direction—from designed to spontaneous TEL communities. It examines how designed learning environments, or communities, are rapidly changing to incorporate new methodologies, tools, norms, practices, perceptions, or habits of mind that originate from spontaneous processes in the networked society. Schofield Clark's introduction to this section sets the stage by introducing how everyday uses of digital media shape our identities and aspirations in the spontaneous learning arena (Chap. 8). Then, in Chap. 9, Kent, Rechavi, and Rafaeli use social learning analytics to explain how communities of learners co-create knowledge in online conversations. By appending analytics to social learning, they derive quantifiable measures based on well-accepted social learning theories and extract interactional patterns of learning among learners, learning resources, and the resulting learning process. By doing so, they illustrate that to understand how people learn in current designed environments, new methodologies are required that explain spontaneous processes in a networked society. In Chap. 10, Har Carmel, Olsher, Elkin-Koren, and Yerushalmy examine the appropriateness of the institutional and legal norms that govern the use and authorship of current textbooks. Their examination offers insights on new challenges, for both educational practice and policy making, brought about by the emergence of eTextbooks. In Chap. 11, Hod and colleagues explore the notion of Future Learning Spaces (FLSs). Drawing on what is known about learning spaces from the past several decades of educational research, as well as about learning in a networked society, the authors explore several FLS examples to offer new insights about this generative and timely concept. Mishol-Shauli, Shacham, and Golan's work concludes Part III in Chap. 12, exploring how traditionally inclined societies infuse new technologies that may ultimately alter their worldviews and identities. Using the case of the Jewish Ultra-Orthodox (Haredi) community in Israel, the authors show how grassroots ICT practices may bridge digital and economic gaps, offering new insights regarding marginalization processes in today's networked society. This case illustrates how communities with pre-existing (designed) norms and practices are changing, with the infusion of new tools and practices stemming from spontaneous processes in our society.

The LINKS book ends with Part IV, comprising Chap. 13, in which Cress concludes by examining the term "networks" by illustrating how, in each of the book chapters, individuals define the activity of the whole network, but networks also influence the activity of its members.

Bibliography

Asher, I., Nasser, S., Ganaim, L., Tabak, I., Kollias, V., Kyza, E. A., et al. (2010). The educative and scalable functions of authoring tools to support inquiry-based science learning. In *Learning in the disciplines: Proceedings of the 9th International Conference of the Learning Sciences* (Vol. 2, pp. 236–243). Chicago, IL: International Society of the Learning Sciences.

Barab, S. A., Gresalfi, M., & Ingram-Goble, A. (2010). Transformational play using games to position person, content, and context. *Educational Researcher, 39*(7), 525–536.

Barabási, A.-L., & Albert, R. (1999). Emergence of scaling in random networks. *Science, 286*(5439), 509–512.

Basil-Shachar, J., Ben-Zvi, D., & Hod, Y. (2014). Characterizing group norms in a technology-enhanced learning community. In Y. Yair & E. Shmueli (Eds.), *Proceedings of the 12th Annual Conference of MEITAL* (pp. 72–76). Tel Aviv, Israel: Levinsky College of Education.

Bell, P., Tzou, C., Bricker, L., & Baines, A. D. (2012). Learning in diversities of structures of social practice: Accounting for how, why and where people learn science. *Human Development, 55*(5-6), 269–284.

Berry, J. W. (2007). Acculturation. In J. E. Grusec & P. D. Hastings (Eds.), *Handbook of socialization: Theory and research* (pp. 520–540). New York, NY: Guilford Press.

Biagi, F., & Loi, M. (2013). Measuring ICT use and learning outcomes: Evidence from recent econometric studies. *European Journal of Education, 48*(1), 28–42.

Biehler, R., Ben-Zvi, D., Bakker, A., & Makar, K. (2013). Technology for enhancing statistical reasoning at the school level. In M. A. Clements, A. Bishop, C. Keitel, J. Kilpatrick, & F. Leung (Eds.), *Third international handbook of mathematics education* (pp. 643–690). Dordrecht: Springer.

Bransford, J. D., Brown, A., & Cocking, R. R. (Eds.). (2000). *How people learn: Brain, mind, experience and schools.* Washington, DC: National Academy Press.

Brown, A. L., & Campione, J. C. (1994). Guided discovery in a community of learners. In K. McGilly (Ed.), *Classroom lessons: Integrating cognitive theory and classroom practice* (pp. 229–270). Cambridge, MA: MIT Press.

Castells, M. (2007). Communication, power and counter-power in the network society. *International Journal of Communication, 1*(1), 238–266.

Cialdini, R., & Trost, M. (1998). Social influence: Social norms, conformity, and compliance. In D. Gilbert, S. Fiske, & G. Lindzey (Eds.), *The handbook of social psychology* (Vol. 2, 4th ed., pp. 151–192). New York, NY: McGraw-Hill.

Cobb, P., & Jackson, K. (2011). Towards an empirically grounded theory of action for improving the quality of mathematics teaching at scale. *Mathematics Teacher Education and Development, 13*(1), 6–33.

Cobb, S., Millen, L., Glover, T., Parsons, S., Garib-Penna, S., Weiss, P., et al. (2010). Integrative approach for designing collaborative technologies for social competence training in children with autism spectrum conditions. In P. Sharkey & J. Sanchez (Eds.), *Proceedings of the 8ᵗʰ International Conference on Disability, Virtual Reality and Associated Technologies* (pp. 295–298). Reading, UK: University of Reading.

Coburn, C. E., & Penuel, W. R. (2016). Research-practice partnerships in education: Outcomes, dynamics, and open questions. *Educational Researcher, 45*(1), 48–54.

Collins, A. (2017). *What's worth teaching? Rethinking curriculum in the age of technology.* New York, NY: Teachers College Press.

Collins, A., & Halverson, R. (2009). *Rethinking education in the age of technology: The digital revolution and the schools.* New York, NY: Teachers College Press.

Comi, S. L., Argentin, G., Gui, M., Origo, F., & Pagani, L. (2017). Is it the way they use it? Teachers, ICT and student achievement. *Economics of Education Review, 56*, 24–39. https://doi.org/10.1016/j.econedurev.2016.11.007

Denis, A. B., & Kalekin-Fishman, D. (2009). *The ISA handbook in contemporary sociology: Conflict, competition, cooperation* (Vol. 57). Thousand Oaks, CA: Sage.

Dewey, J. (1916). *Democracy and education: An introduction to the philosophy of education.* New York, NY: Macmillan.

Elias, N., & Lemish, D. (2009). Spinning the web of identity: The roles of the internet in the lives of immigrant adolescents. *New Media & Society, 11*(4), 533–551.

Farnsworth, V., Kleanthous, I., & Wenger-Trayner, E. (2016). Communities of practice as a Social theory of learning: A conversation with Etienne Wenger. *British Journal of Educational Studies, 64*(2), 139–160.

Fiesler, C., Morrison, S., Shapiro, R. B., & Bruckman, A. S. (2017). *Growing their own: Legitimate peripheral participation for computational learning in an online fandom community.* Paper presented at the CSCW.

Gee, J. P., & Green, J. L. (1998). Discourse analysis, learning, and social practice: A methodological study. *Review of Research in Education, 23*(1), 119–169.

Goodyear, P., & Dimitriadis, Y. (2013). *In medias:* Reframing design for learning. *Research in Learning Technology, 21.* https://doi.org/10.3402/rlt.v21i0.19909

Gutiérrez, K. D., & Penuel, W. R. (2014). Relevance to practice as a criterion for rigor. *Educational Researcher, 43*(1), 19–23.

Hod, Y., & Ben-Zvi, D. (2014). A group psychotherapeutic perspective on transforming participation in a learning community. *Instructional Science, 42*(6), 949–970.

Hod, Y., & Ben-Zvi, D. (forthcoming). The co-development of knowledge, experience, and self in humanistic knowledge building communities. *Instructional Science.*

Kali, Y., Eylon, B.-S., McKenney, S., & Kidron, A. (forthcoming). Design-centric research-practice partnerships: Building productive bridges between theory and practice. In M. Spector, B. Lockee, & M. D. Childress (Eds.), *Learning, design, and technology: An international compendium of theory, research, practice and policy.* Dordrecht: Springer.

Kali, Y., & Linn, M. C. (2007). Technology-enhanced support strategies for inquiry learning. In J. M. Spector, M. D. Merrill, J. van Merrienboer, & M. P. Driscoll (Eds.), *Handbook of research on educational communications and technology* (3rd ed., pp. 445–490). New York, NY: Laurence Erlbaum Associates.

Kali, Y., Linn, M. C., & Roseman, J. E. (Eds.). (2008). *Designing coherent science education: Implications for curriculum, instruction, and policy.* New York: Teachers College Press.

Kali, Y., Tabak, I., Ben-Zvi, D., Kidron, A., et al. (2015). Technology-enhanced learning communities on a continuum between ambient to designed: What can we learn by synthesizing multiple research perspectives? In O. Lindwall, P. Koschman, T. Tchounikine, & S. Ludvigsen (Eds.), *Exploring the material conditions of learning: The Computer Supported Collaborative Learning Conference (CSCL), Volume II* (pp. 615–622). Gothenburg, Sweden: The International Society of the Learning Sciences.

Kim, J., & Hastak, M. (2018). Social network analysis: Characteristics of online social networks after a disaster. *International Journal of Information Management, 38*(1), 86–96. https://doi.org/10.1016/j.ijinfomgt.2017.08.003

Kolikant, Y. (2009). Students' perceptions of the appropriateness and usefulness of the internet for schoolwork and the value of school. *Journal of Educational Computing Research, 41*(4), 407–429.

Kulik, J. A. (2003). *Effects of using instructional technology in elementary and secondary schools: What controlled evaluation studies say (P10446.001).* Arlington, VA: Science and Technology Policy Program of SRI International.

Kumar, A., Tewari, A., Shroff, G., Chittamuru, D., Kam, M., & Canny, J. (2010). *An exploratory study of unsupervised mobile learning in rural India.* Paper presented at the Proceedings of the SIGCHI Conference on Human Factors in Computing Systems.

Lam, W. S. E., & Smirnov, N. (2017). Identity in mediated contexts of transnationalism and mobility. In S. Thorne & S. May (Eds.), *Language, education and technology* (pp. 1–13). Cham: Springer.

Levy, F., & Murnane, R. J. (2006). Why the changing American economy calls for twenty-first century learning: Answers to educators' questions. *New Directions for Youth Development, 2006*(110), 53–62.

Levy, S. T., & Wilensky, U. (2008). Inventing a "mid level" to make ends meet: Reasoning between the levels of complexity. *Cognition and Instruction, 26*(1), 1–47.

Lewis, S., Pea, R., & Rosen, J. (2010). Beyond participation to co-creation of meaning: mobile social media in generative learning communities. *Social Science Information, 49*(3), 351–369.

Lu, W., & Hampton, K. N. (2017). Beyond the power of networks: Differentiating network structure from social media affordances for perceived social support. *New Media & Society, 19*(6), 861–879. https://doi.org/10.1177/1461444815621514

Malone, T. W. (2004). *The future of work: How the new order of business will shape your organization, your management style and your life.* Boston, MA: Harvard Business Review Press.

Matthews, J. C. (2016). Historical inquiry in an informal fan community: Online source usage and the tv show the tudors. *Journal of the Learning Sciences, 25*(1), 4–50. https://doi.org/10.1080/10508406.2015.1112285

McKenney, S. (2016). Researcher-practitioner collaboration in educational design research: Processes, roles, values & expectations. In M. A. Evans, M. J. Packer, & R. K. Sawyer (Eds.), *Reflections on the learning sciences* (pp. 155–188). New York, NY: Cambridge University Press.

Nachmias, R., Miodusar, D., Forkosh-Baruch, A., & Tubin, D. (2003). National policies and practices on ICT in education - Israel. In T. Plomp, R. E. Anderson, N. Law, & A. Quale (Eds.), *Cross national policies and practices on information and communication technology in education* (pp. 403–422). Charlotte, NC: Information Age Publishing.

Oleksy, T., & Wnuk, A. (2017). Catch them all and increase your place attachment! The role of location-based augmented reality games in changing people - place relations. *Computers in Human Behavior, 76,* 3–8.

Penuel, W. R., Roschelle, J., & Shechtman, N. (2007). Designing formative assessment software with teachers: An analysis of the co-design process. *Research and Practice in Technology Enhanced Learning, 2*(1), 51–74.

Rogoff, B. (1994). Developing understanding of the idea of communities of learners. *Mind, Culture, & Activity: An international journal, 1*(4), 209–229.

Rogoff, B., Bartlett, L., & Turkanis, C. (2001). Lessons about learning as a community. In B. Rogoff, C. Turkanis, & L. Bartlett (Eds.), *Learning together: Children and adults in a school community* (pp. 3–17). New York, NY: Oxford University Press.

Roschelle, J., Grover, S., & Bakia, M. (2016). Introducing the U.S. Cyberlearning Community. In K. Verbert, M. Sharples, & T. Klobučar (Eds.), *Adaptive and Adaptable Learning: Proceedings of the 11th European Conference on Technology Enhanced Learning, EC-TEL 2016, Lyon, France, September 13–16, 2016* (pp. 644–647). Cham: Springer.

Roschelle, J., Tatar, D., & Kaput, J. (2008). Getting to scale with innovations that restructure deeply how students learn mathematics. In A. E. Kelly, R. A. Lesh, & J. Y. Baek (Eds.), *Handbook of design research in mathematics, science and technology education: Innovations in science, technology, engineering, and mathematics learning and teaching* (pp. 369–395). New York, NY: Routledge.

Salomon, G., & Ben-Zvi, D. (2006). The difficult marriage between education and technology: Is the marriage doomed? In L. Verschaffel, F. Dochy, M. Boekaerts, & S. Vosniadou (Eds.), *Instructional psychology: Past, present and future trends (Essays in honor of Erik De Corte)* (pp. 209–222). Amsterdam, Netherlands: Elsevier.

Scardamalia, M., & Bereiter, C. (1994). Computer support for knowledge-building communities. *Journal of the Learning Sciences, 3*(3), 265–283.

Schelling, T. C. (1978). *Micromotives and macrobehavior.* London, UK: W. W. Norton & Company.

Selwyn, N. (2006). Exploring the 'digital disconnect' between net-savvy students and their schools. *Learning, Media and Technology, 31*(1), 5–17.

Selwyn, N. (2014). *Distrusting educational technology: Critical questions for changing times.* New York, NY: Routledge.

Squire, K. D., & Jan, M. (2007). Mad city mystery: Developing scientific argumentation skills with a place-based augmented reality game on handheld computers. *Journal of Science Education and Technology, 16*(1), 5–29.

Steinkuehler, C., & Williams, C. (2009). Math as narrative in WoW forum discussions. *International Journal of Learning and Media, 1*(3). https://doi.org/10.1162/ijlm_a_00028

Tabak, I. (2009). Information processing to no end: A critical review of computers in education. *Alpayim* [Two Thousand], *34*(special issue on education), 194–215. [Hebrew].

Tabak, I., & Reiser, B. (2008). Software-realized inquiry support for cultivating a disciplinary stance. *Pragmatics & Cognition, 16*(2), 307–355.

Tsetsi, E., & Rains, S. A. (2017). Smartphone internet access and use: Extending the digital divide and usage gap. *Mobile Media & Communication., 5*(3), 239–255. https://doi.org/10.1177/2050157917708329

van Deursen, A. J. A. M., & van Dijk, J. A. G. M. (2013). The digital divide shifts to differences in usage. *New Media & Society, 16*(3), 507–526.

Warschauer, M., & Matuchniak, T. (2010). New technology and digital worlds: Analyzing evidence of equity in access, use, and outcomes. *Review of Research in Education, 34*(1), 179–225.

Wasko, M. M., Teigland, R., & Faraj, S. (2009). The provision of online public goods: Examining social structure in an electronic network of practice. *Decision Support Systems, 47*(3), 254–265.

Wenger, E. (1998). *Communities of practice learning, meaning, and identity.* Cambridge, UK: Cambridge University Press.

Weninger, C. (2018). Problematising the notion of 'authentic school learning': Insights from student perspectives on media/literacy education. *Research Papers in Education, 33*(2), 239–254. https://doi.org/10.1080/02671522.2017.1286683

Xu, W. W., Park, J.-y., & Park, H. W. (2017). Longitudinal dynamics of the cultural diffusion of kpop on youtube. *Quality & Quantity, 51*(4), 1859–1875. https://doi.org/10.1007/s11135-016-0371-9

Yerushalmy, M., & Botzer, G. (2011). Guiding mathematical inquiry in mobile settings. In O. Zaslavsky & P. Sullivan (Eds.), *Constructing knowledge for teaching secondary mathematics* (Vol. 6, pp. 191–207). New York: Springer.

Ziegler, M. F., Paulus, T., & Woodside, M. (2013). Understanding informal group learning in online communities through discourse analysis. *Adult Education Quarterly, 64*(1), 60–78.

Chapter 3
Forming Socio-intellectual Capital: The Case of LINKS

Daphne R. Raban and Dorit Geifman

Abstract This chapter traces the formation of socio-intellectual value by the LINKS research center, which focuses on studying the co-creation of knowledge in spontaneous and designed learning environments, in the community at large and at educational facilities. By analyzing academic publications before and during LINKS activity using topic modeling, we identify evolving research areas. Topic modeling is a statistical algorithm which extracts the underlying thematic structure of a collection of documents, automatically identifying latent topical structures within the documents.

We received 447 articles published by 15 LINKS PIs from 2009 to 2016. The corpus for analysis consisted of the title, keywords, and abstracts of these articles. Three of the pre-LINKS topics persisted during LINKS were: Content Exchange, Gamification & Virtual Reality, and STEM Education. We observed a shift in focus from Curriculum Design, Online Communities, and Diversity Online pre-LINKS to Collaborative Learning, Learning Communities, and an increased interest in STEM Education thereafter.

Keywords Socio-intellectual capital · Co-creation of knowledge · Spontaneous and designed learning environments · Topic modeling · Content exchange · Gamification · Virtual reality · STEM education · Collaborative learning · Learning communities

Social capital is a value that results from belonging to a network of people—a social network (Coleman, 1988). The value can be tangible, such as easy access to resources (e.g., research and teaching facilities) available to peers in the network, or intangible, such as advice or generation of reputation. Value can be direct, when derived from strong ties, close friends, and relatives, or indirect, when obtained from friends of friends. We propose the term *socio-intellectual value* for the value a

D. R. Raban (✉) · D. Geifman
University of Haifa, Department of Business Administration, Haifa, Israel
e-mail: draban@univ.haifa.ac.il

© Springer Nature Switzerland AG 2019
Y. Kali et al. (eds.), *Learning In a Networked Society*, Computer-Supported Collaborative Learning Series 17, https://doi.org/10.1007/978-3-030-14610-8_3

network derives from common intellectual interests, thereby underscoring the specific dimension of social capital to be examined below. This chapter traces the formation of socio-intellectual value by Learning In a NetworKed Society (LINKS), an Israeli Center of Research Excellence (I-CORE), which focuses on studying the co-creation of knowledge in spontaneous and designed learning environments, in the community at large and at educational facilities (see Tabak, Ben-Zvi, & Kali, Chap. 2). We examine fifteen LINKS researchers (PIs) working at four academic institutions, representing a broad spectrum of scientific inquiry, including education, human–computer interaction, law, occupational therapy, information science, management, and communications.

LINKS was established by a group of researchers who were somewhat acquainted with one another. The idea was to bring together researchers interested in a common challenge and to investigate it from different points of view, using various methodologies (see Hoadley and Kali, Chap. 1). It may be perceived as an example of weak ties used for the formation of an interdisciplinary, inter-university, synergetic research task force. Where weak ties come to play, social capital is likely to form. Previous research suggests that expectations for success of a new network of researchers should be moderate because of substantial differences in theories, understanding of issues and methodological approaches (Wellman, Dimitrova, Hayat, Mo, & Smale, 2014). It maintains that digital communications do not provide full compensation for geographical distance and lack of in-person meetings. Indeed, the interaction among the LINKS researchers extended beyond digital communications.

The 15 LINKS PIs conducted quarterly meetings, during the first 4 years of the project. The smaller executive management team, consisting of six researchers, met monthly. Once a year, in the fall, the whole LINKS community, consisting of the PIs and dozens of graduate students, convened for a 2-day conference at one of the participating campuses. In addition, smaller groups of researchers consisting of PIs and graduate students collaborated on specific projects, and in some cases joint advising of graduate students was conducted.

Socio-intellectual value may be explicit or implicit. Explicit manifestations occurred during the LINKS Center's regular research meetings, seminars, and conferences, but its longest lasting effects will be determined by the power of the research community formed and its relevance to the three themes on which the LINKS community was founded: (a) the development of shared knowledge and understanding in technology-enhanced communities; (b) how technology-enhanced communities build shared practices, norms, and regulations; and (c) how technology fosters learning within and among diverse people from various sectors of society (see Fig. 1 in Chap. 1).

One method of creating long-term impact is scholarly publishing. Writing is accomplished individually and collaboratively, but during the first few years, most published works reflected mentor–graduate student relationships. Forming these relationships has apparently been more typical, easier, or faster than bridging among disciplines and between researchers from different institutions. New research bonds require time for brainstorming, research planning, implementation, and publication.

This study was conducted during the fourth year of LINKS Center activity. Its aim was to observe the development of internal synergies and assess their relationship with the original themes, thereby exploring the formation of the LINKS research core and uncovering the implicit intellectual ties produced by Center activity. We expect this study, which is based on a small group of researchers and a short timeframe, to provide a foundation for more extensive research on knowledge formation in large research projects. To gain an early glimpse at the maturation of weak ties into future research links (or LINKS), we analyzed the common interests that surfaced during the Center's activity.

Research questions include:

- How is LINKS socio-intellectual value structured?
- What topics were covered in material published by LINKS researchers during its first 3 years?
- Do these topics reflect the evolution of subjects studied by the same people before LINKS was established?
- Which new topics have evolved?

Scientific achievements are often measured by bibliometric indices, such as various forms of individual or publication-based impact factors and citation counts; such metrics, however, must rely on the tectonic rate of formal academic publication. By contrast, this study investigates the continuous evolution of socio-intellectual capital at LINKS, analyzing academic publications before and during Center activity using the topic modeling method to help identify evolving research areas. Analysis is followed by brief background to explain the approach applied.

Analytical Approach

Topic modeling is a family of statistical algorithms used to extract the underlying thematic structure of a large collection of documents. It refines the semantic classification of a document beyond rudimentary analysis of its raw terms, automatically identifying latent topical structures within the document by evaluating the distribution of each topic over a fixed vocabulary of the whole corpus (Blei, 2012).

Topic modeling is a generative, unsupervised machine learning algorithm that requires no prior annotation or labeling of the documents or the terms within them. This study uses Latent Dirichlet Allocation (LDA), the most popular application of the topic modeling algorithm. The algorithm infers the corpus's hidden topic structure by computing the topic structure's conditional distribution according to the wording of the relevant documents. It then identifies the document's thematic structure by calculating the proportion of each topic within the document. The process yields a dual outcome: a set of topics, each identified by the distribution of raw terms, and a distribution of the topics running through each document. The semantic

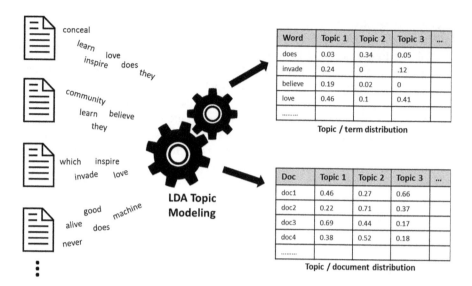

Fig. 3.1 The LDA topic modeling process

meaning of a topic is observed qualitatively according to words ranked with high probability. Figure 3.1 provides a graphic representation of the process.

Method

Text analysis of large corpuses requires automated processing, but such procedures cannot fully address the linguistic and semantic complexities of text. Manual intervention is needed for a more thorough understanding of the text, especially the semantic aspects thereof. In this study, several R packages were used to analyze the corpus of text, and manual processes were introduced to enhance the quality and performance of the automated analysis. This section describes the data collection, preprocessing, and topic modeling analysis used in this research.

Data Collection

Fifteen LINKS PIs responded to a call to provide their LINKS-related peer-reviewed publications, extracted from their individual Google Scholar accounts. Manual searches were employed when partial data required completion. Several articles were removed after a PI indicated that they related to a completely different area of research, leaving a collection of 447 articles published by the PIs from 2009 to

2016. The corpus for analysis consisted of the title, keywords, and abstracts of these articles. A total of 42 papers had title data only.

Preprocessing

The preprocessing step involved stop word removal and stemming. Stop words are neutral words, such as "and," "the," "actually," etc., that do not contribute to the specific context of analysis despite their high frequency and are removed from the corpus to preclude biased analysis. Stemming is the process of combining morphological variants of the same words by reducing them to a common root. In most cases, words with the same root have similar meaning, and by stemming the corpus, the collection of words becomes smaller and more accurate. For example, words such as "community," "communities," "communal" are all stemmed to same root—*commun*—and counted as only one term, a favorable outcome.

The *tidytext* R package that includes a list of 1147 standard stop words was used for stop word removal. The standard list was extended with context-specific words relevant to the special characteristics of the corpus that consisted primarily of academic article abstracts largely concerned with research methods. Such text is irrelevant, however, when trying to understand the context of research. To correct this imbalance, we removed method-oriented words such as "research," "author," "results," "methods," etc. while ensuring that context-related words remained.

For stemming the corpus, we used the Porter word stemming algorithm as implemented in the *SnowballC* R package. Stemming is a process with known deficiencies (Hull, 1996):

- Words with different meanings are combined to the same root, e.g., "new" and "news."
- Words with similar meanings stem to different roots, e.g., "learn," "learned."
- After stemming, many words lose a recognizable form and cannot always be reconstructed, as the stemming process is irreversible.

To address these deficiencies, we created a process that combines automatic and manual processing:

1. Applying the stemming algorithm to the full corpus.
2. Reviewing transformation of the 500 most frequent words in the corpus (60% of the unique words) to identify inconsistencies in the stemming process. For example, words such as "informal" and "information" were inappropriately stemmed to the same root, while words such as "man" and "men" were not combined.
3. Re-applying the stemming process to the corpus, eliminating exceptional words.
4. Transforming the outcome back to a recognizable form by selecting the most frequent original word that formed each stemmed word.

The preprocessing step resulted in a corpus of 3510 words.

Topic Modeling

To compare pre-LINKS research topics with emergent LINKS areas of research, the corpus was divided into two partitions: Pre-LINKS (2009–2013: 250 publications, 2687 words) and LINKS (2014–2016: 197 publications, 2309 words). The LDA topic modeling algorithm, as implemented in the *topicmodels* R package (Hornik & Grün, 2011), was applied separately to each partition, using the Gibbs method and the default parameters.

The number of topics to be generated is essential to the algorithm, yet no guidelines have been stipulated to help define this parameter. An excessive value may yield topics that cannot be distinguished from one another in any meaningful way, while a figure too small may combine several topics that should be distinct into one. Following best practices in the field (DiMaggio, Nag, & Blei, 2013), we experimented with different numbers of topics and found six to be most appropriate in the present case.

The outcome of this step yielded two tables: one, listing the distribution of words over the topics, and the other, indicating the representational strength of each topic in each document (Fig. 3.1). The results are presented and interpreted below.

Results and Interpretation

Topic modeling is a type of statistical analysis that places terms into *buckets* (topics), irrespective of their meaning and context. The observations resulting from this analysis are mostly qualitative in nature. The following results reflect the richness of information that can be derived from this analysis.

Table 3.1 displays the division of the corpus into six topics for each of the two periods: Pre-LINKS and LINKS. Each topic has a list of terms associated with it based on probabilities. Topic titles attempt to describe the idea common to most terms in each. Terms are shown in Figs. 3.2 and 3.3.

Table 3.1 displays a gradual change over the years. While STEM Education, Content Exchange, and Gamification and Virtual Reality continue to play a central role, the other three topics display a stronger focus on aspects of learning in the LINKS years than in the earlier period. Figures 3.2 and 3.3 depict the distribution of

Table 3.1 Pre-LINKS topics and LINKS topics

Pre-LINKS topics (2009–2013)	LINKS topics (2014–2016)
Curriculum Design	Collaborative Learning
Online Communities	Learning Communities
Content Exchange	Content Exchange
Gamification and Virtual Reality	Gamification and Assistive Technology
STEM Education	STEM Education 1
Diversity Online	STEM Education 2

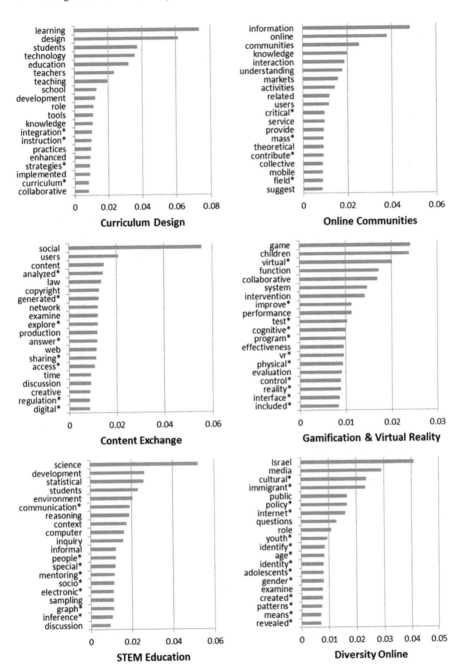

Fig. 3.2 Probabilities of terms per topic in the Pre-LINKS corpus. *denotes a term that appeared in the pre-LINKS corpus only

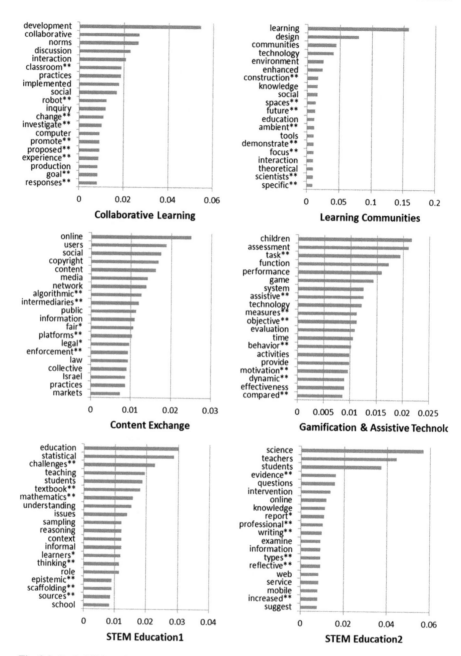

Fig. 3.3 Probabilities of terms per topic in the LINKS corpus. **denotes a new term appearing in the LINKS corpus

Table 3.2 Research agenda during the Pre-LINKS period

PI	Curriculum Design	Online Communities	Content Exchange	Gamification & Virtual Reality	Diversity Online	STEM Education
Baram-Tsabari	5	1	0	0	6	6
Barzilai[a]	3	0	0	0	0	1
Ben-Zvi	13	1	0	0	0	18
Elias	0	0	0	0	19	0
Elkin-Koren	0	0	13	0	0	0
Golan[a]	0	1	0	0	5	0
Hod[a]	3	0	0	0	0	0
Kali	23	1	0	0	1	1
Raban	0	15	6	1	0	0
Rafaeli	0	12	4	0	1	0
Schejter	0	1	3	0	15	0
Tabak	5	0	0	0	0	6
Weiss	1	0	0	33	1	6
Yerushalmy	13	1	0	0	1	0
Zuckerman	1	1	0	2	0	0

[a]denotes young scholars

the terms over the topics found in Table 3.1, providing a visual display of the significance of these terms to their respective topics:

Another product of the LDA algorithm is the probability distribution of topics within each article in the corpus. By identifying the highest scoring topic for each article and averaging it by topic for each PI, we derived a measure of the level of the PI's involvement in a specific topic. Tables 3.2 and 3.3 and Figs. 3.4 and 3.5 provide two perspectives on the research agenda of LINKS PIs in the pre-LINKS and LINKS periods. The tables list the number of articles written by the PIs in the respective topics, while the figures show the convergence of researchers surrounding mutual research interests.

By linking PIs and topics, Figs. 3.4 and 3.5 represent the socio-intellectual network during the pre-LINKS and LINKS periods, respectively. Researchers are connected to their respective topical interests. The width or weight of the edge reflects the average probability of the topics ranking highest in the PI's papers, representing the intensity of the PI's involvement in this topic.

Discussion

This introductory chapter studies the formation of socio-intellectual capital at a newly formed research center, LINKS. By applying a topic modeling approach, we uncover latent topics that form intellectual links among LINKS researchers. Below,

Table 3.3 Research agenda during the LINKS period

PI	Collaborative Learning	Learning Communities	Content Exchange	Gamification & Assistive Technology	STEM Education 1	STEM Education 2
Baram-Tsabari	0	1	3	0	1	7
Barzilai	0	1	0	0	7	1
Ben-Zvi	10	6	0	0	13	0
Elias	0	1	1	0	0	0
Elkin-Koren	0	0	12	0	1	0
Golan	1	0	1	1	0	0
Hod	7	5	0	0	1	0
Kali	1	11	1	0	1	4
Raban	0	1	6	2	0	1
Rafaeli	4	2	2	3	0	2
Schejter	1	0	8	0	0	0
Tabak	2	4	0	0	7	3
Weiss	7	2	0	14	0	0
Yerushalmy	0	0	0	2	8	0
Zuckerman	5	0	0	10	0	2

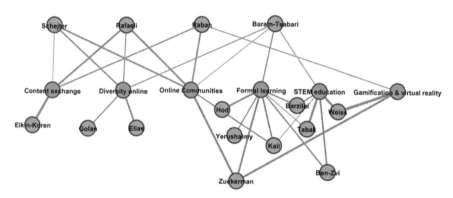

Fig. 3.4 The socio-intellectual network during the pre-LINKS period

we present several insights derived from the above findings, relating to topic titles, terms used, researchers' foci, and the newly formed socio-intellectual capital, concluding with observations concerning the original LINKS themes described in the Introduction.

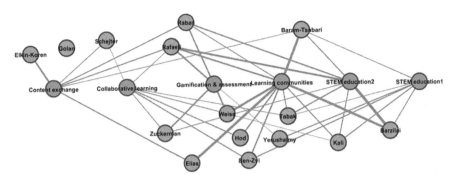

Fig. 3.5 The socio-intellectual network during the LINKS period

Topic Titles

Topic titles presented in Table 3.1 were defined according to the high-probability terms characterizing each topic, as shown in Figs. 3.2 and 3.3. Following approval by the authors of this chapter, the proposed titles were presented and discussed at a LINKS Center research meeting. The titles are broad enough to cover most of the terms associated with them. For example, the topic title Content Exchange covers legal, social, and market terms, as would be expected from this broad topic (Raban, Gordon, & Geifman, 2011).

Three of the original six topics defined for the pre-LINKS period persisted during the LINKS period: Content Exchange, Gamification and Virtual Reality, and STEM Education. In fact, STEM Education became more dominant during the LINKS period. While this persistence in itself may not be surprising because LINKS is about learning in a networked society, it does lend some validation to application of the topic modeling method in our research. During the pre-LINKS period, STEM Education was studied by one leading researcher and five colleagues somewhat less involved in this field, whereas during the LINKS period, it extended over two topics with six researchers publishing relevant material frequently and another six less often. Similarly, the number of researchers focusing on Content Exchange increased from four in the earlier period to eight in the later one.

The slight change in the Gamification topic indicates a shift in terminology rather than topic. This domain was led by one dominant researcher and two others in the pre-LINKS period. Research doubled during the LINKS period to two dominant and four additional researchers.

The emergent topic titles display a shift in research focus from Curriculum Design, Online Communities, and Diversity Online in the pre-LINKS era to Collaborative Learning and Learning Communities and an increased interest in STEM Education thereafter. Overall, we observe continuing strong focus on Gamification and Virtual Reality and Content Exchange, with intensification of research on STEM Education and technology-enhanced, collaborative forms of learning.

Terms Used

The evolution of terms constitutes a research agenda description that is also interesting from a semantic point of view, considering the terminological changes that took place over time. For example, *virtual reality* has become less common, having been supplanted by *assistive technology*, as confirmed by the relevant researchers. This nuanced change is reflected in the topic title alone: the topic remained of interest, but its terminology changed. Another semantic change is the apparent replacement of *mentoring* by *scaffolding*. Finally, the rather general term *online communities* morphed into the more learning-oriented *learning communities*.

From a research agenda perspective, the disappearance of certain terms and their replacement with new ones is a telling phenomenon. Disappearing terms are marked with one asterisk in Fig. 3.2 and new terms with two asterisks in Fig. 3.3. The most prominent terminological change occurred in the Diversity Online topic: 14 out of the top 20 terms in this topic from pre-LINKS data are not highly ranked in the LINKS period. Terms such as *immigrant, gender,* and *identity* received little research attention after the Research Center was established. The terms have not disappeared altogether, but they were assigned lower probability of appearing in LINKS articles because of the emergence of new research ideas and terminology. A stronger technological agenda is apparent in the LINKS period, wherein terms are easily constructed into concepts such as *future learning spaces, technology-enhanced learning,* and *algorithmic intermediaries*, all of which are examples of the prevailing trend, as reflected in LINKS publications.

Forty-two of the 112 unique terms in the 6 topics of the pre-LINKS period were replaced by newer ones during the LINKS period. This change may represent the pace of innovation at the LINKS Center of Research Excellence: According to the turnover rate of significant terms over a 3-year period, two thirds of the Center's output consists of solid research terminology and one third innovation.

Researchers' Foci

Tables 3.2 and 3.3 provide a bird's-eye view of the researchers' topical foci. Three researchers— Barzilai, Golan, and Hod—entered the LINKS period as young scholars beginning their careers; as such, their presence naturally appears stronger in Table 3.3 than in Table 3.2. Moreover, these researchers introduced some of the research innovation reflected in the new terminology. Furthermore, while discussion is limited to principal research foci, each researcher has additional research interests, designated by the lower values in Tables 3.2 and 3.3.

STEM Education emerged as a core LINKS topic. Beginning as one pre-LINKS topic with six researchers, it expanded into two topics during the LINKS period with no fewer than 10 out of 15 researchers contributing to publications in this broad area of interest. Ben-Zvi combined STEM Education research with studies of

Curriculum Design during the pre-LINKS period and with Collaborative Learning and Learning Communities thereafter. Similarly, Kali's research topic shifted from Curriculum Design to Learning Communities. Most (13 out of 15) PIs are involved in the two network-related topics (Collaborative Learning and Learning Communities) conforming with the LINKS research agenda (Learning in a Network Society). Four researchers—Elkin-Koren, Raban, Rafaeli, and Schejter—showed an interest in Content Exchange in the pre-LINKS period and continued to focus on the topic during the LINKS period, probably because of its status as a core topic for the project. Four additional researchers—Baram-Tsabari, Elias, Golan, and Kali—concentrated on the topic during the LINKS period as well.

The main actor of the pre-LINKS Gamification & Virtual Reality topic was Weiss, who was joined by Zuckerman in the LINKS project, resulting in the topic's evolution and restatement as Gamification & Assistive Technology. The topic is of significance not only for its research synergy value but also because of its substantial social contribution to people with special needs. Thus, although diversity disappeared from the topic titles, it maintains its presence in publication terminology.

Previous interest in Curriculum Design fueled the newly formed topic of Collaborative Learning, both involving nine researchers. It also funneled into the expanded interest in STEM Education. Baram-Tsabari provides a sound example of this shift.

Schejter and Elias, who were the champions of diversity online, mostly found their way into the LINKS period Content Exchange topic. Weiss, whose publications were almost exclusively about Gamification and Virtual Reality, remained loyal to this research agenda but expanded considerably into Collaborative Learning. Rafaeli and Raban, who were mostly associated with Online Communities, Content Exchange, and Gamification during the pre-LINKS period, largely remained with their original topics, although Rafaeli's interests also extended to Collaborative Learning.

Figures 3.4 and 3.5 offer a clearer view of research topic changes and the common interests of researchers working on them, as detailed below.

Socio-intellectual Capital

Figure 3.4, representing the years preceding the formation of LINKS, clearly distinguishes researchers whose intellectual home is the Department of Education from all others to whom the figure refers. Education researchers concentrated on Curriculum Design and STEM Education. In the pre-LINKS period, these topics were of little interest to the remaining researchers, who provided the Center with their knowledge about Diversity Online, Content Exchange, Gamification and Virtual Reality, and Online Communities, wherein the last topic constituted a bridge between the two groups of researchers.

Figure 3.5 constitutes a lucid graphic representation of several newly formed research synergies, especially when viewed in contrast with Fig. 3.4. Its most salient feature, however, is its display of the potential for additional new collaborations based on shared topical interests. For example, it shows that most LINKS researchers manifest a strong affinity to Learning Communities, an emerging topic that captured interest and sparked research productivity, demonstrating the intensifying synergy surrounding a topic that is central to the LINKS mission. Learning Communities is thus a *connector topic* for the LINKS Research Center, as suggested at a recent conference symposium (Kali et al., 2015).

Overall, each of the other topics generated interest for researchers from various backgrounds. In Fig. 3.5, each topic was linked with five to seven researchers, expanding the more limited picture observed in Fig. 3.4. This shared interest may be partly attributed to collaborative projects and shared graduate student mentoring, constituting potential for future research collaboration by linking PIs who have not worked together but display similar or complementary research interests and approaches.

Previous studies of research networks have shown that despite their desire to work with colleagues from distant places and different disciplines, researchers actually collaborate with colleagues from the same discipline and geographical vicinity (Mo, Hayat, & Wellman, 2015). Such studies continue to suggest that institutional intervention may be used to enhance geographically dispersed, multidisciplinary collaboration, as demonstrated by LINKS, whose proactive management and project meeting series resulted in productive interdisciplinary research ties.

LINKS Themes

LINKS Center focuses on three themes: (A) development of shared knowledge and understanding in technology-enhanced communities; (B) institution of shared practices, norms, and regulations in technology-enhanced communities; and (C) technology-fostered learning within and among diverse people from various sectors of society.

The range of topics, the terms included in those topics, and the reshuffling of terms between the pre-LINKS and LINKS periods attest to the researchers' focus on these three themes. Technology (Theme A) appears in all topics, expressed in terms such as *technology-enhanced, technology, network, digital, new media*, and the like. Terms addressing norms and regulations (Theme B) appear primarily in the Collaborative Learning and STEM Education topics, including *norms, practices, copyright, law, fair*, etc. By contrast, the Learning Communities and Content Exchange topics imply adoption of norms even if the relevant expressions were not represented in the lists of top 20 terms per topic (Fig. 3.3). Diversity (Theme C) found its way from explicit mention in the pre-LINKS topics to presence in the revised LINKS topic of Gamification & Assistive Technology.

Study Limitations and Future Work

The primary limitation of this study is the relatively small quantity of data it addresses: the titles, keywords, and abstracts of 447 publications, divided into 2 unequal parts. Other studies using topic modeling often use larger amounts of data. From an intuitive and practical point of view, large data sets generally prove beneficial to such studies, although certain drawbacks may be present nonetheless in them as well. For example, automatic analysis, using methods such as stemming, may result in context errors and sacrifice fine-tuned insights. In our case, however, the small sample allowed us to actually read the lists of terms and apply our judgment and knowledge of the project to understand what we saw. We also discussed and verified the terms and topics with the researchers themselves.

The data was divided into two unequal parts, according to the relevant periods—pre-LINKS (about 5 years) and LINKS (about 3 years). The number of pre-LINKS publications was approximately 25% greater than the corresponding figure for LINKS data, although LINKS researchers appeared to have been more prolific than their earlier counterparts (65 vs. 50 publications per year, respectively). To achieve proper data balance, we perceived value in analyzing a longer historical period for pre-LINKS research.

When this chapter was written, the LINKS period covered only three of the project's 5-year period. While our research noted the effects of collaboration among researchers regarding the respective topics, it is still too early to identify any major research agenda shifts. A follow-up study can be conducted at the end of the LINKS period to observe additional changes. It would also be worthwhile to interview PIs and determine whether their subjective experiences match the observations resulting from the data.

Conclusion

LINKS has evolved around three core topics, STEM Education, Content Exchange, and Gamification and Virtual Reality/Assistive Technology. Three new topics emerged: Learning Communities, Collaborative Learning, and further expansion of STEM Education. We observed a solid core with a steady rate of research innovation, achieved by bridging among scientists from various backgrounds. All together, these topics cover multifaceted research about learning, including normative, behavioral, cognitive, and practical and social aspects. While previous studies identified difficulties in achieving multidisciplinary and multi-institutional academic collaboration through virtual networks, we maintain that the tighter face-to-face interactions among LINKS PIs have engendered research synergies that lead the Center towards its pre-defined research agenda. Several outcomes of this multifaceted approach are described in chapters of this book discussing educational policy issues, the shape and meaning of physical spaces, the promises and perils of networks and new media, and other matters of contemporary interest.

References

Blei, D. M. (2012). Probabilistic topic models. *Communications of the ACM, 55*(4), 77–84.

Coleman, J. S. (1988). Social capital in the creation of human capital. *American Journal of Sociology, 94*, S95–S120.

DiMaggio, P., Nag, M., & Blei, D. (2013). Exploiting affinities between topic modeling and the sociological perspective on culture: Application to newspaper coverage of US government arts funding. *Poetics, 41*(6), 570–606.

Hornik, K., & Grün, B. (2011). Topicmodels: An R package for fitting topic models. *Journal of Statistical Software, 40*(13), 1–30.

Hull, D. A. (1996). Stemming algorithms: A case study for detailed evaluation. *JASIS, 47*(1), 70–84.

Kali, Y., Tabak, I., Ben-Zvi, D., Kidron, A., Amzaleg, M., Baram-Tsabari, A., et al. (2015). Technology-enhanced learning communities on a continuum between ambient to designed: What can we learn by synthesizing multiple research perspectives. In *The 11th international conference on the Computer Supported Collaborative Learning (CSCL)* (Vol. 1, pp. 615–622).

Mo, G. Y., Hayat, Z., & Wellman, B. (2015). How far can scholarly networks go? examining the relationships between distance, disciplines, motivations, and clusters. In *Communication and information technologies annual* (pp. 107–133). Bingley, UK: Emerald Group Publishing.

Raban, D. R., Gordon, A., & Geifman, D. (2011). The information society: The development of a scientific specialty. *Information, Communication & Society, 14*(3), 375–399.

Wellman, B., Dimitrova, D., Hayat, Z., Mo, G. Y., & Smale, L. (2014). Networking scholars in a networked organization. In *Contemporary perspectives on organizational social networks* (pp. 479–497). Bingley, UK: Emerald Group Publishing.

Part II
From Spontaneous to Designed TEL Communities

Chapter 4
Epistemic Thinking in a Networked Society: Contemporary Challenges and Educational Responses

Sarit Barzilai and Clark A. Chinn

Abstract The development and spread of new media and technologies are creating new challenges and opportunities for education. One of the key challenges, to which education needs to respond, is the wide-ranging impact of new media on people's capabilities to engage in reliable epistemic processes for achieving epistemic aims. As a result of this impact, participation in networked knowledge societies requires a greater degree of epistemic competence in order to successfully achieve epistemic aims. Therefore, we argue that education should promote learners' apt epistemic performance, i.e., their capabilities to achieve epistemic aims through competence, so that they are better prepared for navigating "post-truth" landscapes. We describe some educational approaches for achieving this objective. To conclude, we discuss the Knowledge Society Sandbox, a digital learning environment that supports knowledge construction from multiple information sources, and analyze how this environment is designed to promote learners' apt epistemic performance.

Keywords Epistemic education · Epistemic cognition · Apt epistemic performance · Networked society · New media · "Post-truth" · Knowledge Society Sandbox

The chapters in Part II of this book—From Spontaneous to Designed Technology Enhanced Learning (TEL) Communities—share a deep concern with how the affordances of new media are impacting democratic societies. These affordances are described by Baram-Tsabari and Schejter as a "double-edged sword" (Chap. 5). Wielded carelessly, they can endanger their bearers and society at large; wielded wisely, they promise great benefits for personal and social well-being and growth. The role of education, to continue this metaphor, is to train the bearers of this sword,

S. Barzilai (✉)
University of Haifa, Faculty of Education, Haifa, Israel
e-mail: sarit.barzilai@edtech.haifa.ac.il

C. A. Chinn
Rutgers University, Graduate School of Education, New Brunswick, NJ, USA

© Springer Nature Switzerland AG 2019
Y. Kali et al. (eds.), *Learning In a Networked Society*, Computer-Supported Collaborative Learning Series 17, https://doi.org/10.1007/978-3-030-14610-8_4

so that their arms are strong and nimble enough and their minds thoughtful enough, to wield it with accuracy, precision, and benevolence. Thus, the chapters in this section, including our own, discuss how *spontaneously* occurring changes, arising from the development and spread of new media and technologies, are creating new challenges and opportunities for education, and, consequently, how education can be *designed* to address these challenges and opportunities.

In this introductory chapter, we apply an epistemic thinking lens to the tales told by this set of chapters. Epistemic thinking, or epistemic cognition, is concerned with people's ways of knowing and their understandings of how people know (Barzilai & Chinn, 2018). Many of the challenges and opportunities discussed in the chapters of Part II of this book bear directly on people's ways of knowing. More specifically, we first show that the chapters describe many ways in which new media can increase as well as decrease people's capabilities to engage in reliable epistemic processes. Next, we analyze the educational implications of these developments. We argue that participation in networked knowledge societies requires a greater degree of epistemic competence in order to successfully achieve epistemic aims and that education should hence promote learners' capabilities to engage in *apt epistemic performance*. We then review some of the educational responses suggested by the chapters and suggest how they may contribute to addressing this goal. Finally, as one way to address the issues we have discussed, we describe the *Knowledge Society Sandbox*, a digital learning environment that supports knowledge construction from multiple information sources and analyze how the design of this environment is intended to promote learners' apt epistemic performance.

New Media in the Balance: Epistemic Risks and Opportunities

The chapters in this section examine spontaneously occurring learning in networked societies as a point of reference for defining educational goals and designing educational practices. Specifically, they look at public engagement with science (Baram-Tsabari and Schejter, Chap. 5), public participation in science (Sagy et al., Chap. 6), and pubic engagement in democratic discourse (Kidron et al., Chap. 7) as important forms of civic participation in networked societies and ask what role can education play in preparing students to engage in such civic participation. Collectively, the chapters point to ways in which new media can, on the one hand, enable and enrich civic participation and, on the other hand, limit or thwart participation.

Central to these analyses are the epistemic affordances of new media: All of the aforementioned forms of civic participation entail processes of accessing, producing, and communicating information and knowledge. The outcomes of these processes can be evaluated by examining whether individuals, groups, or society at large have gained new knowledge or new ways of knowing that can valuably contribute to individual and collective flourishing. Thus the outcomes of these processes correspond with the outcomes of "Eudaemonic Learning," which Hoadley and Kali (Chap. 1) describe as learning that enables individuals and society to mutually develop and flourish.

In what follows, we build on the descriptions of new media in the chapters of this section to analyze the impact of new media on epistemic processes that individuals and groups can engage in. Our analysis is grounded in the AIR model of epistemic thinking (Chinn & Rinehart, 2016; Chinn, Rinehart, & Buckland, 2014). This model includes three components: epistemic aims and value, epistemic ideals, and reliable epistemic processes. In brief, *epistemic aims* are goals of cognition and action that have a representational nature, such as acquiring true beliefs, avoiding error, justifying claims, or developing explanations and models. The *epistemic value* or importance that people assign to epistemic aims affects how they approach the achievement of these aims. For example, people who value accurate information about vaccines are likely to go to greater lengths to acquire such information. *Epistemic ideals* are criteria or norms for evaluating whether epistemic aims have been achieved. Epistemic ideals are used for evaluating epistemic products and justifying their acceptance—for example, for evaluating the quality of scientific models or the trustworthiness of websites. *Reliable epistemic processes* are cognitive and sociocognitive processes that dependably result in achievement of epistemic aims; examples are argumentation and evaluation of testimony. Sources of knowledge such as observation, memory, and testimony can also be viewed as reliable processes for producing knowledge.

Goldman (1986, 1987) proposed several epistemic criteria for evaluating individual and social epistemic processes: reliability, power, fecundity, speed, and efficiency. The *reliability* of an epistemic process or practice is reflected in the proportion of true beliefs among the beliefs it produces. The more reliable a process is, the higher the ratio of true beliefs it produces. *Power* reflects the problem-solving or question-answering capacity of epistemic processes. Powerful processes are ones that can produce a large number of valuable true beliefs. *Fecundity* reflects the extent to which the process can be employed by many people and not just by small groups of experts. Fecund processes are ones that enable larger groups of people to engage in knowledge production. Finally, *speed* refers to question answering speed and *efficiency* to the costs involved in answering questions.

In what follows, we explore the impact of new media on the reliability, power, fecundity, speed, and efficiency of knowledge acquisition and production processes. To do so, we follow the chapters of this section in building on Schejter and Tirosh's (2016) analysis of the nature of new media. Schejter and Tirosh argued that new media differ from older forms of communication in four fundamental ways: abundance, mobility, interactivity, and multimediality. We next discuss how each of these characteristics impacts knowledge acquisition and production processes. Our analysis is not meant to be exhaustive but rather to demonstrate some of the ways in which new media can change people's ways of knowing. For a summary, see Table 4.1.

Table 4.1 The impact of new media on knowledge production and acquisition processes

Property of new media	Criteria for evaluating epistemic processes			
	Reliability	Power	Fecundity	Speed and efficiency
Abundance	↑ By corroborating multiple sources of information, people may avoid adopting erroneous beliefs. ↓ People can find it more difficult to discern information trustworthiness and may be more susceptible to erroneous beliefs.	↑ People can obtain larger amounts of information, and this information can be more diverse. ↓ Difficulties with integrating information from multiple sources and analyzing large amounts of data can make it hard to find answers.	↑ More people can engage in knowledge production and dissemination. ↓ Gaps in digital access and skills can limit participation in knowledge production and curtail the spread of information across society.	↑ The abundance of information can enable faster access with fewer costs. ↓ Drawing reasonable conclusions from abundant but inconsistent information can require more time, effort, and resources.
Mobility	↑ People can collect data on the spot and share it swiftly. This can increase the accuracy and precision of available information. ↓ Information seeking on mobile devices may be short and perfunctory and may hence increase risk of error.	↑ Mobile devices increase opportunities to access and share information. Hence, people can find answers to a greater number of questions. ↓ Information produced on mobile devices tends to be of limited scope and depth, reducing its capacity to provide adequate answers.	↑ Mobile devices are widespread and relatively affordable, enabling more people to produce and acquire knowledge. ↓ Despite relative affordability, there are nonetheless people who lack mobile devices and needed bandwidth, limiting fecundity.	↑ People can more quickly and easily obtain information when they need it and where they need it. ↓ Getting high-quality information quickly on small, slower mobile devices may be difficult.

Interactivity	↑ People have more tools and resources for individual and collective knowledge validation processes. ↓ Tailoring and filtering of information environments can reduce exposure to alternative ideas and viewpoints, thus creating greater risk of error.	↑ Collaborative knowledge building can result in knowledge that is enriched by the interaction of multiple voices and perspectives. ↓ Difficulties in participating in multivoiced discourse may lead to exclusion of important voices, which are needed to for powerful knowledge production.	↑ Collaborations between groups that usually do not have opportunities to interact create new opportunities for participation in diverse epistemic communities and practices. ↓ Interactive discourse may also result in the marginalization and exclusion of people and groups from various epistemic practices.	↑ Tailoring of information environments can increase the speed and efficiency of gaining personally useful information. ↓ Interactivity may reduce speed and efficiency of knowledge acquisition and production because it can require prolonged active engagement.
Multimediality	↑ Under proper conditions, multimedia can improve the accuracy of knowledge acquisition. ↓ Multimedia messages may be evaluated less critically, contributing to the spread of inaccurate information.	↑ Combination of text and images can improve learning and enhance interest, thereby promoting more extensive knowledge acquisition. ↓ Inappropriate uses of multimedia can impair knowledge acquisition.	↑ Digital tools and devices enable a greater number of people to create and share images and videos that can provide important information and documentation. ↓ Creation of multimedia messages may require technical resources and know-how that are not available to all.	↑ Digital devices, tools, and networks lower image and video production and sharing costs and enable swift and efficient access. ↓ Multimedia representations can increase cognitive load and require slower and more effortful processing.

Note. An upward facing arrow (↑) indicates positive effects, and a downward facing arrow (↓) indicates negative effects.

Abundance

Access to information, to the channels through which it travels, and to means of storing it used to be scarce and costly (Schejter & Tirosh, 2016). This scarcity led to systems of control of communication processes. In contrast, new media are characterized by an abundance of means for producing, communicating, and storing information. The increase in epistemic power is dramatic: People can now use a variety of digital tools and resources to obtain larger amounts of information and can find more answers to more questions that interest them (Baram-Tsabari & Schejter, Chap. 5; Kidron et al., Chap. 7). The information has also become more diverse, reflecting more viewpoints and data sources (Coady, 2012). The ability to corroborate information from multiple sources can increase reliability by identifying inaccuracies or errors. The increase in people engaging in knowledge production and dissemination reflects an increase in fecundity (Sagy et al., Chap. 6); and more sophisticated search tools enable accessing information in greater speed and efficiency.

On the other hand, much of the information available online is inaccurate, and diverse sources can make it more difficult to distinguish between trustworthy and untrustworthy information (Baram-Tsabari & Schejter, Chap. 5; Kidron et al., Chap. 7; Bromme, Stadtler, & Scharrer, 2018). As a result, people may fall into error. Additionally, people may find it difficult to integrate information from the abundant information sources (Bråten, Braasch, & Salmerón, in press; Stadtler, Bromme, & Rouet, 2018) and to draw reasonable conclusions from large amounts of data (Sagy et al., Chap. 6). These difficulties reduce the power, speed, and efficiency of knowledge acquisition. Finally, there is a danger that this abundant information may be available only to those who have digital access and the requisite digital information skills (Hargittai & Hsieh, 2013; Kidron et al., 2018/this volume). As a result, information may be unevenly spread across society.

Mobility

Whereas former electronic media were largely stationary, new media are increasingly mobile (i.e., cellular phones, tablets, and wearable devices). This enables communicating at will from diverse locations and produces changes in norms and patterns of communication (Schejter & Tirosh, 2016). Mobility can increase epistemic power, speed, and efficiency by overcoming limits of time and place. People are more likely to find relevant information they need when they need it (Baram-Tsabari & Schejter, Chap. 5). In terms of information production, mobile devices enable collecting data from any place and sharing it swiftly (Baram-Tsabari & Schejter, Chap. 5). This can increase the amount, accuracy, and currency available of data, contributing to both power and reliability. Mobile devices may also increase fecundity in virtue of their being widespread in the population (Schejter & Tirosh,

2016). This enables more people to contribute to citizen science data collection initiatives (Sagy et al., Chap. 6), to share information about emerging political, social, and environmental events, and to immediately discuss this information with others, potentially learning other perspectives.

However, information seeking on mobile devices may have limited reliability and power compared to stationary devices. For example, search queries are shorter on mobile devices, and people tend to look at fewer information sources and examine these in a more cursory manner (Napoli & Obar, 2014). Also, because of their limited input tools (e.g., smaller keypads), content creation on mobile devices tends to be of limited scope and depth (Napoli & Obar, 2014). This may lower accuracy and comprehensiveness. Finally, not all people may have access to mobile devices and adequate bandwidth.

Interactivity

Interactivity, in Schejter and Tirosh's (2016) framework, refers to "users' capability to design for themselves their own media environments, including the identity of those they converse with, and the ability to contribute their own content to these environments" (p. 16). In older media (e.g., television, newspapers), content was created by few and passively received by many. New media lower the barriers for active production and sharing of information; people can react, actively contribute content, engage in extensive discussions, and tailor their own information environments (Baram-Tsabari & Schejter, Chap. 5). Interactivity can promote knowledge acquisition through helping people learn from each other and enabling collaborative knowledge construction (Kidron et al., 2018, Chap. 7). Furthermore, the quality of knowledge can be enriched when people bring new information and ideas from their various spheres into the conversation (Baram-Tsabari & Schejter, Chap. 5). All these opportunities increase people's capabilities to gain knowledge—that is, they increase epistemic power. Interactivity can also increase the reliability of knowledge acquisition by enabling individuals and groups to screen and validate the knowledge that they find online. For example, people can google authors to examine their track records or refer to collaborative fact checking websites (Caulfield, 2017). New media can also enable collaborations between groups that usually do not have opportunities to interact, such as citizens and scientists, thus increasing fecundity by offering greater opportunities for participation in diverse communities and practices (Sagy et al., Chap. 6).

Nonetheless, the promise of interactivity may fail to materialize. Some people may not be motivated or may find it difficult to engage in multivoiced discourse; as a result, not all voices may be heard and included in knowledge building (Kidron et al., Chap. 7). Additionally, both intentional and automated tailoring of information environments can result in "information bubbles" or "echo chambers" in which people expose themselves only to a restricted set of congenial ideas (Bakshy, Messing, & Adamic, 2015; Baram-Tsabari & Schejter, 2018/this volume). This might reduce both power and reliability by lowering exposure to alternative ideas and viewpoints (Lynch, 2016).

Multimediality

Multimediality refers to the capability to create or transmit messages using a variety of forms of expression—text, static images, dynamic images, and sound (Schejter & Tirosh, 2016). Multimediality can increase the power of knowledge acquisition because the combination of text and images can improve people's capacities and inclinations to learn about complex concepts and processes (Baram-Tsabari & Schejter, 2018/this volume; Kidron et al., 2018/this volume; Mayer, 2014). Multimediality enables people to convey social presence (Schejter & Tirosh, 2016) and can thus promote knowledge-producing social interactions. Digital tools and devices enable a greater number of people to create and share images and videos that can provide important, often accurate information. The ease and speed of accessing these multimedia resources have dramatically increased due to image and video sharing networks, such as Snapchat and YouTube.

Conversely, researchers have found that multimedia is beneficial only when texts and images are combined in particular ways; otherwise, it can increase cognitive load and decrease comprehension (Baram-Tsabari & Schejter, 2018/this volume; Mayer, 2014). Finally, people may find it difficult to evaluate the trustworthiness and quality of multimedia messages such as digital images (Barzilai & Eilam, 2018; Wineburg, McGrew, Breakstone, & Ortega, 2016) and digital games (Barzilai, 2017). Thus, multimedia messages—which are often especially persuasive—may be evaluated less critically and can decrease reliability through the spread of inaccurate information (Lynch, 2016; Sagy et al., 2018/this volume).

Envisioning New Goals for Epistemic Education

As the preceding analysis illustrates, new media can both increase and decrease the reliability, power, fecundity, speed, and efficiency of people's epistemic processes. This can have a wide-reaching impact on people's capabilities to achieve valuable epistemic aims. How should education respond to this challenge? Elsewhere, we have argued that participation in networked knowledge societies requires a greater degree of epistemic competence in order to successfully achieve epistemic aims and that education should, therefore, focus on promoting students' capabilities to engage in *apt epistemic performance* (Barzilai & Chinn, 2018). In this section we briefly explain this notion.

According to philosopher Ernest Sosa (2011, 2015), epistemic performances such as forming a belief or making a judgment can be judged by their epistemic success, for example, by whether the belief is accurate or the judgment is the most reasonable one that can be achieved. Epistemic performances can also be judged according to their competence, for example, according to whether the belief or the judgment was well formed by appropriately considering all the relevant information. An apt epistemic performance is one in which the agent successfully achieves her epistemic aims through the exercise of her epistemic competence and not by luck or chance. Competent epistemic performance is valuable because it is less likely to fail.

To ensure fully apt performance, agents must also possess the epistemic meta-competence of determining whether they are capable of performing aptly in a particular situation. For example, a person who successfully evaluates the validity of information on a health website does so aptly when she is adept at evaluating online information, and her success arises from her adeptness. She does so fully aptly if she knows when her competence is sufficient to successfully evaluate information on websites on her own and when her competence is insufficient so that she should defer to experts or withhold judgment (Barzilai & Zohar, 2016; Bromme & Goldman, 2014).

Building on Sosa's account, we have proposed that the overarching purpose of epistemic education should be to *promote fully apt epistemic performance* (Barzilai & Chinn, 2018). This means that the primary objective of epistemic education should be to enable learners to reliably succeed, through epistemic competence, in activities such as forming accurate judgments or evaluating arguments, across a range of situations, as well as to appraise accurately through epistemic meta-competence when success can be achieved reliably enough.

Although apt epistemic performance has always been important, the impact of new media has increased its importance. New media can enable greater epistemic success while also threatening to make people significantly less successful. Consequently, education should enable students to perform aptly with new media despite the challenges described in Table 4.1. Furthermore, to handle the "double-edged sword" of new media, students also need meta-competence that will enable them to regulate their epistemic performance. For example, they need to realize that by integrating multiple sources of information, they can achieve a more accurate and comprehensive understanding and that failure to consider multiple perspectives and to compare and weigh these can lead to poorer understanding. Such meta-level understanding can inform the regulation of these epistemic processes (e.g., "Did I consider all the important perspectives? Did I compare and contrast them?") and may make the difference between successful and unsuccessful epistemic performance.

What Does It Take to Promote Apt Epistemic Performance?

To further unpack the notion of promoting apt epistemic performance, we have proposed that educators need to attend to five aspects of such performance (Barzilai & Chinn, 2018). These aspects specify the nature of apt epistemic performance vis-à-vis the three key components of the AIR model (Chinn et al., 2014)—epistemic aims and value, epistemic ideals, and reliable epistemic processes. Hence, we have dubbed this framework as the Apt-AIR framework:

- *Aspect 1 - Cognitive engagement in epistemic performance.* Learners should be able to identify valuable epistemic aims and to engage in processes that can reliably achieve these aims, in accordance with epistemic ideals (e.g., aiming to find if vaccines are safe and skillfully searching for an evidence-based answer).

- *Aspect 2 - Adapting epistemic performance.* Learners should be able to achieve these epistemic aims in an adaptive manner that takes into account the type of aim, the type of information available, the area- and domain-specific standards and practices, and the affordances of the media in diverse situations (e.g., reliable processes of finding out if vaccines are safe are not the same as reliable processes of finding out which local candidate has the best record of achievement).

- *Aspect 3 - Understanding and regulating epistemic performance.* Learners should be capable of successfully managing and coordinating their epistemic performance. This requires metacognitive skills for monitoring one's personal knowledge and appropriately selecting and managing epistemic processes for improving that knowledge as well as metacognitive knowledge about various epistemic ideals and processes (including social processes) that people can use to achieve their epistemic aims (e.g., knowledge about how to evaluate the trustworthiness of online information sources and about important evaluation criteria). This metacognitive knowledge includes an appreciation of the reasons why particular aims and ideals are valuable (e.g., why finding accurate information is vital to achieving other goals such as better health or a flourishing democracy) and why particular processes should be viewed as reliable or not (e.g., why studies published in peer reviewed journals are generally more reliable than studies that have not undergone peer review).

- *Aspect 4 - Caring about and enjoying epistemic performance.* Apt epistemic performance can be effortful, and hence learners should ideally have motivational-affective dispositions to achieve valuable epistemic aims. This includes caring about how epistemic aims are achieved, wanting to achieve them in a good kind of way, and even enjoying achieving valuable epistemic aims (e.g., wanting to understand the causes of pollution in one's area enough to make the effort to combine multiple sources of information in a careful and responsible manner).

- *Aspect 5 - Participating in epistemic performance together with others.* Finally, apt epistemic performance requires capabilities for achieving epistemic aims in varied social configurations and settings (e.g., engaging in collaborative knowledge building on Wikis) as well as understanding the fundamentally social nature of knowledge production and dissemination (e.g., appreciating that scientific consensus is formed through socially established community processes, such as systematic reviews and expert panels, and that although these are fallible, they are nonetheless more reliable than relying on the testimony of an individual expert).

In school, students are still typically expected to perform in an epistemically "safe" climate in which the information they receive is carefully monitored and regulated to ensure its trustworthiness, quality, and appropriateness (Goldberg, 2013). However, the epistemic climate that awaits student outside of school is decidedly "unsafe" and is characterized by abundant information that can be inaccurate, diverse, and complex to process. Students who are capable of engaging in apt epistemic performance stand to gain substantial benefits. In contrast, students who are incapable of doing so face risks such as being poorly informed, making ill-informed decisions, and failing to make their perspective count aptly in social knowledge-building processes.

Thus, it is no surprise that a sense of urgency and responsibility underlies the papers in this section. For example, Kidron et al. write, "we argue that in face of the possible threats described, contemporary media's added value to democratic processes is not obvious and that only careful design of the way these media are used, especially in the context of educational interventions, can lead to positive change and a better future in terms of democracy and education" (p. X, this volume). Furthermore, all of the chapters call for transformative—even radical—changes in how education approaches the task of helping prepare students for participation in knowledge societies. For example, Sagy et al. call for breaking the boundaries between schools and science by involving students in citizen science, and Kidron et al. seek to transform the traditional structure of a university course by breaking boundaries between disciplines and learners.

In both chapters, the authors pay attention to engaging students in activities that will foster their abilities to cognitively engage in epistemic processes that are important for functioning in networked societies (Aspect 1 of Apt-Air). For example, Sagy et al. call for developing students' abilities to draw inferences from big data, and Kidron et al. call for fostering students' capabilities to integrate ideas from different disciplines to address complex problems. Both chapters also foreground the importance of developing students' capabilities of engaging in such epistemic performances together with others (Aspect 5 of Apt-Air). For example, Sagy et al. envision citizen science as a community effort that requires developing the skills of engaging in knowledge building in communities whose participants have diverse areas and levels of expertise. Kidron et al. propose engaging students in collaborative knowledge-building activities and peer-review processes.

In the next section, we present another example of an instructional approach to addressing the challenges of learning in spontaneous networked societies. We discuss the "Knowledge Society Sandbox"—a digital educational environment that aims to promote students' apt epistemic performance.

The Knowledge Society Sandbox: Promoting Apt Epistemic Performance

As we have described, a main challenge to learning in a networked society is draw-ing reasonable conclusions and developing coherent understandings from abundant information sources reflecting diverse purposes and viewpoints (Alexander & DRLRL, 2012; Leu, Kinzer, Coiro, Castek, & Henry, 2013). Making sense of mul-tiple information sources requires constructing coherent meaning from texts that may present complementary, inconsistent, or conflicting information on the same situation, issue, or phenomenon (Bråten et al., in press). Doing so well involves performance of multiple processes or strategies—chiefly, task interpretation, search-ing for information sources, evaluating the quality and trustworthiness of informa-tion sources, analyzing these documents, integrating information, and communicating the analysis and its conclusion in a coherent and responsible manner (Goldman, Lawless, & Manning, 2013; Rouet & Britt, 2011).

Numerous studies have demonstrated that many students find it difficult to engage in such meaning making from multiple information sources. For example, students may fail to actively evaluate source trustworthiness and may be unfamiliar with appropriate criteria for doing so (e.g., Barzilai, Tzadok, & Eshet-Alkalai, 2015; Coiro, Coscarelli, Maykel, & Forzani, 2015). Students may experience difficulties comparing, weighing, and integrating information from multiple sources (e.g., Barzilai & Ka'adan, 2017; Solé, Miras, Castells, Espino, & Minguela, 2013). Furthermore, students' epistemic assumptions regarding the characteristics of desir-able sources of knowledge, standards for justifying and accepting knowledge, and strategies for knowing can influence how they go about constructing knowledge from these sources (Barzilai & Eshet-Alkalai, 2015; Bråten, Britt, Strømsø, & Rouet, 2011; Kammerer, Bråten, Gerjets, & Strømsø, 2013).

In response to these challenges, Barzilai and the Center for Educational Technology[1] (CET) have developed a digital learning environment for secondary school students called "The Knowledge Society Sandbox." The development of the Sandbox environment is part of the research initiatives of the LINKS Israeli Center of Research Excellence (I-CORE) that serve the public at large. The Sandbox is currently available online to all of the public secondary schools in Israel. The over-arching aim of the Sandbox is to promote students' abilities to critically construct knowledge from multiple information sources and to foster their epistemic under-standings regarding knowledge construction and evaluation.

As suggested by its name, the Sandbox is a digital environment in which students can engage with authentically diverse information sources in a "safe" space, which enables exploration and learning, with dedicated supports and lower risks. The Sandbox simulates the learning that occurs in spontaneous knowledge societies, yet within a designed environment whose aim is to prepare students for meeting future

---

[1] http://www.home.cet.ac.il/

challenges. Thus, the Sandbox bridges between the spontaneous learning that occurs in networked societies and the highly designed learning that occurs at school.

The Sandbox incudes three main components:

1. *A collection of tasks* that require evaluation, analysis, and integration of multiple information sources. Each includes a task statement and a set of information sources carefully chosen to represent diverse viewpoints, genres, credibility, quality, and more. Students and teachers can add and remove information sources and create their own tasks.
2. *Cognitive scaffolds* that support knowledge construction processes. These scaffolds help students evaluate the credibility and relevance of the information sources, identify their claims and supporting reasons, map the network of links among sources and claims, and write based on multiple information sources.
3. *Metacognitive scaffolds and supports* that promote regulation and understanding of knowledge construction and evaluation. These scaffolds include metacognitive monitoring and evaluation prompts, short explanations about relevant epistemic concepts (e.g., "credibility"), and longer units that engage students in learning about when, why, and how one evaluates and integrates multiple information sources, and other relevant issues.

In the next paragraphs we take a closer look at how the design of the sandbox is intended to promote apt epistemic performance along the five aspects of the Apt-AIR framework.

Promoting Cognitive Engagement in Epistemic Performance (Aspect 1)

The design of the Sandbox is based on current theoretical models of multiple document comprehension (Braasch & Bråten, 2017; Britt, Rouet, & Braasch, 2013; Rouet & Britt, 2011; Rouet, Britt, & Durik, 2017) and supports students through several phases of knowledge construction: understanding the task and its requirements, evaluating and selecting information sources, analyzing information sources, creating an integrative representation, producing a written product, and evaluating and revising this product. Here we focus on how the Sandbox supports engagement with two central epistemic strategies—evaluation and integration of multiple information sources.

The evaluation scaffold addresses students' tendency to neglect to evaluate information sources and, if they do so, to focus primarily on criteria of relevance and communicative quality and less on criteria of information validity and source credibility (e.g., Barzilai & Zohar, 2012; Kiili, Laurinen, & Marttunen, 2008). The evaluation scaffold includes a set of questions about each information source (e.g., "Is the author an expert?"). Based on these questions, students rate the credibility and relevance of the information sources. These ratings impact the visual representation

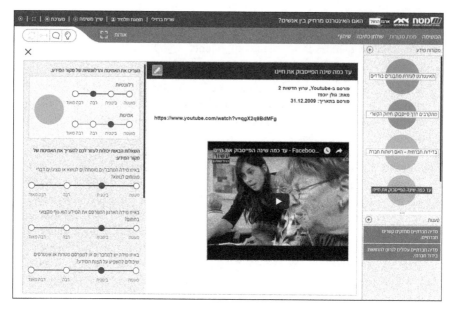

Fig. 4.1 Information source evaluation scaffold

of the information sources (color and size respectively), thus making students' evaluations visible and salient through the knowledge construction process (see Fig. 4.1).

The integration scaffold includes a visual map based on the Documents Model framework (Britt & Rouet, 2012; Rouet, 2006). Briefly, this framework posits that in order to comprehend multiple information sources dealing with the same issue, readers need to (a) build a coherent mental representation of the situations described in the texts, (b) represent the sources of that information, (c) track the relations between sources and contents (source-content links), and (d) understand how the sources are related to each other (source-source links).

The integration scaffold supports construction of documents models by enabling students to create main claims, link them to sources, define the nature of these links (attribution, support, or opposition), and enter reasons for these links (e.g., why the source supports the claim). Students can also create links among sources and among claims (see Fig. 4.2). The integration scaffold supports integration by making sources, main claims, and their connections visible and salient, enabling students to keep track of these elements as they read through multiple information sources, and by concentrating this information in a single display. These features can help students identify, corroborate, and weigh claims.

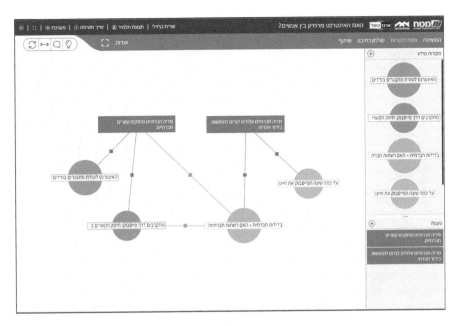

Fig. 4.2 Information source integration scaffold

Fig. 4.3 Disciplinary diverse multiple source units: from the crusaders to vaccinations

Promoting Adaptive Epistemic Performance (Aspect 2)

The Sandbox design aims to promote adaptive epistemic performance in two ways. First, the Sandbox offers a wide range of units that address multiple issues from different disciplinary areas (language arts, history, geography, citizenship, science, and social studies) (see Fig. 4.3). Further, these differ in their task types (e.g., summary or argument tasks), types of information sources (e.g., newspaper articles, social media postings, YouTube videos, charts, and more), and relations among the information sources (e.g., conflicting or complementary). In this way, students can learn that evaluation and integration have some commonalities across tasks, topics, and disciplines, yet that there are also important differences in how information sources are evaluated and integrated in these contexts. Through engaging with diverse units, students can learn to adapt their evaluation and integration performance and can develop sensitivity to how different task conditions may require attending to different epistemic criteria and processes (Barzilai & Chinn, 2018). Reflective activities in class can draw attention to these similarities and differences.

Second, the evaluation prompts and the metacognitive scaffolds (see the next section) can be tailored for each unit. For example, the information source evaluation questions in science, history, and citizenship units have some commonalities (e.g., examining author expertise) but also some differences (e.g., examining the availability and quality of empirical support for claims in science units and examining the identity of the author and the context in which the document was produced in history units). This design further highlights that different epistemic criteria may be important in different contexts.

Promoting Regulation and Understanding of Epistemic Performance (Aspect 3)

One of the aims of the Sandbox is to help students regulate their epistemic performance and to develop their metacognitive understanding of the nature, value, and uses of epistemic aims, ideals, and processes. Building on prior research on metacognitive scaffolds for inquiry (e.g., Bannert & Reimann, 2012; Quintana, Zhang, & Krajcik, 2005; Stadtler & Bromme, 2008), the Sandbox includes three types of metacognitive scaffolds and supports: meta-epistemic regulation prompts, meta-epistemic explanations, and meta-epistemic learning units.

The *meta-epistemic regulation prompts* support regulation of epistemic performance through cueing metacognitive planning, monitoring, and evaluation during knowledge construction and evaluation. For example, in the evaluation phase, students are asked, "Did I evaluate the credibility and relevance of the information source?" and more. During the integration phase, students are asked, "Did I identify if the information sources agree with each other?" (see Fig. 4.4).

The *meta-epistemic explanations* provide short, just-in-time explanations about concepts, criteria, and processes that students encounter as they work in the Sandbox. For example, in the evaluation phase, students can read brief explanations about why it is important to evaluate information sources, how to evaluate the credibility and relevance, how to identify the viewpoint of the author, and more. During the integration phase, students can read brief explanations about what source-content

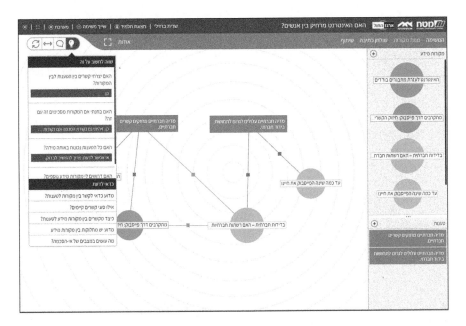

Fig. 4.4 Meta-epistemic prompts and explanations

links are, why they are important, how to create them, and more (Fig. 4.4). These brief meta-epistemic explanations link to *meta-epistemic units*. These units include learning sequences that span one to two lessons and that address evaluation, integration, and writing with multiple information sources in greater depth. These meta-cognitive supports are designed to support meaningful discussion and understanding of epistemic aims, ideals, and processes.

Promoting Caring About and Enjoying Epistemic Performance (Aspect 4)

In order to foster students' motivation to engage in knowledge construction and evaluation, the topics chosen for the Sandbox units are intended to evoke adolescents' interest by exploring meaningful issues or provocative dilemmas with personal or social relevance. For example, units explore issues such as whether youth should be required to volunteer, whether there is equality between women and men in Israel, whether one should try to counter globalization, and whether playing computer games increases violence. When students investigate meaningful and relevant problems, they are more likely to care about whether epistemic aims are achieved and how well they are achieved.

Another way in which the Sandbox aims to increase motivation is by fostering students' autonomy. Students have a large degree of control over their knowledge construction and evaluation processes: They are free to add or remove information sources at will, to evaluate these information sources as they see fit, and to focus on the claims that they deem to be most relevant. The metacognitive scaffolds support student autonomy by offering relevant cues and information that can help students take charge of their own learning.

A third motivation mechanism is the social structure of the Sandbox. Students share their maps and their essays with their classmates and teachers and receive feedback from them. Class discussions about how to evaluate and integrate multiple information sources can also create a greater sense of commitment to engaging in these reliable processes and applying appropriate epistemic ideals.

Finally, the Sandbox is also meant to make the intimidating task of working with multiple information sources more appealing and pleasurable. This is achieved by breaking down and scaffolding this task to make it easier and by offering engaging visual tools. Preliminary observations and feedback suggest that students indeed enjoy using these visual tools to create their own integration maps.

Promoting Participation in Epistemic Performance Together with Others (Aspect 5)

Knowledge production, sharing, and consumption in networked societies are deeply social (Goldman, 2011). In the Sandbox, students learn how to deal with information created by others: They learn how to evaluate information from diverse sources as well as how to integrate information that reflects diverse purposes and viewpoints. Thus, students learn how to engage in individual epistemic processes that address social epistemic processes of information production.

Students also have opportunities to engage in group epistemic processes in dyads or small groups. As mentioned, the products of the Sandbox can be shared, and classmates can provide comments on these products. Thus, students learn how to give and receive peer feedback—a valuable social process for improving epistemic products. This provides opportunities for students to learn how to engage in shared knowledge development through argumentation and other forms of co-construction.

The meta-epistemic prompts encourage students to engage in discussion of their shared epistemic ideals and processes (cf. Chinn, Duncan, & Rinehart, 2018). For example, they can discuss and compare how they evaluated sources and how they formed their judgments. Students also have opportunities to jointly develop epistemic criteria. Such social epistemic processes are requisites for forming knowledge producing communities (Longino, 1990). For example, the quality of knowledge on Wikipedia is regulated by the ongoing discussion and development of socially accepted epistemic norms that govern knowledge production (Oeberst, Halatchliyski, Kimmerle, & Cress, 2014). Hence, participating in discussions about epistemic criteria is a valuable social epistemic process.

Education in a Networked Society: Capitalizing on the Opportunities, Overcoming the Challenges

All the chapters in this section, including our own, chart new opportunities and challenges of learning in a networked society. Although the chapters have different foci, they converge in arguing that education must cultivate learners' capabilities to produce and evaluate knowledge in order to reap the potentially transformative benefits of information and communication technologies, while avoiding the risks that they pose. These benefits include increasing the reliability, power, fecundity, speed, and efficacy of knowledge-producing processes; the risks involve decreasing all of these. We have suggested that education for a networked society requires promoting learners' apt epistemic performance—that is, promoting their capabilities and dispositions to successfully achieve valuable epistemic aims through competence. We have described five aspects that we believe are essential for promoting such apt epistemic performance: engaging in reliable cognitive processes that lead to achievement of epistemic aims, adapting epistemic performance to diverse situations, metacognitively regulating and understanding epistemic performance, caring about and enjoying epistemic performance, and participating in epistemic performance together with others. Promoting these ends will require educational designs that enable both individuals and groups to gain adeptness in all five aspects, whether designing for public engagement in science, for citizen science, or for engagement in public engagement in democratic discourse.

Bibliography

Alexander, P. A., & DRLRL. (2012). Reading into the future: Competence for the 21st century. *Educational Psychologist, 47*(4), 259–280.

Bakshy, E., Messing, S., & Adamic, L. (2015). Exposure to ideologically diverse news and opinion on facebook. *Science* 348(6239), 1130–1132.

Bannert, M., & Reimann, P. (2012). Supporting self-regulated hypermedia learning through prompts. *Instructional Science, 40*(1), 193–211.

Barzilai, S. (2017). "Half-reliable": A qualitative analysis of epistemic thinking in and about a digital game. *Contemporary Educational Psychology, 51*, 51–66.

Barzilai, S., & Chinn, C. A. (2018). On the goals of epistemic education: Promoting apt epistemic performance. *Journal of the Learning Sciences, 27*, 353–389.

Barzilai, S., & Eilam, B. (2018). Learners' epistemic criteria and strategies for evaluating scientific visual representations. *Learning and Instruction, 58*, 137–147.

Barzilai, S., & Eshet-Alkalai, Y. (2015). The role of epistemic perspectives in comprehension of multiple author viewpoints. *Learning and Instruction, 36*, 86–103.

Barzilai, S., & Ka'adan, I. (2017). Learning to integrate divergent information sources: The interplay of epistemic cognition and epistemic metacognition. *Metacognition and Learning, 12*, 193–232.

Barzilai, S., Tzadok, E., & Eshet-Alkalai, Y. (2015). Sourcing while reading divergent expert accounts: Pathways from views of knowing to written argumentation. *Instructional Science, 43*(6), 737–766.

Barzilai, S., & Zohar, A. (2012). Epistemic thinking in action: Evaluating and integrating online sources. *Cognition and Instruction, 30*(1), 39–85.

Barzilai, S., & Zohar, A. (2016). Epistemic (meta)cognition: Ways of thinking about knowledge and knowing. In J. A. Greene, W. A. Sandoval, & I. Bråten (Eds.), *Handbook of epistemic cognition* (pp. 409–424). New York: Routledge.

Braasch, J. L. G., & Bråten, I. (2017). The discrepancy-induced source comprehension (D-ISC) model: Basic assumptions and preliminary evidence. *Educational Psychologist, 52*(3), 167–181.

Bråten, I., Braasch, J., & Salmerón, L. (in press). Reading multiple and non-traditional texts: New opportunities and new challenges. In E. B. Moje, P. Afflerbach, P. Enciso, & N. K. Lesaux (Eds.), *Handbook of reading research* (Vol. V). New York: Routledge.

Bråten, I., Britt, M. A., Strømsø, H. I., & Rouet, J.-F. (2011). The role of epistemic beliefs in the comprehension of multiple expository texts: Toward an integrated model. *Educational Psychologist, 46*(1), 48–70.

Britt, M. A., & Rouet, J.-F. (2012). Learning with multiple documents: Component skills and their acquisition. In J. R. Kirby & M. J. Lawson (Eds.), *Enhancing the quality of learning: Dispositions, instruction, and learning processes* (pp. 276–314). New York: Cambridge University Press.

Britt, M. A., Rouet, J.-F., & Braasch, J. L. G. (2013). Documents as entities: Extending the situation model theory of comprehension. In M. A. Britt, S. R. Goldman, & J.-F. Rouet (Eds.), *Reading - from words to multiple texts* (pp. 160–179). New York: Routledge.

Bromme, R., & Goldman, S. R. (2014). The public's bounded understanding of science. *Educational Psychologist, 49*(2), 59–69.

Bromme, R., Stadtler, M., & Scharrer, L. (2018). The provenance of certainty: Multiple source use and the public engagement with science. In J. L. G. Braasch, I. Bråten, & M. T. McCrudden (Eds.), *Handbook of multiple source use* (pp. 269–284). New York: Routledge.

Caulfield, M. A. (2017). *Web literacy for student fact checkers*. Retrieved from https://webliteracy. pressbooks.com/

Chinn, C. A., & Rinehart, R. W. (2016). Epistemic cognition and philosophy: Developing a new framework for epistemic cognition. In J. A. Greene, W. A. Sandoval, & I. Bråten (Eds.), *Handbook of epistemic cognition* (pp. 460–478). New York: Routledge.

Chinn, C. A., Rinehart, R. W., & Buckland, L. A. (2014). Epistemic cognition and evaluating information: Applying the air model of epistemic cognition. In D. Rapp & J. Braasch (Eds.), *Processing inaccurate information* (pp. 425–454). Cambridge, MA: MIT Press.

Chinn, C. A., Duncan, R. G., & Rinehart, R. W. (2018). Epistemic design: Design to promote transferable epistemic growth in the PRACCIS project. In E. Manalo, Y. Uesaka & C. A. Chinn (Eds.), *Promoting spontaneous use of learning and reasoning strategies: Theory, research, and practice for effective transfer* (pp. 242–259). New York, NY: Routledge.

Coady, D. (2012). *What to believe now: Applying epistemology to contemporary issues*. Malden, MA: Wiley-Blackwell.

Coiro, J., Coscarelli, C., Maykel, C., & Forzani, E. (2015). Investigating criteria that seventh graders use to evaluate the quality of online information. *Journal of Adolescent & Adult Literacy, 59*(3), 287–297.

Goldman, A. I. (1986). *Epistemology and cognition*. Cambridge, MA: Harvard University Press.

Goldman, A. I. (1987). Foundations of social epistemics. *Synthese, 73*(1), 109–144.

Goldman, A. I. (2011). A guide to social epistemology. In A. I. Goldman & D. Whitcomb (Eds.), *Social epistemology: Essential readings* (pp. 11–37). New York: Oxford University Press.

Goldman, S. R., Lawless, K., & Manning, F. (2013). Research and development of multiple source comprehension assessment. In M. A. Britt, S. R. Goldman, & J.-F. Rouet (Eds.), *Reading - from words to multiple texts* (pp. 160–179). New York: Routledge.

Goldberg, S. (2013) Epistemic Dependence in Testimonial Belief, in the Classroom and Beyond. *Journal of Philosophy of Education, 47*(2), 168–186.

Hargittai, E., & Hsieh, Y. P. (2013). Digital inequality. In W. H. Dutton (Ed.), *Oxford handbook of internet studies* (pp. 129–150). Oxford, UK: Oxford University Press.

Kammerer, Y., Bråten, I., Gerjets, P., & Strømsø, H. I. (2013). The role of Internet-specific epistemic beliefs in laypersons' source evaluations and decisions during web search on a medical issue. *Computers in Human Behavior, 29*(3), 1193–1203.

Kiili, C., Laurinen, L., & Marttunen, M. (2008). Students evaluating Internet sources: From versatile evaluators to uncritical readers. *Journal of Educational Computing Research, 39*(1), 75–95.

Leu, D. J., Kinzer, C. K., Coiro, J., Castek, J., & Henry, L. A. (2013). New literacies: A dual level theory of the changing nature of literacy, instruction, and assessment. In D. E. Alvermann, N. J. Unrau, & R. B. Ruddell (Eds.), *Theoretical models and processes of reading* (6th ed., pp. 1150–1181). Newark, DE: International Reading Association.

Longino, H. E. (1990). *Science as social knowledge: Values and objectivity in scientific inquiry.* Princeton, NJ: Princeton University Press.

Lynch, M. P. (2016). *The internet of us: Knowing more and understanding less in the age of big data.* New York: WW Norton & Company.

Mayer, R. E. (Ed.). (2014). *Cambridge handbook of multimedia learning* (2nd ed.). New York: Cambridge University Press.

Napoli, P. M., & Obar, J. A. (2014). The emerging mobile internet underclass: A critique of mobile internet access. *The Information Society, 30*(5), 323–334.

Oeberst, A., Halatchliyski, I., Kimmerle, J., & Cress, U. (2014). Knowledge construction in Wikipedia: A systemic-constructivist analysis. *Journal of the Learning Sciences, 23*(2), 149–176.

Quintana, C., Zhang, M., & Krajcik, J. (2005). A framework for supporting metacognitive aspects of online inquiry through software-based scaffolding. *Educational Psychologist, 40*(4), 235–244.

Rouet, J.-F. (2006). *The skills of document use: From text comprehension to web-based learning.* Mahwah, NJ: Lawrence Erlbaum Associates.

Rouet, J.-F., & Britt, M. A. (2011). Relevance processes in multiple document comprehension. In M. T. McCrudden, J. P. Magliano, & G. Schraw (Eds.), *Text relevance and learning from text* (pp. 19–52). Charlotte, NC: Information Age Publishing.

Rouet, J.-F., Britt, M. A., & Durik, A. M. (2017). RESOLV: Readers' representation of reading contexts and tasks. *Educational Psychologist, 52(3)*, 200–215.

Solé, I., Miras, M., Castells, N., Espino, S., & Minguela, M. (2013). Integrating information: An analysis of the processes involved and the products generated in a written synthesis task. *Written Communication, 30*(1), 63–90.

Sosa, E. (2011). *Knowing full well.* Princeton, NJ: Princeton University Press.

Sosa, E. (2015). *Judgment and agency.* Oxford, UK: Oxford University Press.

Stadtler, M., & Bromme, R. (2008). Effects of the metacognitive computer-tool met.a.ware on the web search of laypersons. *Computers in Human Behavior, 24*(3), 716–737.

Stadtler, M., Bromme, R., & Rouet, J.-F. (2018). Learning from multiple documents: How can we foster multiple document literacy skills in a sustainable way? In E. Manalo, Y. Uesaka & C. A. Chinn (Eds.), *Promoting spontaneous use of learning and reasoning strategies: Theory, research, and practice* (pp. 46–61). Singapore: Routledge.

Schejter, A. M., & Tirosh, N. (2016). *A justice-based approach for new media policy: In the paths of righteousness.* Cham, Switzerland: Palgrave Macmillan.

Wineburg, S., McGrew, S., Breakstone, J., & Ortega, T. (2016). *Evaluating information: The cornerstone of civic online reasoning,* Stanford Digital Repository.

Chapter 5
New Media: A Double-Edged Sword in Support of Public Engagement with Science

Ayelet Baram-Tsabari and Amit M. Schejter

Abstract Modern life requires individuals with little formal educational background in the sciences to daily make science and technology-based decisions, ranging from vaccinating one's children and consuming genetically modified food to buying a house near a nuclear power plant. The main information source for many such decisions are contemporary media that have become the public's primary reference concerning science and technology. Indeed, these media increasingly shape public engagement with science. This chapter addresses the role of new media in personal and civic decision-making. It argues that many of its characteristics – abundance of content, interactivity, mobility, and multimediality – act as a double-edged sword, providing enhanced affordance over traditional media, while rendering it more difficult for a non-expert audience to reach informed, science-related decisions. Higher and lower thinking skills are discussed as they pertain to the usage of new media while taking into account public deliberation and distributive justice concerns.

Keywords New media · Traditional media · Public engagement with science · Internet · Search engines · Science-based decisions · Personal and civic decision-making · Thinking skills · Public deliberation · Distributive justice

This chapter explores the special attributes of new media, compared with their "traditional" predecessors, in the context of public engagement with science and specifically with informed decision-making regarding science-related issues.

A. Baram-Tsabari (✉)
Faculty of Education in Science and Technology, Technion – Israel Institute of Technology, Haifa, Israel
e-mail: ayelet@technion.ac.il

A. M. Schejter
Department of Communication Studies, Ben-Gurion University of the Negev, Beer Sheva, Israel

Donald P. Bellisario College of Communications, The Pennsylvania State University, State College, PA, USA

© Springer Nature Switzerland AG 2019
Y. Kali et al. (eds.), *Learning In a Networked Society*, Computer-Supported Collaborative Learning Series 17, https://doi.org/10.1007/978-3-030-14610-8_5

Modern life requires individuals with little formal educational background in the sciences to make science and technology-based decisions, which could range from vaccinating one's children, through consuming genetically modified food to buying a house near a nuclear power plant. The chief or sole information source for many such decisions is the Internet that has become the public's primary reference data-base concerning science and technology (Israeli Ministry of Science, 2017; National Science Board, 2016). New media thus increasingly shape public engagement with science (Brossard, 2013; Brossard & Scheufele, 2013; Peters, Dunwoody, Allgaier, Lo, & Brossard, 2014).

The new media landscape is characterized by an abundance of content and chan-nels through which information travels, as well as by interactivity, mobility, and multimediality (Schejter & Tirosh, 2016). New media have the potential to enrich information and make its transference more effective. This chapter tackles both the benefits and the challenges of making informed decisions based on access to these media. We argue that each of these characteristics is a double-edged sword, provid-ing enhanced affordances over traditional media, while rendering it more difficult for a non-expert audience to reach an informed, science-related decision.

We begin by discussing each of these characteristics briefly and then highlight the literature regarding public engagement using the theoretical framework of Habermas's (1996) model for deliberation and Rawls (1971, 2001) and Sen (2004, 2009) theories of justice, applying them to online engagement with science and the challenges it presents. This is accomplished by examining the theory through real-world examples discussing the affordances of new media as they relate to the higher and lower thinking skills needed for effective engagement, based on Bloom, Engelhart, Furst, Hill, & Krathwohl's, (1956) taxonomy.

What's New About New Media?

Media are the go-between apparatus by which humans convey information to each other. Indeed, the technological affordances of the media impact the quality and quantity of the information conveyed as well as its availability, the time it takes for its transfer, the ability to consume it, and the formats through which it travels. Historically, the media themselves have influenced the ways in which we communi-cate, transmit, and consume information and have impacted our ability to under-stand information and process it. Changes in media technology are not neutral: they have implications regarding who gets to communicate with whom and what type of information can be transmitted. The appearance of new forms of media technology may thus have an effect on our understanding of the information they convey. This is why it is important to try and determine what is new about the media we describe as "new media."

The dominant media of the twentieth century, both physical and electronic, oper-ated under conditions of scarcity. They bore relatively little information and the channels through which they traveled were limited (Schejter & Yemini, 2007) and largely stationary. Except for the telephone, that enabled two-way communication, twentieth-century media were primarily unidirectional. The information they transferred was designed by large corporations for mass consumption, consisting of specific types of messages that characterized each medium: newspapers delivered texts and photos in print; radio delivered sound and television moving images and sound.

In certain respects, the media landscape of the twenty-first century is very different from that of the twentieth. First, it provides access to abundant information flowing through virtually unlimited "channels", granted that, accessibility to the information and "channels" alike is confined by the usual suspects—economics, culture, and education. Second, more and more media are mobile. Mobility allows individuals to access information as well as to send it to others whenever it is needed—not only when they are at home or at work but also while on the go.

Unlike traditional media, contemporary media are also interactive, allowing users to design their own media environments.[1] Finally, while in the previous mass media generation, people could hardly transmit information in more than one format, focusing primarily on telephone voice calls, multimedia messages are now sent and received routinely. These features bear both promise and peril, especially with regard to engagement with science-based decision-making.

Theories of Public Engagement and Their Application to Science-Based Decision-Making

Modern life demands science and technology-based decisions from individuals with very little formal educational background in the sciences, the consequences of which may affect themselves, their family members, or their community. Some of these decisions entail the ability to find and understand information and to evaluate its sources, requiring preliminary knowledge and the ability to weigh alternatives, such as consenting to medical treatment or choosing an appropriate diet. Some people need to articulate science-based information when advocating social positions on a national (e.g., food labeling regulations) or local (e.g., Radiation levels from a mobile phone base station at a neighborhood facility) level. While certain individual decisions may appear personal, they actually impact others and affect the community at large (such as a decision not to vaccinate one's child).

Non-experts may also become highly involved in science policymaking as consumers (making science-based decisions themselves), voters (supporting a candidate or party according to avowed positions regarding science-based policies), and activists (protesting or supporting science-based policies) or in many other social roles. In some established democracies, public participation in making decisions, especially those requiring scientific knowledge, is rooted in the political culture. In such cases, public participation takes place within accepted and well-established

---

[1] Note that this differs from our conventional understanding of *interactivity* in educational technology, referring to interface-mediated, two-way flow of information between user and technology.

normative and structured systems. In other democracies, in which public participation is not so deeply ingrained into the system, the public role may be questioned (Mejlgaard, Bloch, Degn, Nielsen, & Ravn, 2012). In both cases, the challenge is one of recognized expertise versus inexpert opinions, and the weight each is assigned in public discourse.

Making science and technology-based decisions appears intuitively challenging, as scientific and technological knowledge are indeed complex and possess an aura that distances them from persons not deemed "expert" in the respective fields. On the other hand, imbuing certain types of knowledge with "expertise" as a condition for discussing them and participating in the relevant decision-making may also be interpreted as an exclusionary practice. Scientization of the public debate regarding science may seem trivial, almost tautologous. Nevertheless, in any decision-making process in which the public participates, there is always a certain trepidation that expertise and its attendant terminology (often referred to as "expert-language") will be used as an excuse to exclude participation of persons systematically placed in a disadvantaged position. Indeed,

> … ordinary citizens will increasingly be asked to make judgements about matters under-pinned by science knowledge or technological capability, but overlaid with much wider considerations. Those without a basic understanding of the ways in which science and tech-nology are impacted by, and impact upon, the physical and the sociopolitical environment will be effectively disempowered and susceptible to being seriously misled in exercising their rights within a democratic, technologically-dependent society. (Hodson, 2003, p. 650)

Habermas (1996) regards positioning science and technology as ideology as leading to the depoliticization of the public, by excluding lay members of the citizenry from partaking in science-based debates. He observes that democratic decision-making and deliberation of values are disregarded when values are determined by experts who assume a position of power by excluding non-experts from the debate. While one may argue that the capability to assess and address scientific and technological information does indeed require knowledge and training, the challenge facing a society aiming at inclusion of all its members is not the quest for exclusion criteria but rather the creation of inclusion mechanisms. This can be accomplished primarily by carrying out two major activities: (1) enhancing the capabilities for learning and for being informed of all members of society, especially the least advantaged and least capable of interpreting and discussing science and technology, and (2) rewriting the rules of public deliberation in a manner that legitimizes additional forms of speech and relevant contributions. Such would be, for example, the case of citizen science, as discussed in Chap. 6.

Inclusion mechanisms should not be confused with disregard of science but rather perceived as a rejection of ideological positions presented as though they had emerged directly from scientific "truths." In other words, allowing nonscientific arguments in a debate does not necessarily question the science thereof yet may nonetheless legitimize other types of arguments.

While mechanisms for enhancing the capabilities for learning and being informed of all members of society may be installed in the formal public education system, they also appear in environments that were not designed to support learning, such as the mass and new media. For decades, the goal of formal science education has been to achieve scientific literacy that includes individual abilities, such as possession of content, along with procedural and epistemic knowledge (OECD, 2015). Recent views of scientific literacy also perceive it as an outcome of the environment that enables it (Snow & Dibner, 2016). Indeed, participatory enhancing mechanisms cannot be limited to conversations surrounding the acquisition of scientific literacy but must also be rooted in creating opportunities to learn, requiring installation of mechanisms for redistribution of knowledge, first and foremost among those who currently have the least access to it. While scientific learning is largely thought of in the context of formal schooling, studying the sciences is an ongoing, lifelong pursuit that should be supported, considering the constant influx of new knowledge. Such remedial policies are consistent with the LINKS conceptualization of learning on the continuum between spontaneous and designed (see Tabak, Ben-Zvi, & Kali, Chap. 2) and can be viewed through the lens of redistributive justice literature, most commonly associated with the writings of John Rawls and Amartya Sen.

The theory of justice developed by Rawls (1971) regulates the procedures according to which a society determines the rules that pertain to its basic structure—and its fundamental institutions, such as the law and the economy (Schejter & Tirosh, 2016). The principles that regulate agreements among citizens, explains Rawls, should create the conditions for all such decisions to be reached in a rational manner. Theoretically, this can be achieved only if the participants are unaware of their own circumstances and how they themselves will fare as a result of the decision reached (Rawls, 1971). However, states Rawls (1999), rational decision-making is still bounded by two conditions: the need to guarantee each individual's basic liberties (that he terms the primary goods) and the need to ensure that the outcome of the deliberation will provide the greatest advantage to those mostly disadvantaged.

Freedom of expression is a basic primary good. In the Rawlsian vocabulary, political liberties accord all a "fair opportunity" to take part in political life, whether as competitors for public office or as people who affect the outcome of public deliberations (Rawls, 2001, p. 149). To reach the goal of equal distribution of liberties, among them participation in public decision-making, mechanisms rewriting the rules of public deliberation are needed. One source for rules of deliberative decision-making takes us back to the philosophy of Jürgen Habermas. As Wilson et al. (2003) submit, "discussion is the foundational element of rationality, at the center of the process by which knowledge and values are reconciled" (p. 356).

In a non-dominated discussion, one in which all are free to engage and all those engaged are free to express themselves, stating their wishes and needs, decisions can be reached that truly take each individual's need into account. This type of discussion constructs a discursive bridge between such individual needs and the joint decision reached that reflects them. For the relevant discussion to emerge without a dominant participant, however, access to all forms of speech, including privileged forms such as scientific jargon, has to be equal. Under such circumstances, either all can understand the jargon or have an opportunity to learn what it means, or said jargon will be replaced with terminology of greater frequency and comprehensibility (Rakedzon, Segev, Chapnik, Yosef, & Baram-Tsabari, 2017).

Jargon is only one symptom of the accessibility problem. Non-experts would also find it extremely difficult to debate the suitability of methods or analysis. Their lack of preliminary knowledge required to evaluate results would leave them with a permanently limited understanding of science (Bromme & Goldman, 2014). Under such conditions, Amartya Sen's theory of justice—the Capabilities Approach—can be applied.

Sen's (1990) Capabilities Approach proposes a path that takes individual needs into account, seeks to improve the position of the least advantaged, and accepts egalitarian discourse as the basis for such decision-making. In this respect, Sen's objectives may conflict with those of Rawlsian justice because of the former's focus on individually defined needs rather than a set list of primary goods. Sen believes that the goal of correcting measures in society should center on enabling people "to lead the kind of lives they have reason to value" (Sen, 1990, p. 460) and not necessarily those deemed desirable by prevailing norms. He also prioritizes people's actual capability to make use of the goods, services, and opportunities available to them rather than mere access to or ownership of those goods (Sen, 1980).

Promotion of a person's desired capabilities is the challenge Sen's concept of social justice is designed to encounter: "A theory of justice based on fairness must be deeply and directly connected with the actual freedoms enjoyed by different persons" (Sen 1990, p.112) and not just the opportunity to have them. Within the context of this chapter, putting the freedom to participate in decision-making to good use may be perceived as such a capability. It requires developing individual capabilities to use the goods, services, and opportunities made available through science-based information in the ways they desire.

Lower and Higher Thinking Skills in Using New Media

New media are key technologies whose unique characteristics are personalizable and consequently possess the potential to provide individuals with access to the knowledge they need, when they need it and in the appropriately comprehensible format. Nevertheless, discovery, comprehension, evaluation, and use of information in such complex ways do not comprise a monolithic competence. Besides access, they also require fundamental and digital literacies, as well as different levels of thinking skills.

Several taxonomies, which have been developed within educational theory, have been proposed to classify such thinking skills, as types of knowledge and the cognitive processes associated with them. These taxonomies enable us to think systematically about formal knowledge. The primary motivation for their development was evaluation of students' knowledge, as well as the cognitive demands of educational tasks. One of the most widely cited attempts was Bloom et al. (1956) "Classification of Educational Goals." Bloom and his associates proposed six hierarchical types of goals for education: knowledge, comprehension, application, analysis, synthesis, and evaluation. This cognitive taxonomy was revised by Anderson, Krathwohl, and Bloom (2001) to include remembering, understanding, applying, analyzing, evaluating, and creating. The modifications are called for replacing nouns with actions, changing some terminology (e.g., from *knowledge* to *remembering*), and, most importantly, replacing *synthesis* with *creating* in an effort to make the taxonomy more relevant to the twenty-first century.

The taxonomy proposed by Anderson et al. (2001) divides the cognitive range into lower- and higher-order thinking skills, wherein the lower range includes remembering and understanding factual and conceptual knowledge and applying them to familiar situations and contexts, while the higher one is comprised of more sophisticated application, analysis, evaluation, and creativity. Generally speaking, higher-order thinking skills tend to be complex, uncertain, and non-algorithmic: the total path is not "visible" from any single point in the process. Problems often have more than one solution, each with its own costs and benefits, entailing the application of numerous criteria and nuanced judgment (Resnick, 1987).

In 2008, Andrew Churches added *digital verbs* to each of the key terms, thereby creating Bloom's Digital Taxonomy, in which, for example, *remembering* includes searching and googling; *understanding*, annotating; *applying*, uploading and editing; *analyzing*, linking and tagging; and *evaluating*, reviewing, commenting, and alpha and beta testing, while *creating* includes programming and producing podcasts (Churches, 2008).

To illustrate the application of different thinking skills to real-life situations of public engagement with science online, imagine a woman who heard about Angelina Jolie's double mastectomy and is now both intrigued and worried. She searches for and finds the meaning of "BRCA mutation" using the first Google search result that comes up (remembering, lower-order skills). At first, she is puzzled by the unfamiliar jargon on the National Cancer Institute and Wikipedia websites (first two results) but after some reading is able to make sense of the term "tumor suppressor proteins" and understands why a mutation in BRCA genes may be harmful (understanding, lower-order skill). She reads about the ethnic populations in which BRCA1 and BRCA2 mutations are more prevalent and about screening for family history. She then realizes that she might be at risk and should consider testing for the mutation (application, lower-order skill). She searches online for more information, including patients' forums, medical portals, mass media publications, and commercial testing providers. She also speaks to a female cousin who had lost her mother to breast cancer several years ago, to find out if she had been tested, using all this information to determine whether she should be tested and, if so, what her options are for doing so (analyzing, higher-order skill). In the meantime, she also called her doctor for an appointment that was to take place 6 weeks later. Instead of waiting all that time, she evaluates the information sources and decides to take a commercial test (evaluation, higher-order skill). When the test scores arrive, she finds out she cannot understand them on her own. Again, she goes online, enters the results she received, and finds out what they mean (understanding and application, lower-order skill). Finally, she posts a message describing her journey, so that other women may follow (creating, higher-order skill). By now, her doctor's appointment is only 2 weeks away.

This example demonstrates progression from a passive, to an active, consumer role and producer of knowledge. It assesses the thinking skills employed as processes and not according to their results. It may well be that the heroine of our story used irrelevant information sources or did not understand what she read and misapplied it to her situation. Perhaps she misinterpreted her test results, and her post will only cause harm to those who follow in her footsteps. But the analysis evaluates the thinking levels people use, not their outcomes.

The example described a case of personally useful engagement with science, rather than civic deliberation. The notion of capacity building—the skills, tools, and knowledge needed for participation in civic life—was suggested as a means of reframing the democratic potential of public engagement with activities involving science and technology (Selin et al., 2017).

We use the adaptations and new understandings of Bloom's taxonomy as an analytical framework to study the types of cognitive processes and actions people perform when they have to make science-related decisions in a digital environment. In the next section, we explore how these cognitive processes interact with the four characteristics of new media, thereby shedding light on ways in which new media may enable or hinder democratic discourse and science-related, non-expert decision-making.

What's New About Public Engagement with New Media?

In what ways do the characteristics of new media affect the public's ability to reach informed decisions? Table 5.1 uses Schejter and Tirosh's (2016) characteristics of new media and the revised version of Bloom's taxonomy (Anderson et al., 2001) to analyze how new media may both support and hinder different levels of cognitive processes people may be performing while engaging with science online. Below, we describe and demonstrate several of these interactions.

Abundance

Accessibility to abundant amounts of information may empower those who had been unable to obtain it before, but new risks may well emerge unless they possess the requisite means and skills for proper evaluation of expertise and trustworthiness. The notion of *abundance* may also constitute only an illusion of empowerment to some extent, with adverse consequences likely. For example, although information sources are abundant, users tend to use only one search engine and to make do with its first results page alone (Granka, Joachims, & Gay, 2004; Jansen & Spink, 2006; Jansen, Spink, & Saracevic, 2000; Pan et al., 2007; Segev, 2010). Even

Table 5.1 New media characteristics as they relate to low and high thinking skills

| New media characteristics | Benefits and challenges | Low-level thinking skills: Recall of information or the application of concepts or knowledge to familiar situations and contexts | | | High-level thinking skills: Non-algorithmic, complex, often yields multiple solutions, involve the application of multiple criteria, uncertainty, and self-regulation | | |
		Remembering (technologically assisted)	*Understanding*	*Applying (in a familiar context)*	*Analyzing*	*Evaluating*	*Creating*
Abundance	Upside	Easy access	Content at multiple levels	Access to use made by others	There are more points of view to consider	There are more points of view to consider, including the original scientific work. Access to many sources allows for more comparative input	Supports the ability to do things yourself because of access to the original materials
	Downside	In the lack of tools for verification of information and no inherent authority structure or gatekeeping mechanism, an abundance of information challenges both low-level and high-level thinking processes					
Mobility	Upside	Accessible everywhere. The information is there when one needs it					One can take part in conversing and debating the issues by collecting information in relevant settings
	Downside	Dependency on mobile devices creates a vacuum when inaccessible					

(continued)

Table 5.1 (Continued)

		Low-level thinking skills: Recall of information or the application of concepts or knowledge to familiar situations and contexts			High-level thinking skills: Non-algorithmic, complex, often yields multiple solutions, involve the application of multiple criteria, uncertainty, and self-regulation		
Interactivity	Upside	Relevance	Environment adapted to one's needs	One can create familiarized contexts	The ability to converse with experts and lay experts, test one's insights	Exposure of research to public and professional scrutiny	Fewer barriers to producing and sharing
	Downside	Designing one's environment may create a filter bubble, knowingly by choice of sources or unknowingly as dictated by search engines or social media algorithms as a result of the characteristics of the information you seek, the group you joined, previous interactions, etc.					
Multimediality	Upside	Many formats for information, accessible to different users with different needs and learning preferences					Many ways to express oneself
	Downside	May attract people to messages that are easier to immerse in and call for less effort, thus leading to a more superficial understanding of the phenomenon. Access to information that is in richer media may be limited to those with richer access networks					

undergraduate student research rarely proceeds beyond the first Google results page (Georgas, 2014). Furthermore, information may be far less abundant to persons who cannot read English fluently and have very little online content available in their mother tongue (e.g., only 0.2% of the top ten million websites are in Hebrew (Wikipedia, 2017)). In addition, richness and abundance of relevant and less relevant information may result in cognitive load and challenge information processing.

Abundance supports public engagement with science in different ways. Most straightforwardly, it provides easy access to information, making technologically assisted memory easier than ever to manage. It supports and demands higher-level thinking skills by providing many points of view, including access to original scientific papers, enabling evaluation and even reconstruction of studies. Its downside, however, is highly fundamental and may affect thinking processes at all levels: the basic information provided may be unreliable. Without tools for verification of information, an inherent authority structure or gatekeeping mechanisms, abundance of information challenges both low- and high-level thinking processes. No analysis and synthesis process can be of value if the knowledge base is faulty ab initio.

The most obvious problem is that of information resources. A Google Search[2] (in Hebrew) for "should I vaccinate" yielded first page results from two popular news sites, two women's magazines, a doula site, a commercial site for parents, a portal of pregnancy and baby-related service providers, two New Age natural lifestyle sites, and—toward the bottom of the page—one link to a commercial medical portal. Considering Google Search's huge market share of 80.5% (according to (NetMarketShare, 2017)) and the general tendency to use only the first page of results, abundance does not necessarily yield greater clarity. Even if reliable, updated, and scientifically accurate information were available and accessible from any desktop computer or mobile phone, it does not mean that the general public would find it and use it for deliberative activities. In fact, an analysis of science-related discussions on Facebook has found an extremely low percentage (4%) of items using any evidence to back up their claims (Orr & Baram-Tsabari, 2018; Orr, Baram-Tsabari, & Landsman, 2016). The public's capability to make good use of abundant information is limited by social and educational factors, as well as by motivation and prioritizing issues.

Interactivity

Interactivity allows users to personalize their own relevant information environments, with different gains for different thinking skills. Remembering and understanding, for example, will benefit from relevant information selected to fit one's needs, situated in contexts that would support understanding and application. Exposure to public and professional scrutiny allows informed evaluation of

---

[2] February 2017, using an incognito mode

scientific claims. Interactivity lowers barriers for production and sharing, and supports an ethos of creativity and creation, limited of course, by technological features. Interactivity proposes an alternative to passivity in the face of expert knowledge by allowing users to reframe scientific messages and add their own values to socioscientific discussions. Laslo, Baram-Tsabari, and Lewenstein (2011) found that readers' comments to news stories involving animal experimentation echoed many pro and con messages voiced by interest groups and reframed science stories (that ignored the issue) as a basis for a different discussion. Indeed, scientific ideas can grow into unexpected types of discussions when encountered by the public. Laslo et al. (2011) suggest that discourse in new media can be understood by thinking of the audience as a "growth medium" in which seeds planted by individual stories can grow into knowledge of the sort imagined by the writers and also into new branches nurtured by the readership. This may include applying information from other sources or contexts to the current discussion (e.g., by linking or copying/pasting), by analyzing or evaluating claims and by creating new content as well. Interestingly, two to three times more comments referred to content that was brought up by readers rather than to content from the original article. Within a formal context, in Kidron et al. (Chap. 7), university students in an online course felt that interactions with others in their learning community played a major role in their own learning.

The downside of interactivity, like that of abundance, is common to all thinking skills (except creating): building one's environment may result in a filter bubble—a consequence that may occur intentionally as a result of choice of sources or friends on social media (see also Barzilai & Chinn, Chap. 4). Under less fortuitous circumstances, however, it may happen without one's knowledge as the algorithms applied by personalized search engines or social media automatically deem certain information irrelevant (Hannak et al., 2013) because of the information's own characteristics, the group you join, previous interactions with specific content, and the like. Ladwig, Anderson, Brossard, Scheufele, and Shaw (2010) studied Google Suggest automatic suggestions for further searches in the field of nanotechnology. Suggestions are determined by users' previous searches, overall search volume on specific terms, and potentially sponsored content. The study found that besides suggesting health-specific search terms, the results also direct users disproportionately toward health-based links when searching for nanotechnology-related terms, regardless of application of the search term. The authors thus warned of a self-reinforcing spiral that consolidates a link between health and nanotechnology in online news environments, reduces the complexity and detail of the information that users are likely to encounter online, and may also impact the public's perception of science and the range of its applications.

Interactivity causes many people to enter a filter bubble, especially because of participation in social media, resulting from their choice of friends and decisions of the social network's algorithm (Bakshy, Messing, & Adamic, 2015). In the resulting echo chamber, they are exposed mostly to ideas and opinions to which they agree, creating the illusion that "everyone thinks that way." The phenomenon received much attention regarding political opinions (e.g., Bakshy, Messing, & Adamic,

2015) but is also apparent in some science-related issues, such as anti-vaccination communities, climate change denialism, and other issue-specific groups. In these cases, one could be surrounded by a critical mass of like-minded people more easily and more frequently than was possible in the physical world. Sentiments regarding a new vaccine, derived from over 100,000 social media users, revealed that information flows more often between users who share the same sentiments than it would by chance alone. Furthermore, most communities are dominated by either positive or negative sentiments toward the novel vaccine (Salathé & Khandelwal, 2011). The authors warn that simulations of infectious disease transmission show that if clusters of negative vaccine sentiments lead to clusters of unprotected individuals, the likelihood of disease outbreaks is greatly increased.

Additionally, while one may solicit advice from experts or from peers struggling with the same problem, join a learning community, or find other means of support, all these affordances may also provide a fertile field for discourse management by charlatans or conspiracy-driven groups.

Mobility and Multimediality

As mobility provides access to information anywhere at any time, it enables mobile-based learning. Moreover, it allows people to contribute to citizen science projects (see Sagy et al., Chap. 6) or participate in science research to advance understanding and control of their local environment. The limitations of mobile devices, however, with regard to features such as display size, information transfer speed, accessibility challenges in certain locations, and so forth, adversely affect dependence on such devices as chief sources of information. A vacuum may suddenly result when the technology is inaccessible. Higher-level thinking skills may be limited by the silos created using mobile apps that are less likely to support analysis and synthesis of multiple information sources. Indeed, "mobile leapfrogging" has been identified as a potential obstacle to the progress of communities that had lacked access to media technologies before becoming mobile (Napoli & Obar, 2014).

Multimediality offers many information formats that are accessible to different users with differential needs and learning preferences: it enables users to choose how information is to be consumed; helps to render it more relevant, interesting, and coherent for the individual learner; and supports repetition of viewing, listening, and reading content. Its effect on learning is by no means straightforward, however. It may hinder attempts at synthesizing information from different sources (e.g., video and text). In a classic study (Kozma, 2003), science novices experienced difficulty moving across or connecting multiple representations; hence their understanding and discourse were constrained by individual surface representation features. In a review by Mayer (1997), however, consistent evidence was found for a positive multimedia effect, wherein students who received coordinated presentations of explanations in verbal and visual formats generated more creative solutions on problem-solving tests than did those given verbal explanations alone.

Not everyone has access to rich multimodal data: Focus on visualization and video content may attract people to messages that facilitate immersion and minimize effort, thus leading to a more superficial understanding of the phenomenon. Irrelevant illustrations may hinder information processing (Berends & Van Lieshout, 2009; Schnotz & Bannert, 2003) and divert attention from needed facts to reliance on and impressions of visuals. If not properly designed and coordinated (Cook, 2006)—a distinct possibility among material offered gratis to all—multimediality may also lead to cognitive overload. In this case as well, however, empirical evidence appears to yield mixed results. Among low-income parents, for example, embedded multimedia news stories slightly decreased knowledge gains compared with those of online texts (Pincus, Wojcieszak, & Boomgarden, 2017). Another study (Campbell, Goldman, Boccia, & Skinner, 2004) involved participants who relied on video to convey information, as they considered well-produced print media to be "questionable" (Campbell et al., 2004), while Petersen (2011) found that texts may actually exert a more powerful emotional effect than pictures.

Access to information available only in richer media may be limited to those with richer access networks. These challenges are particularly pertinent among marginalized, less educated, and remotely located communities. Consequently, we should pay all due attention to the disparities these communities and others face between the opportunity to access more and richer data and the ability to understand, evaluate, and apply it for their benefit.

Concluding Remarks

In this chapter, we attempted to combine two theoretical frameworks. The first concerns rules for deliberation, the need to ensure they are egalitarian, and the goal of guaranteeing inclusion of the least advantaged members of society. All should have an opportunity to express themselves, their needs, and their desires, when such deliberation concerns science-related decisions. The second component concerns types of knowledge acquired in social interaction and the skills that are required to interpret them. As science-based decision-making calls for both deliberation and the cognitive ability to make sense of the relevant information, we advocated the introduction of new rules of deliberation. These should be egalitarian in nature, thereby improving the position of those traditionally excluded from pubic deliberations and taking their wants and desires into account. We then sought to determine whether new media supports diverse audiences who do not possess the necessary expertise in each scientific field requiring everyday decisions, considering the unique characteristics of the relevant media. We found that new media constitute a double-edged sword and that each of their novel features can either boost or decrease knowledge levels as defined by Bloom.

We discussed the benefits and challenges of using new media for public engagement with science in the context of one's actual ability to use available online resources rather than simply having access to them. These skills concern both higher and lower thinking skills, as demonstrated in the context of four features of new media. Naturally, other relevant features merit attention as well. As early as 1996, Newhagen and Rafaeli suggested criteria differentiating the Internet from other media, including hypertextuality (versus linearity), communication topology (designed to ignore routes), synchronous/asynchronous elasticity, interactivity, and multimediality (Newhagen & Rafaeli, 1996). It would be interesting to determine whether similar conclusions would be obtained using other analytical frameworks, such as hypertextuality and elasticity of synchronicity (for an example see Chap. 4).

Habermas's theory of democratic decision-making and deliberation can be adapted for analysis when applied to the involvement of lay publics—and not only individuals— in science decision-making. Its implementation requires development of mechanisms to enhance the capabilities of all members of society to interpret and converse about science and technology. Those who have the least access to knowledge require the most assistance in its acquisition, as well as in understanding the benefits and dangers of using new media for this purpose. We believe it is they who should constitute the focus of policymaking, in the spirit of Rawlsian redistributive justice principles.

When it comes to science-based decisions in particular, however, one should be aware of individual autonomy and each person's desires in freely seeking opportunities in life. Thus, interpreting *capability* as a goal tailored to an individual's desires, in light of Amartya Sen's Capability Approach, should be the basis for designing those policies. For this to take place, one should pay attention to spontaneous learning and engagement with science online and to enhance our understanding of how new media shape these processes in order to inform design of educational policy.

Bibliography

Anderson, L. W., Krathwohl, D. R., Airasian, P. W., Cruikshank, K. A., Mayer, R. E., Pintrich, P. R., et al. (2001). *A taxonomy for learning, teaching, and assessing: A revision of Bloom's taxonomy of educational objectives* (abridged ed.). White Plains, NY: Longman.

Bakshy, E., Messing, S., & Adamic, L. A. (2015). Exposure to ideologically diverse news and opinion on Facebook. *Science, 348*(6239), 1130–1132.

Berends, I. E., & Van Lieshout, E. C. (2009). The effect of illustrations in arithmetic problem-solving: Effects of increased cognitive load. *Learning and Instruction, 19*(4), 345–353.

Bloom, B. S., Engelhart, M. D., Furst, E. J., Hill, W. H., & Krathwohl, D. R. (1956). *Taxonomy of educational objectives: The classification of educational goals* (Vol. 1, 19th ed.). New York: David McKay.

Bromme, R., & Goldman, S. R. (2014). The public's bounded understanding of science. *Educational Psychologist, 49*(2), 59–69.

Brossard, D. (2013). New media landscapes and the science information consumer. *Proceedings of the National Academy of Sciences, 110.*(Supplement 3, 14096–14101.

Brossard, D., & Scheufele, D. A. (2013). Science, new media, and the public. *Science, 339*(6115), 40–41.

Campbell, F. A., Goldman, B. D., Boccia, M. L., & Skinner, M. (2004). The effect of format modifications and reading comprehension on recall of informed consent information by low-income parents: A comparison of print, video, and computer-based presentations. *Patient Education and Counseling, 53*(2), 205–216.

Churches, A. (2008). Bloom's taxonomy blooms digitally. *Tech & Learning, 1*, 1–6.

Cook, M. P. (2006). Visual representations in science education: The influence of prior knowledge and cognitive load theory on instructional design principles. *Science Education, 90*(6), 1073–1091.

Georgas, H. (2014). Google vs. the library (part II): Student search patterns and behaviors when using Google and a federated search tool. *Portal: Libraries and the Academy, 14*(4), 503–532.

Granka, L. A., Joachims, T., & Gay, G. (2004). *Eye-tracking analysis of user behavior in WWW search.* Paper presented at the Proceedings of the 27th annual international ACM SIGIR conference on Research and development in information retrieval.

Habermas, J. (1996). *Between facts and norms: Contributions to a discourse theory of law and democracy* (trans: Reg, W.). Cambridge, MA: MIT Press.

Hannak, A., Sapiezynski, P., Molavi Kakhki, A., Krishnamurthy, B., Lazer, D., Mislove, A., & Wilson, C. (2013). *Measuring personalization of web search.* Paper presented at the Proceedings of the 22nd international conference on World Wide Web.

Hodson, D. (2003). Time for action: Science education for an alternative future. *International Journal of Science Education, 25*(6), 645–670.

Israeli Ministry of Science. (2017). *Public perceptions and attitudes in Israel: Science, technology and space.* Tel Aviv: GeoCatography for the Israeli Ministry of Science, Technology and Space.

Jansen, B. J., & Spink, A. (2006). How are we searching the World Wide Web? A comparison of nine search engine transaction logs. *Information Processing & Management, 42*(1), 248–263.

Jansen, B. J., Spink, A., & Saracevic, T. (2000). Real life, real users, and real needs: A study and analysis of user queries on the web. *Information Processing & Management, 36*(2), 207–227.

Kozma, R. (2003). The material features of multiple representations and their cognitive and social affordances for science understanding. *Learning and Instruction, 13*(2), 205–226.

Ladwig, P., Anderson, A. A., Brossard, D., Scheufele, D. A., & Shaw, B. (2010). Narrowing the nano discourse? *Materials Today, 13*(5), 52–54.

Laslo, E., Baram-Tsabari, A., & Lewenstein, B. V. (2011). A growth medium for the message: Online science journalism affordances for exploring public discourse of science and ethics. *Journalism: Theory, Practice and Criticism, 12*(7), 847–870.

Mayer, R. E. (1997). Multimedia learning: Are we asking the right questions? *Educational Psychologist, 32*(1), 1–19.

Mejlgaard, N., Bloch, C., Degn, L., Nielsen, M. W., & Ravn, T. (2012). Locating science in society across Europe: Clusters and consequences. *Science and Public Policy, 39*(6), 741–750.

Napoli, P. M., & Obar, J. A. (2014). The emerging mobile Internet underclass: A critique of mobile Internet access. *The Information Society, 30*(5), 323–334.

National Science Board. (2016). Science and engineering indicators.

NetMarketShare. (2017). Desktop search engine market share. Retrieved July, 2017, from https://www.netmarketshare.com/search-engine-market-share.aspx?qprid=4&qpcustomd=0

Newhagen, J. E., & Rafaeli, S. (1996). Why communication researchers should study the Internet: A dialogue. *Journal of Computer-Mediated Communication, 1*(4), 0–0.

OECD. (2015). Draft science framework.

Orr, D., & Baram-Tsabari, A. (2018). Science and politics in the polio vaccination debate on facebook: A mixed-methods approach to public engagement in a science-based dialogue. *Journal of Microbiology and Biology Education, 19*(1). https://doi.org/10.1128/jmbe.v19i1.1500

Orr, D., Baram-Tsabari, A., & Landsman, K. (2016). Social media as a platform for health-related public debates and discussions: The Polio vaccine on Facebook. *Israel Journal of Health Policy Research, 5*(1), 34.

Pan, B., Hembrooke, H., Joachims, T., Lorigo, L., Gay, G., & Granka, L. (2007). In google we trust: Users' decisions on rank, position, and relevance. *Journal of Computer-Mediated Communication, 12*(3), 801–823.

Peters, H. P., Dunwoody, S., Allgaier, J., Lo, Y. Y., & Brossard, D. (2014). Public communication of science 2.0. *EMBO reports*, e201438979.

Petersen, T. (2011). Lasswell's problem and Hovland's dilemma: Split-ballot experiments on the effects of potentially emotionalizing visual elements in media reports. *International Journal of Public Opinion Research, 23*, 251. edq051.

Pincus, H., Wojcieszak, M., & Boomgarden, H. (2017). Do multimedia matter? Cognitive and affective effects of embedded multimedia journalism. *Journalism and Mass Communication Quarterly, 94*(3), 747–771.

Rakedzon, R., Segev, E., Chapnik, N., Yosef, R., & Baram-Tsabari, A. (2017). Automatic jargon identifier for scientists engaging with the public and science communication educators. *PLoS One*.

Rawls, J. (1971). *A theory of justice.* Cambridge, MA: The Belknap Press of Harvard University.

Rawls, J. (2001). In E. Kelly (Ed.), *Justice as fairness: A restatement.* Cambridge, MA: The Belknap Press of Harvard University.

Resnick, L. B. (1987). *Education and learning to think.* Washington, DC: National Academy Press.

Salathé, M., & Khandelwal, S. (2011). Assessing vaccination sentiments with online social media: Implications for infectious disease dynamics and control. *PLoS Computational Biology, 7*(10), e1002199.

Schejter, A. M., & Tirosh, N. (2016). Media policy and theories of justice. In *A justice-based approach for new media policy : In the paths of righteousness* (pp. 51–59). Cham, Switzerland: Palgrave Macmillan.

Schejter, A. M., & Yemini, M. (2007). Justice, and only justice, you shall pursue: Network neutrality, the first amendment and John Rawls's theory of justice. *Michigan Telecommunications and Technology Law Review, 14*, 137.

Schnotz, W., & Bannert, M. (2003). Construction and interference in learning from multiple representations. *Learning and Instruction, 13*(2), 141–156.

Segev, E. (2010). *Google and the digital divide: The bias of online knowledge.* Oxford, UK: Chandos Publishing

Selin, C., Rawlings, K. C., de Ridder-Vignone, K., Sadowski, J., Altamirano Allende, C., Gano, G., et al. (2017). Experiments in engagement: Designing public engagement with science and technology for capacity building. *Public Understanding of Science, 26*(6), 634–649.

Sen, A. (1980). Equality of what? In S. M. McMurring (Ed.), *Tanner lectures on human values* (Vol. I, pp. 197–220). Cambridge, UK: Cambridge University Press.

Sen, A. (1990). Justice: Means versus freedoms. *Philosophy & Public Affairs, 19*(2), 111–121.

Sen, A. (2004). Elements of a theory of human rights. *Philosophy & Public Affairs, 32*(4), 315–356.

Sen, A. (2009). *The idea of justice.* Cambridge, MA: Harvard University Press.

Snow, C. E., & Dibner, K. A. (2016). *Science literacy: Concepts, contexts, and consequences.* National Academies Press.

Wikipedia. (2017). Languages used on the Internet. Retrieved June, 2017, from https://en.wikipedia.org/wiki/Languages_used_on_the_Internet

Wilson, R., Payne, M., & Smith, E. (2003). Does discussion enhance rationality? A report from transportation planning practice. *Journal of the American Planning Society, 69*(4), 354–367.

Chapter 6
Citizen Science: An Opportunity for Learning in the Networked Society

Ornit Sagy, Yaela Naomi Golumbic, Hava Ben-Horin Abramsky, Maya Benichou, Osnat Atias, Hana Manor Braham, Ayelet Baram-Tsabari, Yael Kali, Dani Ben-Zvi, Yotam Hod, and Dror Angel

Abstract Seeking to promote science communication, civic engagement, and informal education, citizen science is a genre of research that connects scientists and non-scientists around projects involving science. This meeting point creates opportunities for potential benefits to both sides. Scientists may advance their research and obtain prestigious funding while non-scientists stand to gain enjoyment, new skills, and knowledge. To learn more how these inspiring outcomes can be promoted, we conceptualize citizen science and its myriad stakeholders as an ecology. We complement this metaphor with the term mutualism to express our desire for interactions in which all parties benefit from their involvement and propose a Mutualistic Ecology of Citizen Science (MECS) as an analytic framework that can potentially contribute to the design and conceptualization of learning in citizen science projects. In this chapter, we operationalize this framework, using four lenses that span several disciplines to look at potential benefits to different participants.

Keywords Citizen science · Public participation in research · Science communication · Learning communities · Statistical education · Science literacy · Socioscientific issues · Scientists · Mutualistic Ecology of Citizen Science · Learning in citizen science

O. Sagy (✉) · H. Ben-Horin Abramsky · M. Benichou · O. Atias · H. Manor Braham · Y. Kali
D. Ben-Zvi · Y. Hod
Department of Learning, Instruction, and Teacher Education, Faculty of Education,
University of Haifa, Haifa, Israel
e-mail: dbenzvi@univ.haifa.ac.il; yhod@edu.haifa.ac.il; yael.kali@edtech.haifa.ac.il

Y. N. Golumbic · A. Baram-Tsabari
Faculty of Education in Science and Technology, Technion – Israel Institute of Technology,
Haifa, Israel
e-mail: yaelago@technion.ac.il; ayelet@technion.ac.il

D. Angel
Department of Maritime Civilizations, Charney School of Marine Science,
University of Haifa, Haifa, Israel

© Springer Nature Switzerland AG 2019
Y. Kali et al. (eds.), *Learning In a Networked Society*, Computer-Supported
Collaborative Learning Series 17, https://doi.org/10.1007/978-3-030-14610-8_6

One key benefit of the networked society is connectivity between people and communities that might otherwise have little interaction. Seeking to promote science communication, civic engagement, and informal education, citizen science is a genre of research that connects scientists and non-scientists around projects involving science. Two recent issues of the *Journal of Science Communication* referred to citizen science as "one of the most dramatic developments in science communication in the last generation" (Lewenstein, 2016, p. 1) that plays a role in "environmental science, public health, physics, biochemistry, community development, social justice, democracy, and beyond" (Bonney, Cooper, & Ballard, 2016, p. 1). On the one hand, citizen science has been around for a long time (Cooper & Lewenstein, 2016) such as the work of Frank Chapman, who initiated an annual Christmas Bird Count in 1900 (Silvertown, 2009). On the other hand, research on citizen science is still in its infancy (Bonney et al., 2016; Bonney, Phillips, Ballard, & Enck, 2015; Lewenstein, 2016). Although citizen science projects have grown extensively in number and quality, especially during the past decade, much of the knowledge about it accumulated so far is diffuse (Golumbic, 2015; Pettibone et al., 2016).

This chapter consolidates different research strands dealing with citizen science by providing a new conceptual framework that can advance our understanding of this genre of research. We start with a quick glimpse into *the making of science* and the role that citizen science plays in this context. After briefly describing the benefits to scientists who initiate and take part in citizen science projects, we focus our attention on non-scientists. Specifically, we examine how theoretical frameworks in the fields of science communication, science education, data science education, and learning communities can shed light on participants' learning processes.

The Making of Science and the Role of Citizen Science

It is helpful to think of citizen science in the greater context of the scientific endeavor, specifically—big science and little science. Most scientific advances in the current era have been achieved by participants in *big science*—professional scientists working at scholarly institutions who communicate mostly through journals and conferences. In comparison, *little science* is advanced through personal interactions of diverse participants (Lievrouw, 2010). Darwin, for example, made immensely significant contributions to science as an unpaid ship's naturalist, advancing his ideas through letter writing and discussions with friends (Silvertown, 2009).

Advances in information technologies that gave birth to the networked society have contributed to public engagement with both big and little science, blurring the differences between them (for their affordances and challenges, see Baram-Tsabari and Schejter in Chap. 5 of this book). They offer opportunities for the public to participate in scientific activities such as data collection (Del Savio, Prainsack, & Buyx, 2016); increase the accessibility of data, tools, and communication methods to the public (Aristeidou, Scanlon, & Sharples, 2013; Bizer, 2009; Teacher, Griffiths,

Hodgson, & Inger, 2013); and enable communities of amateurs to engage in science as a serious leisure activity (Stebbins, 1997).

Citizen science projects may be classified as *global*, often representing big science, or *local*, often largely manifesting the characteristics of little science. Global projects include initiatives such as eBird, which involves people in identifying and reporting observations of bird species (ebird.org), or Galaxy Zoo, in which the public classifies galaxies (galaxyzoo.org) and assists science by gathering and interpreting data on a global (or even cosmic) scale. Local projects are represented by endeavors such as the Shermans Creek Conservation Association—a community effort to monitor and protect a creek in Pennsylvania (facebook.com/ShermansCreekConservationAssociation)—with scientists providing answers to citizens' concerns (Irwin, 1995) and engaging in dialogue with the public through social media (Bonney et al., 2015).

Potential Benefits of Citizen Science

Potential beneficiaries of citizen science can be divided into three major groups: Those whose job is to advance knowledge (i.e., scientists), those who participate on an individual basis (i.e., the public, amateurs), and those situated in formal educational settings (i.e., teachers and students).

Potential Benefits to Scientists

The contribution most often mentioned for science and scientists concerns scientific discoveries and consequently the vast number of publications resulting from them, i.e., those that use citizen science data (Yoho & Vanmali, 2016). In 2015 alone, 402 peer-reviewed articles were published that addressed or used such data. The figures are increasing exponentially (Kullenberg & Kasperowski, 2016), as scientists' motivations for participating in citizen science often include promoting scientific research, obtaining prestigious funding, and publishing scientific papers (Golumbic, Baram-Tsabari, & Fishbain, 2017). Personal communication with other scientists has indicated some less obvious motivations as well: "Scientists stand to gain a lot from citizen science: Humility, the need to be more accurate" (Personal communication, 2018).

Potential Benefits to Participating Citizens

Contributions to individual participants in citizen science include enjoyment, community building, acquiring new skills and knowledge, and hands-on understanding of scientific processes (Brossard, Lewenstein, & Bonney, 2005; Dickinson et al., 2012; Raddick et al., 2009). In some cases, especially when projects address environmental hazards (such as pollution or contamination), participants gain important information about their local environment (Golumbic, Fishbain, & Baram-Tsabari, Forthcoming). Participants can also take action, get involved in nature protection and conservation activities, and influence policymakers to institute change. One example is provided by eBird participants, who used the eBird database for protecting local parks and nature sites and preventing further development of altered landscapes (Sullivan et al., 2017).

Potential Benefits to Teachers and Students

Besides the benefits described above, illustrating the individual contribution of citizen science to participants, additional benefits may apply with respect to educational settings. These include various new opportunities for scientific education, enabling students to engage in hands-on authentic research and learn about science from a broad perspective (Bonney, Phillips, Enck, Shirk, & Trautmann, 2014). Research evaluating student learning outcomes in several citizen science projects revealed an increase in content knowledge, a heightened awareness, and an intensified understanding of the scientific research process following student participation (Ballard, Dixon, & Harris, 2017; Golumbic et al., 2016; Kountoupes & Oberhauser, 2008; Silva et al., 2016). Moreover, students involved in the Lost Ladybug Project expressed a sense of pride in their research products and a sense of belonging and connection because they are working on something of major significance (Sickler & Cherry, 2012). Although these outcomes were optimistic and inspiring, the evidence is sparse, and few studies have evaluated broad learning outcomes in a systematic manner. Much work is still needed to understand student learning outcomes in citizen science and to better design learning environments and pedagogical guidance to maximize these outcomes. Recently, several initiatives have embarked on this mission and are examining citizen science in the context of the learning that evolves. Such initiatives include the BSCS Science Learning Workshop on Designing Citizen Science for Both Science and Education (Edelson, Kirn, & workshop participants, 2018), the Board on Science Education within the National Academies of Sciences, Engineering, and Medicine Report on Designing Citizen Science to Support Science Learning[1] and the new Taking Citizen Science to School Research Center (www.tcss.center).

So far, we have reviewed benefits on an individual level, but citizen science has the potential for making science itself more relevant and open for active participation while rendering society more democratic and providing citizens with the ability to influence and promote freedom of expression (see Kidron, Tirosh, Kali, and Schejter's notions on democracy in a networked society, Chap. 7).

While most citizen science projects are targeted at advancing science, many have additional goals of supporting science education, science communication,

---

[1] https://sites.nationalacademies.org/DBASSE/BOSE/CurrentProjects/DBASSE_178572

and evidenced-based decision-making (Golumbic, 2015; Golumbic, Orr, Baram-Tsabari, & Fishbain, 2017). Public participants also have their own rationales for taking part in the initiative. Some of them align well with the goals of the scientists, as in ecological data collection projects, but some far less, such as in Foldit, in which scientists are interested in identifying protein folding structures. Some participants may be interested only in game playing, enjoyment, and internal competition (Curtis, 2015). Unfortunately, many citizen science projects primarily address the goals of one party (Barron, Martin, Mertl, & Yassine, 2016; Bonney et al., 2015). For example, projects may be oriented to benefit scientists who engage the public in collecting data, with only minimal gain to those who contribute the data (Galloway et al., 2015). Other projects, such as S'COOL—Students Cloud Observations On-Line (scool.larc.nasa.gov, now part of Globe: www.globe.gov/web/s-cool/home/participate)—or the EarthEcho Water Challenge (worldwatermonitoringday.org), are oriented toward education or local activism and may have little value for advancement of science (Andújar et al., 2015). Although citizen science projects often engage diverse participants, benefits are not always equally distributed among stakeholders.

Mutualistic Ecology of Citizen Science

To address the interactions among diverse participants in citizen science and their many potential benefits, we conceptualize citizen science and its myriad stakeholders as an ecology. Environments with multiple reciprocal interactions invite this metaphor, as it describes study of the complex interplay among organisms and between them and their habitat. This analogy has been used previously in contexts such as psychology (Kulikowich & Young, 2001), learning (Barron, 2006), and knowledge and innovation (Benkler, 2006). Relationships between parties within the citizen science ecology refer to interaction among scientists, project participants, educational institutions, policymakers, etc. Indeed, participants' interactions have been shown to affect others' participation as well. For example, Cooper and Lewenstein (2016) report a case in which data contributed by a citizen spawned a new research direction that led to novel paths of public participation.

While the ecology metaphor reflects the complexity of multiparty interactions, it does not yet address benefits to participants. Additional metaphors available from biological ecosystems to represent relationships among parties within this ecology could include mutualism, commensalism, or parasitism, which, respectively, provide benefit for both parties, affect one party beneficially with no effect on the other, or benefit one party while adversely affecting the other. Consequently, we complement the ecology metaphor with the term *mutualism* to express our desire for interactions in which all parties benefit from their involvement (Bronstein, 1994). With these two metaphors in mind, we propose a Mutualistic Ecology of Citizen Science (MECS) as an analytic framework for characterizing citizen science endeavors, with the ideal of maximizing benefits to *all participants*. This ideal of mutualism is consistent with Hoadley and Kali's notion of eudæmonic learning (Chap. 1), in which learning in a networked society is conceptualized as a component of how individuals and society mutually develop each other (in this case, participants in citizen science can be viewed as a society).

MECS as an analytic framework can potentially contribute to both conceptualization and design of citizen science projects. To operationalize this framework, we use four lenses, spanning several disciplines that allow us to look at potential benefits to different participants. Seeking to contribute to scholarship on *Learning In the NetworKed Society*, we focus our characterization on benefits associated with learning, i.e., personal growth or advancement of knowledge. In the following section, we elaborate the four lenses that provide us with ways to examine the benefits to different participants—scientists, the general public, and those in formal education settings: (1) the learning community lens illuminates learning opportunities and challenges that may be relevant for all types of participants in different settings; (2) science communication focuses on interactions between scientists and the public and thus highlights related potential for growth; (3) statistical education and data science education aim at supporting the development of data literacy, which may be required and enhanced for citizen science participants, with emphasis on those in formal education; (4) science education is another lens mostly relevant to formal education, as it concerns promotion of scientific literacy.

Learning Communities

Citizen science projects, by design, engage various types of participants whose multiple goals and needs are not necessarily aligned. Many can be thought of as members of different *communities of practice* (Wenger, 1998), defined as groups of people who share a craft and/or profession. This can apply to groups of scientists, citizens focused on a specific socioscientific issue or a particular scientific topic, educators, students, and so forth. Communities of practice are characterized by a combination of three elements: (1) a collective understanding of what the community is about, (2) mutual engagement that reflects shared norms and trusted relationships, and (3) a shared repertoire of communal resources, such as language, routines, artifacts, stories, styles, etc. Wenger (2000) refers to communities of practice as the "basic building blocks of a social learning system, because they are the social 'containers' of the competences that make up such a system" (p. 229). Viewing citizen science projects as a mutualistic ecology in which all communities of practice benefit from the interaction is an extension of Wenger's conceptualization. Instead of focusing on one community of practice, mutualistic ecology focuses on the interaction among such communities.

The communities of practice in the context of citizen science can also be characterized as learning communities. These involve learners with diverse expertise and the common objectives of continuously advancing collective knowledge and mechanisms for its distribution (Bielaczyc, Kapur, & Collins, 2013). Engaging in such communities usually requires its members to move out of their comfort zone and adopt new identities, perceptions, and ways of doing things (Bielaczyc et al., 2013; Penuel, Allen, Coburn, & Farrell, 2015). Brown (1994) describes this exchange of roles in a classroom community of learners:

> In our program, although we assuredly aim at conformity on the basics (everyone must read, write, think, reason, etc.), we also aim at nonconformity in the distribution of expertise and interests so everyone can benefit from the subsequent richness of available knowledge. (p. 10)

The process of developing collective community identity and practice in an ecosystem comprising distinct communities of practice can be challenging (Akkerman & Bruining, 2016; Penuel et al., 2015). While acknowledging the complexity, Wenger (2000) points out the opportunities that such interactions can potentially yield:

> There is something disquieting, humbling at times, yet exciting and attractive about such close encounters with the unknown, with the mystery of "otherness": a chance to explore the edge of your competence, learn something entirely new, revisit your little truths, and perhaps expand your horizon. (p. 233)

The most prominent reason for which we suggest the communities context as a lens for highlighting growth opportunities of diverse citizen science participants lies in the contribution of boundary crossing to learning (Akkerman & Bakker, 2011). Barron (2006) highlights border crossings as an important component of learning ecologies, while Azevedo (2013) suggests tracking such crossings as a means of analyzing learning trajectories. To understand this potential, we examine Wenger's (1998) distinction among three types of boundary interconnections between communities. The first is called *boundary encounters*, when members of one community engage in activities with members of another community. The second boundary interconnection is represented by the role of *brokers*—members who join two or more communities and bridge among them by facilitating the translation, coordination, and alignment of perspectives and meanings. In the context of citizen science, participating citizens may work together and form small groups (Kountoupes & Oberhauser, 2008) or collaborate after attending training workshops (Crall et al., 2012) in which the facilitators may potentially act as brokers. Finally, *boundary objects* are artifacts (tools, documents, models), discourses (common language across boundaries), and processes (routines and procedures) that support the connections among different communities of practice (e.g., scientists and science amateurs). These are exemplified by the online gaming platform of the Foldit project or the Facebook pages that serve as a joint platform for sharing ideas and engaging in a mutualistic discussion in Sensing the Air (sensair.net). In these cases, aspects of the project design serve as boundary objects. Another context in which the three boundary interconnections can work together is citizen science in formal education. We envision boundary crossing (Akkerman & Bakker, 2011) as an inherent part of a citizen science learning community that includes both teachers and students.

In summary, the notion of learning communities is a powerful means toward understanding the many cultural and interactional processes that occur in citizen science projects. As such, it supplies us with powerful tools for analysis, thus enriching our understanding of the notion of mutualism in these contexts and providing us with better design ideas for MECS.

Science Communication

The field of science communication addresses the study of public processes of understanding and engaging with science as it examines its interactions with society (Bucchi & Trench, 2014). Models of science communication can be roughly divided into two subgroups: those emphasizing knowledge transfer, such as Public Understanding of Science (PUS, also referred to as the deficit model), and those emphasizing public dialogue, such as Public Engagement with Science (PES). Both are relevant for the study of citizen science projects, while emphasizing different objectives and leading to diverse outcomes (Haywood & Besley, 2014). While PUS focuses on educational outreach and learning opportunities for the public, PES aims at democratizing science, determining public desires and needs, encouraging transparency, and achieving collective decision-making. Science communication also offers theoretical constructs to examine the benefits of citizen science for scientists, as well as processes of trust building.

Although citizen science projects share goals and potential outcomes with other science communication initiatives, few studies have investigated the relationship among them. The majority of studies on citizen science have not emphasized the approach of science communication, but rather focused on scientific or educational approaches. Nonetheless, many successful citizen science projects incorporate science communication ideas within them and benefit from implementing science communication theories.

As a field that promotes collaborations and relationships between citizens and scientists, citizen science can go beyond the deficit and dialogue models discussed above. Indeed, Trench (2008) proposed an analytic framework of science communication that includes three levels of science communication, maintaining the traditional meaning of PUS as the deficit model and dividing the PES model into dialogue and participation (see Table 6.1). In this framework, dialogue aims at either finding how science could be effectively disseminated or consulting stakeholders regarding specific applications. Participation refers to communication with diverse groups, based on the notion that all can contribute and all have a stake in the outcome of the deliberations and discussions (Trench, 2008).

Table 6.1 Science communication models and meanings

Science communication models	Trench (2008)	Meaning
Public Understanding of Science (PUS)	Deficit	Science transmitted by experts to lay audiences
Public Engagement with Science (PES)	Dialogue	Communication between scientists and public representatives for specific applications or consultation
	Participation	Communication with diverse groups on the basis that all can contribute and all have a stake in the outcome of the deliberations and discussions

Considering Trench's (2008) framework, a natural place for citizen science would have been within the participation model, which orients both scientists and the lay public toward taking part in shaping the issue, setting agendas, and negotiating meaning. Citizen science projects are diverse, however, often varying in their level of inclusion (Bonney, Ballard, et al., 2009; Haklay, 2013). Hence, they may in fact align with all three science communication levels (deficit, dialogue, and participation), depending on their level of inclusion. For example, contributory projects that are initiated and managed by scientists and involve participants only in simple tasks of data collection (Bonney, Ballard, et al., 2009) can be seen as using the public as manpower with no knowledge or ability to make any additional contribution to the scientific process (Haklay, 2013). Consequently, such a project could be aligned with the deficit model, which assumes audiences to be deficient in awareness and understanding of science. Alternatively, co-created projects that involve the public in all stages of the research process, including initiation and planning, could be aligned with the participation model, which considers all partners involved as equal stakeholders.

Each science communication model benefits citizen science participants, as each is directed toward different outcomes. By focusing on educational and learning opportunities, the deficit or PUS model highlights citizen science aspects of public outreach. Participants are introduced to a great deal of scientific information through citizen science projects at levels that range from layman content knowledge to more sophisticated theoretical ideas (Sullivan et al., 2014). These are available through projects, blogs, forums, Facebook pages, etc. (Jackson, Østerlund, Maidel, Crowston, & Mugar, 2016). Participants can learn this information as they study the scientific background and findings of the project at hand. Similarly, through active participation in data collection and analysis, participants can learn about the nature of science and inquiry processes (Bonney, Cooper, et al., 2009) (for more information about learning in citizen science, see the Science Education section of this chapter).

PES complements the PUS model in its dialogic nature, focusing on democratizing science and creating mutual relationships. According to this model, citizen science participants are not just scientific data producers, but rather are considered partners who help direct the study. Through dialogue between scientists and citizens, participants can address scientific topics which are relevant to their lives, help form new scientific questions, and guide studies toward greater sensitivity to society's needs (Haywood & Besley, 2014).

Citizen science can be seen as a way to integrate the different science communication models. Combining ideas from both PES and PUS may promote both social and educational goals. One example is the citizen science initiative Sensing the Air (air.net.technion.ac.il), a collaboration between scientists and citizens that aims at facilitating air quality research through active involvement of volunteers and through the collection and interpretation of meaningful air quality data. To do so, ideas from all science communication models were considered and implemented in practice during the project.

Features of Sensing the Air that correspond to the PUS model were air quality data dissemination facilitated through an interactive data presentation platform, explanations about air quality concepts, and research and examination of learning processes throughout participation in the project. Features that correspond with the PES model were hazard reports submitted to scientists and new research ideas raised by participants, providing opportunities for participants to engage in and conduct their own research—making the science relevant to their everyday life—and responding to public concerns.

While these features align with the two science communication models discussed, in practice, many were in fact implemented as a consolidation of models. This combined practice is illustrated in the data presentation platform. While dissemination of information is a one-way transfer model generally considered part of the PUS model, the platform was designed with a user-centered approach that created dialogue and guaranteed the presentation of relevant information—a key feature of the PES model.

In summary, building elements of all traditions of science communication into citizen science practice and combining them into new practices enable projects to be geared to participants' various needs. Using such practices in the design stages of citizen science projects can support different types of audiences by incorporating multiple opportunities and levels of engagement for the benefit of diverse stakeholders.

Statistical Education and Data Science Education

Citizen science projects often involve the collection of large amounts of differential types of data. Data science is the interdisciplinary field that enables extraction of knowledge from such data (Hardin et al., 2015). The growing number of citizen science projects that provide participants with access to accumulating data brings the value of statistical reasoning, thinking, and literacy to the forefront. In societies that are becoming increasingly technological, individuals should be able to make educated decisions concerning scientific issues that affect their personal lives (e.g., causes and effects of air pollution and related policy). Such decision-making requires statistical understanding of the scientific process. Many studies indicate, however, that adults do not think statistically about important issues that affect their lives (Watson, 1997).

Statistical literacy is described as the ability to interpret and critically evaluate statistical information and data-related arguments that people may encounter in diverse contexts. It is also related to the ability to communicate reactions to statistical information and concerns regarding the acceptability of given conclusions (Gal, 2002). These capabilities are grounded in an interrelated set of human knowledge elements, such as statistical literacy, context knowledge, critical skills, and dispositional elements (e.g., critical stance, beliefs).

Statistics educators argue that to develop statistical literacy, it may be necessary to work with learners—ranging from younger students to adults—in ways that go beyond traditional instructional methods. For example, the big data collected in citizen science projects often contains large amounts of data collected by a variety of people with a wide range of specialties. Analyzing such data to answer scientific questions requires measures to understand how reliable and representative the data is. Such cases provide authentic grounds for familiarizing learners with "worry questions" (Gal, 1994) regarding data quality and validity. Examples include: "Where did the data come from? Was a sample used? Is the sample biased in some way? How reliable or accurate were the instruments or measures used to generate data?" Asking about and querying such data enables the development of a critical stance and supporting beliefs about statistical investigation, including the development of learners' inquiry skills. This can be accomplished by engaging students in carefully designed, technology-enhanced exploratory data analysis learning environments (Ben-Zvi, Gravemeijer & Ainley, 2018; Garfield & Ben-Zvi, 2008). Exploratory data analysis aids can also facilitate learners' handling of uncertainties involved in making *Informal Statistical Inferences* (Manor & Ben-Zvi, 2017; Pratt, Johnston-Wilder, Ainley & Mason, 2008), including development of their model-based skills (Dvir & Ben-Zvi, 2018; Manor & Ben-Zvi, 2015).

Moreover, although most statistical analysis in citizen science projects is performed by scientists, projects designed with supports that develop participants' statistical literacy might improve the quality of collected data, while providing an opportunity to engage citizens in the statistical investigative phase of citizen science projects. Scientists in projects that take these features into account may gain more from participating citizens who understand the needs and importance of collecting reliable data. For example, a citizen who is aware of measurement errors might be more careful while measuring and perform repetitive measurements. As a result, scientists will be able to gradually trust citizens' reasoning and involve them in more intricate parts of the research projects. There may even be cases in which citizens with advanced statistical reasoning skills may propose different methods of gathering data and understand their effect on the analysis and inference processes.

The statistical education lens gives us the ability to analyze the data science literacies needed for participating in different citizen science projects and the extent to which this participation supports the development of those literacies, benefiting those who choose to do so. Furthermore, statistical education informs designers regarding possible scaffolds that may aid in the process of developing the relevant data literacies, benefiting all participants and helping projects become MECS.

Science Education: Scientific Literacy and Socioscientific Issues

As a scientific endeavor itself, citizen science is a fitting and exciting context within which to consider science education. The concept of scientific literacy has different meanings and interpretations of what the public ought to know about science and who that "public" is (Laugksch, 2000). Two visions are most prevalent (Roberts & Bybee, 2014): Vision I is based on the idea of the student as a novice scientist who is expected to master the knowledge of science and its methodologies; Vision II of scientific literacy seeks to cultivate future citizens with the skills and knowledge to take part in rational, democratic decision-making processes regarding science-related issues (Aikenhead, 2005; Bybee & DeBoer, 1994; Roberts & Bybee, 2014).

Twenty-first-century citizens are often required to take an active stance and make decisions concerning socioscientific issues—controversial social affairs involving science, such as environmental or public health topics (Sadler, 2011). The quality of those decisions, mostly made by lay people, is of major significance in a democratic society (Kolstø, 2001). The involvement in informed decision-making in society reflects the four tenets of democracy, as described in Kidron and colleagues (Chap. 7): active participation, free movement of voices, equal and just expression, and ability to influence. In line with these understandings, contemporary views of scientific literacy emphasize Vision II and identify the goal of science education as supporting the development of future citizens, rather than primarily promoting the education of future scientists (Vision I). These views describe scientific literacy as the insights and abilities that empower citizens to confront, negotiate, and make decisions in life situations involving science (Bybee, McCrae, & Laurie, 2009; Sadler, 2011). Some researchers (e.g., Hodson, 2003) have taken this concept further, arguing that science education should prepare the individual for sociopolitical action and that a sense of ownership and empowerment is essential for translation of knowledge into action.

The study of science in the context of socioscientific issues can serve as an effective means to support Vision II science education goals (Zeidler, 2015). Instruction based on socioscientific issues has also been shown to promote students' learning of the content and nature of science, both constituents of Vision I, although the empirical base to support this conclusion is limited (Romine, Sadler, & Kinslow, 2016; Sadler, Romine, & Topçu, 2016).

Local citizen science projects, such as the Shermans Creek Monitoring Program (Wilderman, 2004) or Sensing the Air, often involve socioscientific issues related to conflicting agendas concerning local resources (e.g., nature preservation vs. economic growth). Following Hodson's (2003) claims (see above), it is reasonable to assume that higher levels of engagement and participation in such citizen science projects will promote the development of Vision II and of active citizenship. Indeed, citizen science has been suggested as a platform for encouraging public dialogue on socioscientific issues and as a means to engage the public in decision-making processes (McKinley et al., 2017; Mueller, Tippins, & Bryan, 2012; Stilgoe et al., 2014). Current research examining the feasibility of these ideas is lacking, but some work has been accomplished that does display promising results. While several researchers have shown that participation in citizen science projects has failed to change participants' attitudes toward science in general and environmental issues in particular (Brossard et al., 2005; Crall et al., 2012), other citizen science projects have indeed increased local environmental awareness (Evans et al., 2005). Recent research has addressed this problem by formulating specific design elements. For example, Bonney et al. (2015) suggested adding reflective steps to enhance learning by helping participants understand their own role in the scientific process. Ballard et al. (2017) conceptualized a citizen science framework that integrated science education, skill improvement, and personal development, aimed at empowering youth participating in citizen science projects and inspiring behavioral change.

Participation in citizen science initiatives is associated not only with Vision II but also with an enhanced version of Vision I with greater emphasis on the realms of scientific thinking (Evans et al., 2005), understanding the scientific process and related skills (Bonney, Cooper, et al., 2009; Brossard et al., 2005) and improving knowledge of scientific subject matter (Brossard et al., 2005). Given the evidence for the educational potential of practicing authentic science, citizen science initiatives such as monitoring a section of a sandy beach or measuring water quality at home have been introduced recently into formal education settings. The results appear optimistic in terms of building students' capacity to take part in present and future conservation campaigns and the promotion of a positive perception of science and scientists (Ballard et al., 2017; Redondo, Queiruga Dios, Sáiz Manzanares, & Juez Navarro, 2018), thus achieving some of the benefits citizen science embodies for students taking part in such projects.

Several leading reports concerning contemporary directions for science education—such as the NRC Education for Life and Work Report (2013), the Framework for K-12 Science Education (NRC 2012), and the Next Generation Science Standards (NGSS Lead States, 2013)—have been published over the past few years. These reports emphasize shifting from coverage of isolated facts to focusing on the construction of a rich network of connected ideas and interrelated concepts that can be used to explain phenomena and solve problems by engaging in science and engineering practices (Krajcik et al., 2014; Reiser, 2013), declaring that learning must be practiced within the context of relevant and authentic activities (Sadler, Foulk, & Friedrichsen, 2017). These reports, as well as science education in general, refine the tools to promote and evaluate such learning. As such, the science education lens contributes framework evaluation tools to the MECS that provide insights into the extent to which citizen science projects promote the development of scientific literacy and into the manner in which such supplementary benefits may be incorporated into their design.

The MECS Analytic Framework: An Illustrative Summary

At the new Taking Citizen Science to School Research Center (www.tcss.center), we recently proposed an example for a MECS model based on the four lenses described above (Atias, Sagy, Kali, Angel, & Edelist, 2017). The new model, Students as Citizen Science Ambassadors, integrates a citizen science program in a K-12 school as part of its formal science curriculum. Scientific researchers worked closely with educational scholars and teachers to co-design boundary objects, such as curricular resources and student activities. These were used to advance communication with citizens and engage them in their communities. The various players were encouraged to exchange roles and identities by becoming brokers at different phases in the learning process. Educational researchers bridged between scientific researchers and teachers; teachers mediated between researchers and students, while students—when interacting with other citizens—negotiated between their own community and scientists. The model follows the ideas of Vision II discussed above, where science education practices are used as a means to promote active citizenship among students. Activities designed to advance science and data literacies involved learning about the research subject, thereby gaining proficiency in scientific inquiry and data analysis tasks. Most importantly, students assume an advocacy role, communicating information and designing and executing project-related activities for their close community.

This model is expected to intensify the mutualistic nature of citizen science; the students gain data and science literacies, as well as science communication skills, while being empowered to promote change in their own community. The community gains access to relevant scientific information and an option to contribute to scientific research. The scientists benefit from the students' acting as agents promoting public participation in their research, producing increased capacity for data collection and analysis, along with a well-informed, attentive audience.

As illustrated by the Students as Citizen Science Ambassadors model, the four lenses enable us utilize the unique analytic framework of MECS to enhance our conceptualization of learning in citizen science projects, as well as their design. Specifically, the MECS framework helps focus on the various potential benefits within each of these lenses for the different participants involved. The learning community lens provides a means for examining cultural and interactional processes involved in citizen science, with an eye on those interactions that promote learning and growth. Science communication reveals the power of citizen science as a vehicle to enhance the general public's understanding and engagement with science, thereby supporting mutualism between citizens and scientists. Statistics education and data science education address the ubiquitous need to make educated decisions related to scientific issues that affect people's personal lives, possibly supporting the advancement of science at the same time. Finally, science education empowers citizens to take more control of their lives by making informed decisions regarding their active involvement in society, thereby potentially producing benefit for citizens and society alike. The four lenses combined operationalize the MECS analytic framework, enabling a critical stance for both analysis and design. Understanding the different ways citizen science projects benefit diverse participants is a vital step towards designing effective MECS that contribute to all who are involved in them.

Epilogue

Insights that emerged during the writing of this chapter have been further developed and are currently being carried out and explored as part of the Taking Citizen Science to School Center (www.tcss.center), as exemplified by the Students as

Citizen Science Ambassadors model. Leveraging the interdisciplinary approach at the LINKS Center (see Chaps. 1, 2, and 3), the TCSS Center involves researchers from five STEM education disciplines: mathematics, statistics education, biology, earth science, and environmental education. The principal theoretical perspectives guiding TCSS research span learning sciences, science communication, and public engagement with science, informal and outdoor science education, learning communities, data sciences, and technology-enhanced learning. As described in the current chapter, we believe that these theoretical perspectives, embedded within the notion of MECS and operationalizing it as an analytic framework, hold great promise for further conceptualization, as well as design of citizen science endeavors.

References

Aikenhead, G. S. (2005). *Science education for everyday life: Evidence-based practice*. New York: Teachers College.

Akkerman, S. F., & Bakker, A. (2011). Boundary crossing and boundary objects. *Review of Educational Research, 81*(2), 132–169.

Akkerman, S., & Bruining, T. (2016). Multi-level boundary crossing in a professional development school partnership. *Journal of the Learning Sciences, 25*(2), 1–44.

Andújar, B., Campderrós, G., García, M., Marino, M., Mas, M., et al. (2015). Twenty tips for high-school students engaging in research with scientists. *Frontiers for Young Minds, 3*, 7.

Aristeidou, M., Scanlon, E., & Sharples, M. (2013). A design-based study of citizen inquiry for geology. In *Proceedings of the doctoral consortium at the European conference on technology enhanced learning, co-located with the EC-TEL 2013 conference 7–13*. CEUR.

Atias, O., Sagy, O., Kali, Y., Angel, D., & Edelist, D., (2017). *Jellyfish and people—a citizen-science collaboration with mutual benefits to citizens and scientists*. Poster presented at the American Educational Research Association Conference, San Antonio, Texas, April.

Azevedo, F. S. (2013). The tailored practice of hobbies and its implication for the design of interest-driven learning environments. *Journal of the Learning Sciences, 22*(3), 462–510.

Ballard, H. L., Dixon, C. G., & Harris, E. M. (2017). Youth-focused citizen science: Examining the role of environmental science learning and agency for conservation. *Biological Conservation, 208*, 65–75.

Barron, B. (2006). Interest and self-sustained learning as catalysts of development: A learning ecology perspective. *Human Development, 49*(4), 193–224.

Barron, B., Martin, C. K., Mertl, V., & Yassine, M. (2016). Citizen science: Connecting to nature through networks. In U. Cress, J. Moskaliuk, & H. Jeong (Eds.), *Mass collaboration and education* (Computer-Supported Collaborative Learning Series) (Vol. 16, pp. 257–284). New York: Springer.

Benkler, Y. (2006). *The wealth of networks: How social production transforms markets and freedom*. New Haven/London: Yale University Press.

Ben-Zvi, D., Gravemeijer, K., & Ainley, J. (2018). Design of statistics learning environments. In D. Ben-Zvi, K. Makar, & J. Garfield (Eds.), *International handbook of research in statistics education* (pp. 473–502). Cham, Switzerland: Springer.

Bielaczyc, K., Kapur, M., & Collins, A. (2013). In C. E. Hmelo-Silver, C. A. Chinn, C. Chan, & A. M. O'Donnell (Eds.), *International handbook of collaborative learning*. New York: Taylor & Francis.

Bizer, C. (2009). The emerging web of linked data. *IEEE Intelligent Systems, 24*(5), 87–92.

Bonney, R., Ballard, H., Jordan, R., McCallie, E., Phillips, T., Shirk, J., & Wilderman, C. C. (2009). *Public participation in scientific research: Defining the field and assessing its potential for informal science education*. A CAISE Inquiry Group Report, (July), 1–58.

Bonney, R., Cooper, C., & Ballard, H. (2016). The theory and practice of citizen science: Launching a new journal. *Citizen Science: Theory and Practice, 1*(1).

Bonney, R., Cooper, C. B., Dickinson, J., Kelling, S., Phillips, T., Rosenberg, K. V., et al. (2009). Citizen science: A developing tool for expanding science knowledge and scientific literacy. *Bioscience, 59*(11), 977–984.

Bonney, R., Phillips, T., Enck, J., Shirk, J., & Trautmann, N. (2014). *Citizen Science and Youth Education*. Washington, DC: Research Council Committee on Out-of-School Time STEM.

Bonney, R., Phillips, T. B., Ballard, H. L., & Enck, J. W. (2015). Can citizen science enhance public understanding of science? *Public Understanding of Science, 25*(1), 2–16.

Bronstein, J. L. (1994). Our current understanding of mutualism. *The Quarterly Review of Biology, 69*(1), 31–51.

Brossard, D., Lewenstein, B., & Bonney, R. (2005). Scientific knowledge and attitude change: The impact of a citizen science project. *International Journal of Science Education, 27*(9), 1099–1121.

Brown, A. L. (1994). The advancement of learning. *Educational Researcher, 23*(8), 4–12.

Bucchi, M., & Trench, B. (2014). *Routledge handbook of public communication of science and technology*. Abingdon, UK/New York: Routledge.

Bybee, R. W., & DeBoer, G. E. (1994). Research on goals for the science curriculum. In D. L. Gabel (Ed.), *Handbook of research on science teaching and learning* (pp. 357–387). New York: Simon & Schuster Macmillan.

Bybee, R., McCrae, B., & Laurie, R. (2009). PISA 2006: An assessment of scientific literacy. *Journal of Research in Science Teaching, 46*(8), 865–883.

Cooper, C. B., & Lewenstein, B. V. (2016). Two meanings of citizen science. In D. Cavalier & E. B. Kennedy (Eds.), *The rightful place of science: Citizen science* (pp. 51–62). Tempe, AZ: Consortium for Science, Policy & Outcomes.

Crall, A. W., Jordan, R., Holfelder, K., Newman, G. J., Graham, J., & Waller, D. M. (2012). The impacts of an invasive species citizen science training program on participant attitudes, behavior, and science literacy. *Public Understanding of Science, 21*(1), 1–20.

Curtis, V. (2015). *Online citizen science projects: An exploration of motivation, contribution and participation*. Ph.D. dissertation submitted to the Open University (United Kingdom).

Del Savio, L., Prainsack, B., & Buyx, A. (2016). Crowdsourcing the human gut. Is crowdsourcing also "citizen science"? *Journal of Science Communication, 15*(3), 1–16.

Dickinson, J. L., Shirk, J., Bonter, D., Bonney, R., Crain, R. L., Martin, J., et al. (2012). The current state of citizen science as a tool for ecological research and public engagement. *Frontiers in Ecology and the Environment, 10*(6), 291–297.

Dvir, M., & Ben-Zvi, D. (2018). The role of model comparison in young learners' reasoning with statistical models and modeling. *ZDM – International Journal on Mathematics Education, 50*(7), 1183–1196.

Edelson, D. C., Kirn, S. L., & workshop participants. (2018). *Designing citizen science for both science and education: A workshop report*. (Technical Report No. 2018–01). Colorado Springs, CO: BSCS Science Learning.

Evans, C., Abrams, E., Reitsma, R., Roux, K., Salmonsen, L., & Marra, P. P. (2005). The neighborhood nestwatch program: Participant outcomes of a citizen-science ecological research project. *Conservation Biology, 19*(3), 589–594.

Flávio S. Azevedo. (2013). The Tailored Practice of Hobbies and Its Implication for the Design of Interest-Driven Learning Environments. *Journal of the Learning Sciences 22*(3), 462–510.

Gal, I. (1994, September). Assessment of interpretive skills. Summary of working group, Conference on Assessment Issues in Statistics Education. Philadelphia, Pennsylvania.

Gal, I. (2002). Adults' statistical literacy: Meanings, components, responsibilities. *International Statistical Review, 70*(1), 1–25.

Galloway, M. A., Willett, K. W., Fortson, L. F., Cardamone, C. N., Schawinski, K., Cheung, E., et al. (2015). Galaxy zoo: The effect of bar-driven fuelling on the presence of an active galactic nucleus in disc galaxies. *Monthly Notices of the Royal Astronomical Society, 448*(4), 3442–3454.

Garfield, J., & Ben-Zvi, D. (2008). *Developing students' statistical reasoning: Connecting research and teaching practice.* Springer.

Golumbic, Y. N. (2015). *What makes citizen science projects successful, and what can we learn from them for future projects? THE Technion literature review of citizen science projects. Technion Citizen Science Project (TCSP).* Haifa, Israel: The Technion—Israel Institute of Technology.

Golumbic, Y. N., Baram-Tsabari, A., & Fishbain, B. (2016). Increased knowledge and scientific thinking following participation of school students in air-quality research. In Proceedings of Indoor Air 2016.

Golumbic, Y. N., Baram-Tsabari, A., & Fishbain, B. (2017). Why and how should we facilitate scientific information to the public [in Hebrew]. *Ecology and the Environment, 8*(3), 5–6.

Golumbic, Y. N., Orr, D., Baram-Tsabari, A., & Fishbain, B. (2017). Between vision and reality: A case study of scientists' views on citizen science. *Citizen Science Theory and Practice, 2*(1), 1–13.

Golumbic, Y. N., Fishbain, B., & Baram-Tsabari, A. (Forthcoming). User centered design of a citizen science air-quality monitoring project. *International Journal of Science Education, Part B.*

Haklay, M. (2013). Citizen science and volunteered geographic information—overview and typology of participation. In D. Sui, S. Elwood, & M. Goodchild (Eds.), *Crowdsourcing geographic knowledge: Volunteered geographic information (VGI) in theory and practice* (pp. 105–122). Berlin, Germany: Springer.

Hardin, J., Hoerl, R., Horton, N. J., Nolan, D., Baumer, B., Hall-Holt, O., et al. (2015). Data science in statistics curricula: Preparing students to "think with data". *The American Statistician, 69*(4), 343–353.

Haywood, B. K., & Besley, J. C. (2014). Education, outreach, and inclusive engagement: Towards integrated indicators of successful program outcomes in participatory science. *Public Understanding of Science (Bristol, England), 23*(1), 92–106.

Hodson, D. (2003). Time for action: Science education for an alternative future. *International Journal of Science Education, 25*(6), 645–670.

Irwin, A. (1995). *Citizen science. A study of people, expertise and sustainable development.* New York: Routledge.

Jackson, C., Østerlund, C., Maidel, V., Crowston, K., & Mugar, G. (2016). Which way did they go? Newcomer movement through the Zooniverse. In *Proceedings of the 19th ACM conference on computer-supported cooperative work & social computing* (pp. 623–634). New York: ACM Press.

Kolstø, S. D. (2001). Scientific literacy for citizenship: Tools for dealing with the science dimension of controversial socioscientific issues. *Science Education, 85*(3), 291–310.

Kountoupes, D. I., & Oberhauser, K. S. (2008). Citizen science and youth audiences: Educational outcomes of the Monarch Larva Monitoring Project. *Journal of Community Engagement and Scholarship, 1*(1). http://jces.ua.edu/citizen-science-and-youth-audiences-educational-outcomes-of-the-monarch-larva-monitoring-project/

Krajcik, J., Codere, S., Dahsah, C., Bayer, R., & Mun, K. (2014). Planning instruction to meet the intent of the next generation science standards. *Journal of Science Teacher Education, 25*(2), 157–175.

Kulikowich, J. M., & Young, M. F. (2001). Locating an ecological psychology action for situated methodology. *Journal of the Learning Sciences, 10*(1–2), 17–26.

Kullenberg, C., & Kasperowski, D. (2016). What is citizen science?—A scientometric meta-analysis. *PLoS One, 11*(1). https://doi.org/10.1371/journal.pone.0147152

Manor, H., & Ben-Zvi, D. (2015). Students' emergent articulations of models and modeling in making informal statistical inferences. In *Proceedings of the ninth international research forum on statistical reasoning, thinking, and literacy (SRTL9)* (pp. 107–117). Paderborn, Germany: University of Paderborn.

Manor, H., & Ben-Zvi, D. (2017). Students' emergent articulations of statistical models and modeling in making informal statistical inferences. *Statistics Education Research Journal, 16*(2), 116–143.

McKinley, D. C., Miller-Rushing, A. J., Ballard, H. L., Bonney, R., Brown, H., Cook-Patton, S. C., et al. (2017). Citizen science can improve conservation science, natural resource management, and environmental protection. *Biological Conservation, 208*, 15–28.

Laugksch, R. C. (2000). Scientific literacy: A conceptual overview. *Science Education, 84*(1), 71–94.

Lewenstein, B. (2016). Can we understand citizen science? *Journal of Science Communication, 15*(01), 1–5.

Lievrouw, L. A. (2010). Social media and the production of knowledge: A return to little science? *Social Epistemology, 24*(3), 219–237.

Mueller, M. P., Tippins, D., & Bryan, L. (2012). The future of citizen science. *Democracy and Education, 20*(1), 2.

Pettibone, L., Vohland, K., Bonn, A., Richter, A., Bauhus, W., Behrisch, B., Borcherding, R., Brandt, M., Bry, F., Dörler, D., Elbertse, I., Glöckler, F., Göbel, C., Hecker, S., Heigl, F., Herdick, M., Kiefer, S., Kluttig, T., Kühn, E., Kühn, K., Oswald, K., Röller, O., Schefels, C., Schierenberg, A., Scholz, W., Schumann, A., Sieber, A., Smolarski, R., Tochtermann, K., Wende, W. and Ziegler, D. 2016. Citizen science for all – a guide for citizen science practitioners

Penuel, W. R., Allen, A. R., Coburn, C. E., & Farrell. (2015). Conceptualizing research-practice partnerships as joint work at boundaries. *Journal of Education for Students Placed at Risk, 20*(1–2), 182–197.

Pratt, D., Johnston-Wilder, P., Ainley, J., & Mason, J. (2008). Local and global thinking in statistical inference. *Statistics Education Research Journal, 7*(2), 107–129.

Raddick, M. J., Bracey, G., Carney, K., Gyuk, G., Borne, K., Wallin, J., & Jacoby, S. (2009). Citizen science: Status and research directions for the coming decade. Astro2010: The astronomy and astrophysics decadal survey, Position Paper no. 46. http://adsabs.harvard.edu/abs/2009astro2010P..46R

Redondo, M. L., Queiruga Dios, M. A., Sáiz Manzanares, M. C., & Juez Navarro, S. (2018). Citizen science in school. In M. F. P. C. Martins Costa, J. B. Vásquez Dorrío, & J. M. Fernández Novell (Eds.), *Hands-on science. Advancing science. Improving education.* (pp. 194–198). Hands-on Science Network. Braga, Portugal: Copissaurio Repro – Centro Imp. Unip. Lda. Campus de Gualtar, Reprografia Complexo II. http://www.hsci.info/hsci2018/images/pdfs/eBookHSCI2018.pdf

Reiser, B. J. (2013, September). What professional development strategies are needed for successful implementation of the next generation science standards. In paper written for the Invitational research symposium on science assessment (Vol. 24, p. 25).

Roberts, D. A., & Bybee, R. W. (2014). Scientific literacy, science literacy, and science education. In N. Lederman & S. K. Abell (Eds.), *Handbook of research on science education* (Vol. II, pp. 545–558). Abingdon, UK: Routledge.

Romine, W. L., Sadler, T. D., & Kinslow, A. T. (2016). Assessment of scientific literacy: M. F. P. C. (QuASSR). *Journal of Research in Science Teaching, 54*(2), 274–295.

Sadler, T. D. (2011). Situating socio-scientific issues in classrooms as a means of achieving goals of science education. In *Socio-scientific issues in the classroom: Teaching, learning and research* (pp. 1–9). Dordrecht, The Netherlands: Springer.

Sadler, T. D., Romine, W. L., & Topçu, M. S. (2016). Learning science content through socio-scientific issues-based instruction: A multi-level assessment study. *International Journal of Science Education, 38*(10), 1622–1635.

Sadler, T. D., Foulk, J. A., & Friedrichsen, P. J. (2017). Evolution of a model for socio-scientific issue teaching and learning. *International Journal of Education in Mathematics, Science and Technology, 5*(2), 75–87.

Sickler, J., & Cherry, T. M. (2012). *Lost ladybug project summative evaluation report*. Edgewater, MD.

Silva, C., Monteiro, A. J., Manahl, C., Lostal, E., Schäfer, T., Andrade, N., et al. (2016). Cell spotting: Educational and motivational outcomes of cell biology citizen science project in the classroom. *Journal of Science Communication, 15*(01), A02.

Silvertown, J. (2009). A new dawn for citizen science. *Trends in Ecology & Evolution, 24*(9), 467–471.

Stebbins, R. A. (1997). Serious leisure and well-being. In J. T. Haworth (Ed.), *Work, leisure and well-being* (pp. 117–130). London: Routledge.

Stilgoe, J., Lock, S. J., & Wilsdon, J. (2014). Why should we promote public engagement with science? *Public Understanding of Science, 23*(1), 4–15.

Sullivan, B. L., Aycrigg, J. L., Barry, J. H., Bonney, R. E., Bruns, N., Cooper, C. B., et al. (2014). The eBird enterprise: An integrated approach to development and application of citizen science. *Biological Conservation, 169*, 31–40.

Sullivan, B. L., Phillips, T., Dayer, A. A., Wood, C. L., Farnsworth, A., Iliff, M. J., et al. (2017). Using open access observational data for conservation action: A case study for birds. *Biological Conservation, 208*, 5–14.

Teacher, A. G. F., Griffiths, D. J., Hodgson, D. J., & Inger, R. (2013). Smartphones in ecology and evolution: A guide for the apprehensive. *Ecology and Evolution, 3*(16), 5268–5278.

Trench, B. (2008). Towards an analytical framework of science communication models. In D. Cheng, M. Claessens, N. R. J. Gascoigne, T. J. Metcalfe, B. Schiele, & S. Shi (Eds.), *Communicating science in social contexts: new models, new practices* (pp. 119–138). Dordrecht, The Netherlands: Springer.

Watson, J. M. (1997). Assessing statistical thinking using the media. In I. Gal & J. B. Garfield (Eds.), *The assessment challenge in statistics education*. Amsterdam, The Netherlands: IOS Press.

Wenger, E. (1998). *Communities of practice, learning, meaning and identity*. Cambridge, UK: Cambridge University Press.

Wenger, E. (2000). Communities of practice and social learning systems. *Organization Articles, 7*(2), 225–246.

Wilderman, C. C. (2004). *Shermans Creek: A portrait*. Technical Status Report. Carlisle, PA: Alliance for Aquatic Resource Monitoring (ALLARM). Dickinson College.

Yoho, R. A., & Vanmali, B. H. (2016). Controversy in biology classrooms—citizen science approaches to evolution and applications to climate change discussions. *Journal of Microbiology and Biology Education, 17*(1), 110–114.

Zeidler, D. (2015). Socioscientific issues. In *Encyclopedia of science education* (pp. 998–1003). Dordrecht, The Netherlands: Springer.

Chapter 7
Democracy, Communication, and Education in the Twenty-First Century

Adi Kidron, Noam Tirosh, Yael Kali, and Amit M. Schejter

Abstract The dramatic technological advancements that characterize our current networked society have shifted the ways that people communicate, educate, and interact with each other. How could we build on these advancements to enhance the democratic essence of learning processes for the benefit of both society as a whole and its individual members? What are the opportunities? What are the challenges and threats? This chapter explores the added value of communication technologies to democracy and education. It then builds on this analysis in its examination of the relations between democracy and education, as exemplified in a specific case study: a set of two interconnected interdisciplinary courses in higher education, entitled, as the name of this book – Learning in a Networked Society. As such, it demonstrated a strong potential for cross-fostering of ideas between educational scientists – who focus on the interventionist, design-based study of learning – and social scientists, who may also focus on analytic study of spontaneous social phenomena.

Keywords Democracy · Education · Learning community · Participation · Socio-constructivist education · Interdisciplinary understanding · Voice

A century has gone by since John Dewey published *Democracy and Education*, positing that all types of communications are the expression of social life and

A. Kidron (✉) · Y. Kali
Department of Learning, Instruction, and Teacher Education, University of Haifa,
Haifa, Israel
e-mail: yael.kali@edtech.haifa.ac.il

N. Tirosh
Department of Communication Studies, Ben-Gurion University of the Negev,
Beer Sheva, Israel

A. M. Schejter
Department of Communication Studies, Ben-Gurion University of the Negev,
Beer Sheva, Israel

Donald P. Bellisario College of Communications, The Pennsylvania State University,
State College, PA, USA

© Springer Nature Switzerland AG 2019   117
Y. Kali et al. (eds.), *Learning In a Networked Society*, Computer-Supported
Collaborative Learning Series 17, https://doi.org/10.1007/978-3-030-14610-8_7

therefore possess an educative outcome (Dewey, 1916/2012). Dewey claimed that even living together is a process that educates, as it provides the individual with the opportunity to reflect on his or her experiences and extract meaning therefrom. Education, he concluded, "consists primarily in transmission through communication" (Dewey, 1916/2012, p. 13). As such, education is dependent on both democracy and free transmission of information in society; at the same time, it contributes to the democratization of society, as it can improve the quality of the information transmitted.

Indeed, communication studies and education alike have developed from research trajectories that originate in Dewey's philosophy. Nevertheless, the dramatic technological advancements that characterize our current networked society have shifted the ways that people communicate, educate, and interact with each other. "Old media" have been mostly characterized as unidirectional, stationary technologies, limited in their capacity to carry information created by large corporations or governments. Contemporary media are fundamentally different. These innovative information mediation technologies enable a new and unique form of communication—*mass self-communication* (Castells, 2007, p. 248)—that is "self-generated in content, self-directed in emission and self-selected in reception" (ibid). This chapter explores the added value of these advancements in communication technologies to democracy and education. It then builds on this analysis in its examination of the relations between democracy and education, as exemplified in a specific case study: a set of two interconnected courses in higher education, entitled, as the name of this book—*Learning in a Networked Society* (LINKS).

As explained in previous chapters (Barzilai & Chinn, Chap. 4; Baram-Tsabari, & Schejter, Chap. 5), contemporary media can be defined according to four unique characteristics: mobility, abundance, multimediality, and interactivity (Schejter & Tirosh, 2014, 2015, 2016). They enable communication at will from a variety of locations, providing access to abundant amounts of information over a virtually infinite number of "channels," and possess a wealth of space to store this information. Furthermore, individuals can potentially mediate messages using various forms of expression, including text, photos, graphics, sound, and video or any combination thereof. Contemporary media also enable users to contribute and affect not only the content but also the process of communication in which they are involved and, as such, to influence and even create and design their own mediated environment (Schejter & Tirosh, 2014, 2015, 2016).

Given these characteristics, contemporary media offer new opportunities to reflect on our experiences and to extract meaning. In Dewey's terms, they entail new educational opportunities to enhance democratic processes for the benefit of society as a whole and at the same time for individual members of society. This potential of technology is described by Hoadley and Kali (Chap. 1) as eudaemonic—the type of "flourishing that happens when individuals reach their potential through finding their place in society and improving it". Taking a more critical stance, however, these same characteristics, applied with different interests in mind, can become threats to these very democratic notions, as explained by Baram-Tsabari and Schejter in their double-edged sword analogy for analyzing the potential effects of new media (Chap. 5). For example, people might be silenced by the fear that their voice will remain documented and accessible forever. Moreover, capital can influence patterns of presence in contemporary media as well as the strategic ability to control information flow, shape conversation, and manipulate public opinion. In addition, without transparency, it is more difficult to identify interests, agendas, or fake and biased facts that may threaten the public's trust in social discourse (see Barzilai & Chinn, Chap. 4, for an epistemic thinking lens on such issues). Finally, some knowledge (e.g., scholarly articles) is accessible only to certain parts of the public, thereby threatening equality and egalitarian knowledge acquisition. We argue that in face of the possible threats described, contemporary media's added value to democratic processes is not obvious and that only careful design of the way these media are used, especially in the context of educational interventions, can lead to positive change and a better future in terms of democracy and education.

To demonstrate our claims, this chapter focuses on the LINKS courses as a specific example of an educational intervention in which contemporary media were incorporated carefully into the design of the courses in order to support specific pedagogical goals. The courses, offered at the University of Haifa between 2013 and 2017, aimed at supporting the development of students' interdisciplinary understanding of the LINKS theme. We hypothesized that this could be achieved by promoting meaningful dialogue among learners in which a variety of ideas and ways of thinking would be shared. The resulting design of the LINKS courses is an interesting case study in the context of this chapter for the following reasons:

- The courses were developed as an implementation of a generic instructional model— *Boundary Breaking for Interdisciplinary Learning* (BBIL) (Kidron & Kali, 2015)—that aims at promoting interdisciplinary thinking and understanding. The notion of *breaking boundaries* is embodied in the LINKS courses from curricular, pedagogical, and organizational perspectives, thereby echoing various notions of democracy, as we demonstrate below.
- LINKS courses use a *learning community* (LC) approach that builds on Vygotsky's (1978) social development theory, emphasizing collaborative knowledge advancement and the synthesis of diverse individual contributions as a means of personal learning as well as the learning of the whole community. This aspect of LCs stresses the importance of each member's voice for the community and its ability to achieve its shared objective. Similarly, the essential characteristic of democracy, viewed as a normative ideal, is an active citizenry in which members are able to voice their wills and promote their interests equally (Schejter & Tirosh, 2014; Yona, 2006). Therefore, a learning community approach is democratic by nature, as it builds on active expression of individual interests to promote shared ones.
- LINKS courses use *educational technologies* to support the LC approach in ways that comply with the contemporary media characteristics described above.

In summary, our case study will exemplify the new possibilities brought about by contemporary technological capabilities when implementing democratic values, norms, and practices in a designed learning environment. To set the stage to discuss these cases, we first introduce our theoretical tenets.

Theoretical Underpinnings

It is almost impossible to summarize the meaning and significance of the terms *democracy* and *education* within the scope of this chapter. Consequently, rather than presenting a comprehensive overview, we focus on specific perspectives and interpretations that enable the synthesis of notions, exploring the connections between these two concepts.

Democracy

While many perceive a democratic government as a prerequisite to human progress (Yona, 2006), others (e.g., libertarians) perceive as "democratic" only a regime that limits government involvement in individual affairs (Barber, 1995). Indeed, democracy was, and remains, "invented" according to the identity of its inventors and the circumstances in which they operate (Dahl, 2000). Nevertheless, despite the inherent difficulty in describing an idea that has been occupying the best minds of humanity for at least 2000 years, a few characteristics of democracy have already been identified and are commonly accepted as defining a "democratic" regime as such.

Based on what the Greeks, commonly considered the founders of the democratic ideal, perceived as the meaning of the regime they created, democracy is about notions of citizenship, access to public office, and participation in public debates and decisions all of which are shared by the many rather than constituting the exclusive preserve of the few (Jay, 1984). This interpretation bears notions of equality, the need for a proper decision-making process, and acceptance of the rule of law as determined in established formal proceedings.

In line with these assumptions, American political theorist Robert Alan Dahl (2000) suggested an oft-cited definition of democracy, maintaining that it is comprised of five procedures: effective participation in political life; voting equality at a decisive stage; enlightened understanding of topics at stake; the ability to control the public agenda; and the inclusion of all citizens within the regime. Democracy, he continued, is probably the only known regime that prevents tyranny, establishes basic rights for citizens, supports freedom and individual self-determination, and creates political equality, to list only a few of its merits (Dahl, 2000).

Dahl's procedural democracy is indeed useful when trying to measure the possibilities created for individuals in a regime that is self-defined as democratic. Yet, more than a checklist of must-have mechanisms, democracy is first and foremost a normative ideal (Schejter & Tirosh, 2014). Dahl's procedures are thus insufficient. They do not effectively prevent specific groups within a society from gaining control over essential institutions, such as the media or other means of cultural production, enabling them to achieve dominance while marginalizing others (Gordon, 2001). While Dahl (2000) elegantly suggests minimal formalistic procedures that can determine whether a regime is "democratic" or not, especially regarding the manner in which way collective decisions are taken (Jay, 1984)—unless society adheres to the basic moral commitments that stand at the heart of democracy—these procedures are meaningless. As such, besides maintaining specific procedures, democracy is about constructing a knowledgeable and active citizenry (Schejter & Tirosh, 2014) that is able to voice the desires of its members in an egalitarian manner and promote their interests (Yona, 2006). Thus, the question of voice is crucial when describing an "essential democracy" (Habermas, 1996). Indeed, it is freedom of expression, the mechanism that guarantees the free movement of voices in society, that constitutes the core of the democratic idea.

Expression has long been defined in dichotomous terms, i.e., whether it was allowed or denied. The right of expression thus became synonymous with the right of "free expression," a negative right derived from the prohibition on government obstruction thereof (Berlin, 1969). As such, "the free exchange of ideas is linked directly [...] with the effective functioning of democracy" (Schejter, 2013, 121). "Free expression" alone, however, defined exclusively by the absence of obstruction, does not guarantee that all voices will be heard or attended to equally, nor does it necessarily guarantee the granting of a voice to those who were traditionally silenced to a great extent.

Established criticism of contemporary democracy focuses on the active silencing of voices, despite the purportedly unobstructed expression enabled by free mass media (Schejter & Tirosh, 2015). Individuals may be free to express themselves, but what they lack is the ability to have their voices heard when and where it matters. This ability means actual participation in public discussions about specific issues at stake, the ability to capitalize on the different media in which the discussions take place, representation in these media when discussion occurs, and the opportunity to manifest one's own informed perceptions, thus encountering different opinions and possessing basic educational capabilities to help evaluate these varied perspectives. The challenge thus is "not for expression free of obstruction, but rather for expression devoid of opportunity" (Schejter & Tirosh, 2014, 82).

In this chapter, we summarized the above notions as the following tenets of democracy:

1. *Active participation*: Democracy is about constant interactions surrounding ideas and active participation of all citizens who choose to be involved in social discourse.
2. *Free movement of voices*: A democratic society is informed by knowledge that is not produced and dictated by leaders only (top-down knowledge transmission), but rather by citizens who can voice their ideas and express themselves, contributing to a bottom-up process of knowledge building. Information and voices flow openly and freely within democratic society and cultivate knowledgeable interactions surrounding ideas.
3. *Equal and just expression:* Democracy is about making sure that all citizens are capable of participating in social discourse and that no one is left voiceless. As such, a democratic regime should nurture the skills necessary for participation

in the discussion: Citizens should be able to process information that is available to them; they should possess the tools required to form their personal opinions and viewpoints and be given opportunities to express and present these individual ideas.

4. *Ability to influence:* A democratic society creates opportunities and mechanisms for citizens to express their voices "where it matters," that is, where they can be influential regarding specific issues at stake.

Socio-constructivist Education

As explained, this chapter deals with democracy and education. As we now move toward the second tenant of our argument, we will focus on socio-constructivist education and its meaning. According to constructivist notions, the explanation to how individuals construct meaning may be found in one's cognitive processes. The socio-constructivist theory extends constructivist notions of meaning-making to include the social aspect and learning (Woo & Reeves, 2007). The theory, originating in the work of Lev Vygotsky (1978), emphasizes the role of dialogue and interactions, through which people share perspectives and experiences, as core processes for the construction of meaning. Therefore, socio-constructivist pedagogy views peer students as a major resource of student learning (e.g., Kali, Levin-Peled, & Dori, 2009). Instructional materials are designed to support interactions that enable students to learn from each other and help teachers facilitate this process. Building on socio-constructivist notions, the learning community approach emphasizes collaborative efforts of understanding. Bielaczyc, Kapur, and Collins (2013) maintain that a learning community is characterized by "a diversity of expertise among its members, who are valued for their contributions and are given support to develop a shared objective of continually advancing the collective knowledge and skills; an emphasis on learning how to learn; and mechanisms for sharing" (p. 2). In fact, Dewey's view of "common aims, beliefs, aspirations, knowledge—a common understanding" (1916/2012, p. 7) as building blocks of any community or society corresponds to the main tenets of a learning community. The LINKS courses were designed to leverage socio-constructivist processes as a means of promoting an interdisciplinary understanding of the notion of LINKS among students who chose to participate in these courses and thereby took part in the learning community it involved.

In this chapter, our perspective on socio-constructivist pedagogies is exemplified by four meta-level design principles (Kali & Linn, 2007) that support meaning-making through knowledge integration:

- *Help Students Learn from Each Other:* According to Kali and Linn (2007), this meta-design principle calls for designing social supports and embedding them into (technology-enhanced) learning environments, so that learners can benefit from the ideas of others. Encouraging students to listen to and learn from others takes advantage of the collective knowledge in the classroom community in several ways. First, when students interact, they connect to the cultural aspect of learning by bringing to light the alternative views held by learners and the criteria used to interpret ideas. Second, encouraging students to analyze and build on ideas from peers can motivate them to interpret their own ideas and to be more deliberate about their own learning processes.

- *Make Contents Accessible:* This meta-design principle contributes to socio-constructivist learning by building on what students know, thereby creating a personally relevant basis for the exchange of ideas among learners. Making contents accessible involves eliciting students' ideas by contextualizing the contents in ways relevant to the students' world. Once elicited, students are encouraged to keep reconsidering their ideas in the context of new ideas presented to them. Students are given support (e.g., feedback) to distinguish among the different ideas and generate normative connections that are also relevant to everyday life.

- *Make Thinking Visible:* This meta-design principle focuses on scaffolding the processes of integrating ideas and knowledge generation. To make thinking visible involves modeling and evaluating how ideas are connected and sorted out when forming new knowledge webs (Bransford, Brown, & Cocking, 2000; Collins, Brown, & Holum, 1991; Linn, 1995). Teachers, scientists, and students—and even technology—can all model thinking processes (Linn & Hsi, 2000). Thinking that is made visible can add new perspectives and make explicit the interpretive process of combining perspectives to form more coherent knowledge webs. By doing so, learners can understand the nature of knowledge building as well as the cultural characteristics of the relevant community (e.g., the culture that represents the ways scientists work when learning science). By making their ideas visible, students can inspect their own knowledge integration processes and engage in linking, distinguishing, or reconciling ideas, as appropriate, thereby guiding their learning more deliberately.

- *Promote Autonomous Lifelong Learning:* Promoting autonomy so students can become lifelong learners involves establishing a rich, comprehensive knowledge-building process that students can apply to varied problems both in class and throughout their lives. To become autonomous lifelong learners, students need opportunities to generate and recognize new ideas and to connect them to existing ideas. They need to learn to monitor their progress so that they gain more cohesive understanding. They also need to engage in sustained project work, so they can connect personally relevant problems to class topics and reflect on experience in diverse contexts.

Synthesizing Theoretical Notions of Democracy and Education

Based on the theoretical underpinnings presented above, we may point to certain commonalities between the principal tenets of democracy and those of socio-constructivist education. *Active participation* is crucial when trying to achieve genuine democracy as well as meaningful learning. *Equity* among all members of society (or all students in class) is crucial as well. Both constructs challenge the leader/teacher as the only source of *authority* and suggest alternatives (e.g., other people in society or other students in the class).

Taking a democratic stance, the four meta-design principles that promote socio-constructivist education encompass many of the democratic notions described above:

- *Help students learn from each other* focuses on the variety of ideas and perspectives and the importance of exposing students to them to widen and deepen their own ideas through alternative views prevailing in class. This principle echoes the notion of *active participation* and social interactions around ideas. In addition, it encourages *free movement of voices* that can lead to the development of a more knowledgeable citizenry (Schejter & Tirosh, 2014).
- *Make content accessible* addresses activities that elicit all students' ideas and personal perspectives, thereby enriching the repertoire of ideas available for discussion. This principle encourages *equal and just expression* by forming grounds to connect to one's inner voice and opinion formation. At the same time, accessible ideas are easier to share, thereby promoting *free movement of voices* in the community.
- *Make thinking visible* supports students in combining perspectives to form coherent knowledge webs. This principle upholds the notion of *equal and just expression* by modeling thinking processes and making it easier to understand the nature of knowledge building as well as the cultural characteristics of the relevant community. *Make thinking visible* is especially relevant in the case of those who are used to being voiceless and unheard.
- *Promote autonomous lifelong learning* involves the processes students need to master to apply knowledge-building processes in everyday life. In this sense, the principle supports nurturing of the necessary skills needed for *equal and just expression*: information processing through digital literacy, formation of one's personal opinions and viewpoints, and expression and presentation of these personal ideas. Furthermore, lifelong learning promotes *active participation* and constant interactions surrounding ideas. Finally, the principle echoes notions of *ability to influence* by developing the ability and skills to have one's voice heard where it matters.

Contemporary Media: Opportunity or Challenge for Democracy and Education?

We now return to the conceptualization of contemporary media and use it as a critical lens to examine both democracy and education in the networked society, enabling analysis of the LINKS courses in the following section. Contemporary media provide "a unique venue for civic engagement, exposure to information, and opportunity for education" (Schejter, 2013, p. 117) that capitalize on their unique characteristics: interactivity, abundance, multimediality, and mobility (Schejter & Tirosh, 2016). At the same time, however, these characteristics have the potential to yield undesired consequences. The following is a brief mapping of the opportunities, as well as the challenges, entailed in contemporary media with regard to promotion of democracy and socio-constructivist education, respectively.

Can Contemporary Media Support the Development of Democracy?

Contemporary media play a crucial role in maintaining and developing democracy. As *free movement of voices* is a basic value of democracy, the media constitute a central vehicle for expression in society. Contemporary media enable more voices to be expressed than ever before. The media provide potential for enhanced capabilities and opportunities to interact, at any time and from any place, while accessing large quantities of information capable of transmission in a variety of forms (ibid.). Thus, they are potentially more democratic than their predecessors. Critical analysis of each characteristic of contemporary media, however, reveals the challenges and threats that may accompany the potential opportunities:

- *Abundant* content and numerous transmission channels thereof enable a more informed citizenry to participate in public debate and, more importantly, in social movements for change (Howard & Hussain, 2011). At the same time, however, the constantly rising number of channels for expression might challenge the ability to influence in an effective and relevant manner. One might "like" a Facebook page that expresses opinions she wishes to promote, yet without organized political mobilization, "liking" would be a meaningless social act.
- *Mobility* of access to media enables more citizens to engage in democratic deliberations, regardless of where they may be, bearing potential for encouragement of more equal and just expression. On the other hand, preventing the necessary infrastructure required for mobility can silence selected communities and threaten such just expression. Indeed, people living in areas that suffer from digital exclusion (more commonly referred to as the "digital divide") experience more difficulties than others when trying to tell their stories and report their life circumstances.
- *Interactivity* can change human activity from mere sharing to collaboration and even actual co-creation of new content (Dutton, 2008), thereby fostering active participation of all. On the other hand, facilitation of interaction can turn contemporary media into a modern witch hunt venue where people are persecuted for their opinions and undergo "shaming," thereby threatening the free movement of voices.
- *Multi-mediated* forms of expression in contemporary media can free individual creativity and democratize how people produce and perceive information and culture (Benkler, 2003), thereby fostering a variety of means of expression and the free movement of voices. On the other hand, various dangerous messages

can be packaged and disguised as appealing multi-mediated artifacts and attract the public's attention. A lack of critical thinking skills for discernment of creatively designed vicious information online, may threaten the very tenets of democracy.

To unleash the democratic potential of contemporary media, we should actively design media and communication policies that contribute to fulfilling this task (Schejter & Tirosh, 2015, 2016). In the following section, we show that in the context of education and contemporary media, we bear a similar obligation to ensure careful design of educational activities to maximize derivation of the benefits of contemporary media and to avoid its drawbacks as much as possible.

Can Contemporary Media Support Socio-constructivist Tenets?

We refer to educational technologies as an implementation of contemporary media that offers new options, including leveraging, in fulfilling a socio-constructivist vision of learning. The technology itself, however, is only a means to pedagogical ends. When technology becomes the focus, it can easily maintain traditional pedagogies, thereby challenging socio-constructivism. The following are several examples that demonstrate the advantages and challenges that contemporary media characteristics entail for socio-constructivist tenets, as represented by the four meta-level design principles (Kali & Linn, 2007):

- *Abundance* of content enables access and exposure to many more resources that can render learning more relevant and fulfill the tenet of making content accessible. Abundance of storage space enables the creation of learning materials based on the documentation of students' work, thereby helping students learn from each other. Abundance of content, however, could become a cognitive load on learners who have not developed digital literacy and might feel lost in this ocean of information if it is not designed properly (Kirschner, 2002).
- *Mobility* enables expansion of learning beyond the classroom and integrates real-life situations in the learning process, thereby making content more accessible. In addition, students can apply their learning to varied problems in real life, thereby promoting the skills needed to become autonomous lifelong learners. Nevertheless, mobility may also be used to expand formal monitoring and control over students' learning processes outside the classroom and interfere with their informal learning, thereby challenging their sense of autonomy. Furthermore, those who suffer from insufficient media access at home may lag far behind those who can communicate freely and easily outside the class.
- *Interactivity* helps students learn from each other by enabling them to contribute their ideas and actively participate in designed activities. Furthermore, it supports making content accessible by enabling instructors to give students feedback on their ideas and reasoning, motivating them to continue learning and reconsider the ideas they are developing. Alternatively, interactivity can be

implemented differently as an administrative channel only (to send messages or collect students' work).

- *Multimediality* enhances the potential for students to learn from each other because ideas can be represented by different means of expression, thereby addressing varied learning styles. In addition, it supports the creation of models or visualizations to communicate complex concepts, thereby fostering fulfillment of the tenet of making thinking visible. Used as technical means only, however, multimediality might appear to be a new pedagogy, even though the traditional pedagogical approaches are preserved, creating what Bruckman (1999) characterized as "chocolate-covered broccoli" educational environments.

Taking the above observations into account, we should focus on the different ways in which the socio-constructivist potential of contemporary media can be exploited in educational settings, through careful design of technology-enhanced learning environments. Below, we demonstrate how such design was applied in LINKS courses.

Integrating Perspectives: Democracy, Socio-constructivist Education, and Contemporary Media in LINKS Courses

After laying out the foundations, we may now explore the LINKS courses and how they exemplify integration of the various ideas presented. The LINKS courses constitute a set of twin parallel courses—for undergraduate and graduate students, respectively—offered four times between the years 2013 and 2017, with about 160 undergraduate and 60 graduate participants. Some of the lessons learned from those opportunities were that (a) the design of the course promoted students' development of an interdisciplinary understanding of the courses' main theme—Learning in a Networked Society (Kidron & Kali, 2015)—and (b) that the features designed to encourage students to act as a learning community were critical in this respect (Kidron & Kali, forthcoming). In the current chapter, we view the course community as a microcosm of society and focus on the role of technology-enhanced design in promoting the voices of its members, thereby forming an "essential democracy" (Habermas, 1996). In the context of the LINKS courses, development of such voices refers to the emergence of interdisciplinary understanding[1] through the integration of different disciplinary ideas. As such, interdisciplinary understanding may be seen as a pure expression of a personal voice. We argue that the design principles and the technology-enhanced features of the LINKS courses embodied democratic notions that supported the creation of equal opportunities for all students to develop these personal voices (i.e., interdisciplinary understanding). To explain this point of

---

[1] *Interdisciplinary understanding* is described as a "system of thought in reflective equilibrium" (Boix-Mansilla, 2010, p. 295), meaning it is developed not through linear argumentation but rather through a personal process of weighing various possible types of evidence (e.g., findings, statements, observations, analogies, metaphors, and exemplifications) and personal interpretations.

view, we first describe the courses in terms of their design and then analyze them using contemporary media lenses that support both democracy and education.

Description of the LINKS Courses

The twin LINKS courses shared their title—Learning in a Networked Society—and involved six disciplinary knowledge domains: learning sciences, science communication, health sciences, cognitive sciences, media/communication, and information sciences (which partially represent the expertise of the researchers involved in the LINKS endeavor and the disciplinary resources that serve as building blocks for this book, as described in Tabak, Ben-Zvi & Kali, Chap. 2). The undergraduate course was conducted entirely online, while the graduate course was taught in a hybrid format, with weekly meetings and online assignments. Students in both courses were required to make similar interdisciplinary connections between disciplinary resources adapted to their level of expertise. Both courses were one semester in duration and taught simultaneously to enable interactions between them, as explained below. The courses were taught by two moderators from the learning sciences (Kidron and Kali), who were familiar with the cross-cutting theme. Each knowledge domain was taught for 2 weeks, successively, using a sequence of computer-supported collaborative learning (CSCL) activities, or script (Kobbe et al., 2007), which was repeated for each domain. The script was based on different activities in a predefined schedule that students were required to follow.

The LINKS courses were an implementation of the generic BBIL model (Kidron & Kali, 2015). As explained, this model is based on the boundary-breaking design principle that emerged in response to three challenges identified in traditional practices of typical higher education instruction. These challenges are characterized by compartmentalization of disciplines, traditional pedagogy, and traditional hierarchies that parallel levels of expertise. The BBIL model harnesses educational technologies to address these challenges from three perspectives (see Table 7.1 and Fig. 7.1). From the curricular perspective, the model seeks to address the compartmentalization challenge by breaking boundaries between disciplines. This is achieved by technology-enhanced features designed to promote interdisciplinary understanding and focusing on a cross-cutting theme to help learners integrate knowledge from several disciplinary lenses. Pedagogically, the model seeks to address the traditional pedagogy challenge by breaking boundaries among learners, accomplished by including technology-enhanced features designed to promote a learning community culture enabling participants to synthesize different views, solve problems, and advance knowledge collaboratively (Bielaczyc et al., 2013). In terms of organization, the model seeks to address the hierarchy challenge by breaking the traditional boundaries between graduate and undergraduate students, while using technology-enhanced features that implement a cognitive apprenticeship approach (Collins, 2006) to promote productive interactions.

Table 7.1 BBIL model design principles and features

The design principle		Technology-enhanced features
Design principle 1: Breaking boundaries between disciplines This curricular perspective builds on notions of interdisciplinarity (Boix-Mansilla, 2010) and knowledge integration (Linn, 2006; Linn & Eylon, 2011)	1.	Cross-cutting theme
	2.	Guidelines for integrative artifacts
	3.	Integrative lens
	4.	Disciplinary resources
	5.	Deepening and focusing script
	6.	Moderation for interdisciplinarity
	7.	Interdisciplinarity norm prompts
Design principle 2: Breaking boundaries between learners This pedagogical perspective builds primarily on the notion of learning communities (Bielaczyc et al., 2013; Bielaczyc & Collins, 1999)	8.	Collaborative knowledge-building activities
	9.	Reuse of student artifacts
	10.	Peer review activities
	11.	Social infrastructure activities
	12.	Learning community norm prompts
Design principle 3: Breaking boundaries between organizational hierarchies This organizational perspective builds primarily on the notion of cognitive apprenticeship (Collins, 2006)	13.	Personal mentoring
	14.	Modeling artifacts
	15.	Structured feedback activities between communities
	16.	Coaching

Adapted from Authors (2015)

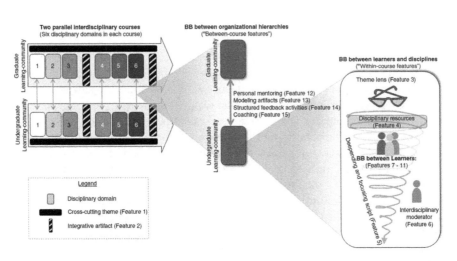

Fig. 7.1 The BBIL model's structure and features (numbers of features refer to their description in Table 7.1). (From Kidron & Kali, 2015)

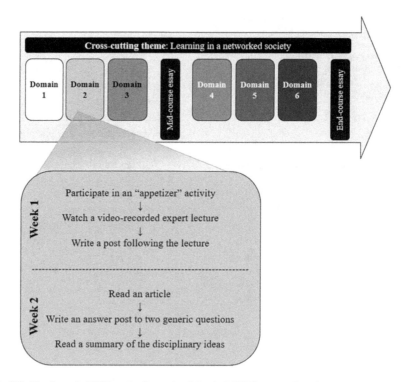

Fig. 7.2 The 2-week CSCL script for each of the six LINKS course domains

The following is a description of the learning sequence in the undergraduate course (Fig. 7.2), which will demonstrate the way the different design principles and features were combined. The sequence started with an "appetizer" activity (Feature 11 in Table 7.1): an activity that exposed students to the domain in an engaging manner and enabled sharing of personal perspectives and experiences. For example, as an "appetizer" for the topic on media and minorities (representing the media and communication disciplinary domain), students collaboratively created a shared online album in which each student visually represented his/her thoughts about media, minorities, and the relations between them. Following this, students were required to watch a video-recorded expert lecture (Feature 4) and share their ideas, insights, and personal perspectives regarding the issues presented in the lecture in an online forum (Feature 8). To encourage interaction, students were guided to respond and comment on each other's posts (Feature 12). Then, in the second week of this script, students read an article on the same topic (Feature 4) written by the same expert and were guided by two generic questions (Feature 3) to create connections between ideas using another forum (Feature 8). The two questions (How are the ideas of this domain related to the main theme? How are they related to ideas of previous disciplinary domains?) were designed to foster interdisciplinarity. Finally, the undergraduates observed a shared Google presentation (Feature 14), prepared for them by the graduate course students, in which the disciplinary ideas were summarized with respect to the generic questions (Feature 3). Undergraduates then sent written shared feedback to the graduate students regarding the presentation's clarity (Feature 15). Twice during the course (halfway into the semester and toward the end of the course), following three such 2-week disciplinary learning scripts, each student submitted a synthesis essay (Feature 2) in which he/she integrated ideas from three disciplinary domains taught earlier to answer a general question derived from the LINKS cross-cutting theme.

Analysis of the LINKS Course Through Contemporary Media Lenses

As noted above, the LINKS courses were based on two principal notions: interdisciplinarity and a learning community approach. As interdisciplinary understanding allows for more than one sole truth, it gains from meaningful dialogues through which a deeper understanding of disciplinary ideas is achieved from a variety of perspectives, laying the groundwork for creative connections among the disciplinary ideas in formation (Kidron & Kali, 2015). Accordingly, in terms of democratic notions, interdisciplinarity encourages free expression of varied ideas and perceptions with respect to their potential contribution to the formation of creative interdisciplinary insights. LINKS students were thus evaluated according to the quality of their participation within the courses' technology-enhanced learning activities. To ensure the voicing of those who are mostly silenced, students received encouraging feedback from the course moderators, who often referred to and highlighted students' productive ideas (e.g., in the summary presentation), focusing on the essence of the idea rather than on its correct articulation (taking language gaps into account). Another important aspect of free expression in the LINKS courses is the safe environment, constructed through learning community norm prompts (e.g., guidelines for respecting others' ways of thinking within posts) presented to the students on different occasions and via various channels (such as the weekly opening message). This demonstrates careful design of new media (i.e., educational technology) implementation informed by the potential threats described earlier in this chapter (e.g., modern witch hunting in which people are persecuted for their opinions and undergo shaming).

Interactions between the graduate and undergraduate LINKS courses, embodying the third design principle of the BBIL model, introduced students to knowledge at different levels of expertise and different ways of thinking, thereby enriching their ideas and comprehension. Taking a democratic stance, this design principle allows knowledge to be "shared among the many, rather than being exclusively the preserve of the few" (Jay, 1984). In the context of learning, this principle calls for breaking traditional boundaries between hierarchies based on levels of expertise, while advocating free access to knowledge instead of traditional segregation thereof (e.g., Davidson & Goldberg, 2009). In a similar sense, knowledge authority is not reserved for teachers alone. Inherently, the LINKS course involves several disciplinary domains (Fig. 7.2), so that no one expert has all the answers. Instead, the traditional teacher becomes a moderator (Feature 6 in Table 7.1) who encourages the students to explore different ideas by themselves while building on a wide range of resources (e.g., disciplinary experts, interdisciplinary moderator, peer ideas, artifacts prepared by the mentor graduate students, and so on). Students' responses to an open-ended question about their learning experience in the course demonstrate the meaningful effect of peers' ideas on their own learning (e.g., "I enjoyed reading different and varied opinions of my peers every week. It expanded my own way of thinking. There were times at which, following the discussion, I could open up to opinions that were originally in contradiction to my own thoughts"). Hence, in light of Dahl's perspective, *political equality* is promoted and *teacher tyranny* prevented.

Analysis of the challenges we faced during the four LINKS enactments (a topic beyond the scope of this chapter) enabled us to refine the different BBIL features in an iterative design process. Collaborative knowledge-building activities encouraged students to participate in a public discussion that may be viewed—within the realm of the microcosmic society as participating in political life. One major LINKS activity consisted of participating in online group discussions designed to encourage the free exchange of ideas, which is also linked to the effective functioning of democracy (Schejter & Tirosh, 2014). Technology in the LINKS courses was designed to guarantee the free movement of voices and enabled inclusion of all students in the community to participate equally without the need to struggle for the right of expression (that often characterizes face-to-face discussions within limited time-framed lessons). Furthermore, norm prompts (Feature 12) guided students toward effective participation in online discussions. For example, students were expected to bring new ideas/voices to the discussion and raise new issues, thereby affecting the public agenda. Students were encouraged to post their ideas in the context of previously posted relevant ideas, so that their voice will be heard where it matters. Finally, we suggested that students base their ideas on learning resources, thereby anchoring their voices within the disciplinary notions and thus developing an informed understanding of topics at stake.

The above analysis shows how the different technology-enhanced BBIL features embodied discrete aspects of the democratic idea and how thoughtful and careful design, which took potential challenges and threats into consideration, led to the formation of a positive learning environment in which these democratic ideas were fulfilled to promote students' learning and the development of interdisciplinary understanding.

Dilemmas and Open Questions: Food for Thought and Further Research

This chapter described how ideas about democracy, society, and communication could contribute to the design of a specific educational intervention. As such, it demonstrated a strong potential for cross-fostering of ideas between educational scientists—who focus on the interventionist, design-based study of learning—and social scientists, who may also focus on analytic study of spontaneous social phenomena (for comprehensive discussions regarding such cross-fertilization between education and social scientists, see Chaps. 1, 2, and 3, each providing a different angle, with Hoadley and Kali illustrating how conceptualizations of knowledge and learning have changed in conjunction with advancements in information technologies in Chap. 1; Tabak et al. explaining the importance of exploring learning in a networked society on the whole spectrum between spontaneous and designed technology-enhanced learning communities; and Raban and Geifmann examining how socio-intellectual capital can be developed in multidisciplinary research collaborations). While we believe that the LINKS courses example and their underlying BBIL design principles demonstrate how contemporary media may enhance the democratic essence of an in-depth learning process, we conclude this chapter with several dilemmas and open questions. We believe that viewing these dilemmas through a spontaneous-designed lens could yield meaningful insights into the understanding of democracy, education, and the role of communication in the twenty-first century.

- *Responsibility:* LINKS course moderators maintain a crucial role in leading the development of a democratic knowledge-building community. Taking society into account, however, leads us to ask whose responsibility it is to promote democracy. What are the technological means for such developments? Can features be designed into contemporary media so that they lead to a more democratic society?
- *Enforced democracy:* LINKS courses are based on the belief that students within a productive learning community will improve their interdisciplinary understanding. As a result, the BBIL design principles and features were meant to promote a democratic learning community. This raises the dilemma on whether using designed or naturally occurring processes affects the value of a democracy when the design is rendered a compulsory part of the system's requirements. How free are the course participants to choose not to be democratic, i.e., not to follow the course norms and expectations? What should the democratic response be to the participants' preference not to be democratic? How can technology be exploited to allow for and promote these processes?
- *Who are the voiceless?* It is interesting to compare the different factors that characterize voiceless members of societies and learning communities, to see how dynamic this situation could become and how technologies could be designed to

change such situations. It appears that in contemporary society and in traditional schooling, the standards for defining influential members are rather rigid (e.g., wealth or superior articulation). By contrast, centrality and peripheriality in a learning community are context-dependent. Certain students may have more to contribute at a given time, meaning that centrality and voice need not remain constant (Bielaczyc & Collins, 1999). Can technology offer such dynamics within larger societies? If so, how?

- *Enforced or free voicelessness:* Being voiceless in a given society is usually a situation enforced by some sort of coercion (e.g., active avoidance of free speech) or a result of limitations (e.g., language gap, economic hardship). In education, by contrast, voicelessness may be the result of free choice. One interesting view of this question may be derived from the notion of legitimate peripheral participation (Lave & Wenger, 1991), a process novices experience when entering a community of experts. First, they practice peripheral tasks that do not require high levels of expertise but enable them to enculturate themselves and become familiar with the community's ways of thinking, acting, and communicating. In the context of our dilemma, legitimate peripheral participation could be expressed by choosing to be voiceless while learning through observation. Another such question inquires whether voices and active participation necessarily place one at the center of influence. It appears that learning communities offer more opportunities for members to have their voices heard where it matters, as the novices' tasks, however peripheral they may be, are necessary for the community's ongoing practice, thereby rendering the novices legitimate members and their voices necessary and important. This situation, too, raises various questions, such as the following: Can some of the everyday practices in a networked society (e.g., commenting on online news or signing online petitions) be considered as peripheral participation in society? To what extent are they essential to society? How does the design of such platforms influence the type of participation and its influence?
- *Should education be democratic?* The leader of a democratic society is chosen to serve citizens' needs, using various social resources to do so, as well as society's technological infrastructures and means of communication (e.g., Donald Trump's use of Twitter). In this manner, democratic leadership constitutes a mechanism for the distribution of resources with respect to society's goals, as selected democratically. In the context of learning, traditional schooling serves goals determined by the educational system, rather than by the students. This raises a question inquiring whether—or to what extent—education should be democratic, and if so, what role can contemporary media play in democratizing education, beyond the principles explored in the present chapter.

Bibliography

Barber, B. R. (1995). Participatory democracy. In *The Encyclopedia of political thought* (pp. 2650–2654). Oakland, CA: University of California Press.

Benkler, Y. (2003). Freedom in the commons: Towards a political economy of information. *Duke Law Journal, 52*(6), 1245–1276.

Berlin, I. (1969). *Two concepts of liberty* (pp. 118–172). Berlin, Germany: I.

Bielaczyc, K., & Collins, A. (1999). Learning communities in classrooms: A reconceptualization of educational practice. In C. M. Reigeluth (Ed.), *Instructional design theories and models* (pp. 269–292). Mahwah, NJ: Lawrence Erlbaum Associates.

Bielaczyc, K., Kapur, M., & Collins, A. (2013). Cultivating a community of learners in K-12 classrooms. In C. E. Hmelo-Silver, C. A. Chinn, C. K. K. Chan, & A. O'Donnell (Eds.), *International handbook of collaborative learning* (pp. 233–249). New York: Routledge.

Boix-Mansilla, V. (2010). Learning to synthesize: The development of interdisciplinary understanding. In R. Frodeman, J. Thompson-Klein, C. Mitcham, & J. B. Holbrook (Eds.), *The Oxford handbook of interdisciplinarity* (pp. 288–306). Oxford: Oxford University Press.

Bransford, J. D., Brown, A. L., & Cocking, R. R. (2000). *How people learn: Brain, mind, experience, and school*. Washington, DC: National Academy Press.

Bruckman, A. (1999). Can educational be fun? In *Game developers conference* (Vol. 99, pp. 75–79).

Castells, M. (2007). Communication, power and counter-power in the network society. *International Journal of Communication, 1*(1), 29.

Collins, A. (2006). Cognitive apprenticeship. In R. K. Sawyer (Ed.), *The Cambridge handbook of the learning sciences* (pp. 47–60). New York: Cambridge University Press.

Collins, A., Brown, J. S., & Holum, A. (1991). Cognitive apprenticeship: Making thinking visible. *American Educator, 15*(3), 6–11.

Dahl, A. R. (2000). *On democracy*. New Haven, CT: Yale University Press.

Davidson, C. N., & Goldberg, D. T. (2009). *The future of learning institutions in a digital age*. Cambridge, MA: MIT Press.

Dewey, J. (1916/2012). *Democracy and education*. Hollywood, FL: Simon and Brown.

Dutton, W. H. (2008). The Wisdom of Collaborative Network Organizations: Capturing the Value of Networked Individuals . *Prometheus, 26*(3), 211–230.

Gordon, N. (2001). Dahl's procedural democracy: A Foucauldian critique. *Democratization, 8*(4), 23–40.

Habermas, J. (1996). *Between facts and norms: Contributions to a discourse theory of law and democracy*. Cambridge, MA: MIT Press.

Howard, P. N., & Hussain, M. M. (2011). The role of digital media. *Journal of Democracy, 22*(3), 35–48.

Jay, M. (1984). *Marxism and totality: The adventures of a concept from Lukács to Habermas*. Berkeley/Los Angeles, CA: University of California Press.

Kali, Y., Levin-Peled, R., & Dori, Y. J. (2009). The role of design-principles in designing courses that promote collaborative learning in higher-education. *Computers in Human Behavior, 25*(5), 1067–1078.

Kali, Y., & Linn, M. C. (2007). Technology-enhanced support strategies for inquiry learning. In J. M. Spector, M. D. Merrill, J. J. G. V. Merriënboer, & M. P. Driscoll (Eds.), *Handbook of research on educational communications and technology* (3rd ed., pp. 445–461). Mahwah, NJ: Lawrence Erlbaum Associates.

Kidron, A., & Kali, Y. (2015). Boundary breaking for interdisciplinary learning. *Research in Learning Technology, 23*(1), Article No: 26496.

Kidron, A., & Kali, Y. (forthcoming). Online learning communities as a pedagogical approach for promoting interdisciplinary understanding through knowledge integration. *Educational Technology Research and Development*.

Kirschner, P. A. (2002). Cognitive load theory: Implications of cognitive load theory on the design of learning. *Learning and Instruction, 12*(1), 1–10.

Kobbe, L., Weinberger, A., Dillenbourg, P., Harrer, A., Hämäläinen, R., Häkkinen, P., et al. (2007). Specifying computer-supported collaboration scripts. *International Journal of Computer-Supported Collaborative Learning, 2*(2), 211–224.

Lave, J., & Wenger, E. (1991). *Situated learning: Legitimate peripheral participation.* Cambridge: Cambridge University Press.

Linn, M. C. (1995). Designing computer-learning environments for engineering and computer science: The scaffolded knowledge integration framework. *Journal of Science Education and Technology, 4*(2), 103–126.

Linn, M. C. (2006). The knowledge integration perspective on learning and instruction. In R. K. Sawyer (Ed.), *The Cambridge handbook of the learning sciences* (pp. 243–264). New York: Cambridge University Press.

Linn, M. C., & Eylon, B.-S. (2011). *Science learning and instruction: Taking advantage of technology to promote knowledge integration.* New York: Routledge.

Linn, M. C., & Hsi, S. (2000). *Computers, teachers, peers: Science learning partners.* New York: Routledge.

Schejter, A. (2013). Rulers of thousands, rulers of hundreds, rulers of fifties, and rulers of tens: Does democracy count? In *Beyond broadband: Developing data-based information policy strategies* (pp. 113–128). New York: Fordham University Press.

Schejter, A., & Tirosh, N. (2014). New media policy: The redistribution of voice. In Y. Liu & R. Picard (Eds.), *Policy and marketing strategies for digital media* (pp. 73–86). London: Routledge.

Schejter, A., & Tirosh, N. (2015). "Seek the meek, seek the just": Social media and social justice. *Telecommunications Policy, 39*, 796–803.

Schejter, A., & Tirosh, N. (2016). *A justice-based approach for new media policy: In the paths of righteousness.* London: Palgrave Macmillan.

Vygotsky, L. S. (1978). Mind in society: The development of higher mental process.

Woo, Y., & Reeves, T. C. (2007). Meaningful interaction in web-based learning: A social constructivist interpretation. *The Internet and Higher Education, 10*(1), 15–25.

Yona, Y. (2006). Democracy. In U. Ram & N. Berkovitz (Eds.), *In/Equality.* Jerusalem: Bialik Institute. [Hebrew].

Part III
From Designed to Spontaneous TEL Communities

Chapter 8
From Designed to Spontaneous Technologically Enhanced Learning Communities: An Introduction

Lynn Schofield Clark and Oren Golan

Abstract With the advent of new media, knowledge has been made accessible on an unprecedented global scale. Given information's ubiquity, questions arise regarding not only how we understand what knowledge is, but also what the responsibilities are for the society that participates in its production. Charting recent educational and social scientific efforts to scaffold learning, the chapter discusses connected learning, an emergent umbrella term that refers to how learners traverse between formal and informal settings. Through this framework, the chapter sets out to address learners' knowledge practices as they navigate between designed and spontaneous or "situated" learning. Accordingly, we identify challenges as educators seek to become agents of positive transformation in the digital age. Online information outlets are, on the one hand, agents for social reproduction and, on the other hand, agents for socioeducational change and individual advancement.

Keywords Knowledge · Designed and spontaneous learning · Social responsibility · Connected learning · Transformational education · Educational systems · Distributed cognition

Knowledge was once considered a scarce resource, but today, thanks largely to unprecedented developments in information and communication technologies, we live in an era of abundant information. What does knowledge mean, and what can it come to mean, in this context of a highly networked and mobile society? Knowledge has changed in terms of how we think of it, as Hoadley and Kali argued in Chap. 2 of this book. Whereas we once thought of knowledge as something that was acquired through the mental processes of thought, experience, and the senses, we are now aware of ourselves as living within complex systems of what Hutchins (1995) has

L. S. Clark (✉)
University of Denver, Department of Media, Film & Journalism Studies, Denver, CO, USA
e-mail: Lynn.Clark@DU.edu

O. Golan
University of Haifa, Faculty of Education, Haifa, Israel

© Springer Nature Switzerland AG 2019
Y. Kali et al. (eds.), *Learning In a Networked Society*, Computer-Supported Collaborative Learning Series 17, https://doi.org/10.1007/978-3-030-14610-8_8

termed *distributed cognition*, recognizing that human cognition is always situated in a complex sociocultural world, and practices of cognition occur in the dynamic relationships between individuals, groups, and the systems in which they participate (Hutchins, 1995; see also Clark & Chalmers, 1998). And in this environment, questions arise regarding not only how we understand what knowledge is but also what the responsibilities are for the society that participates in its production. How do we create the spaces to ensure that knowledge, as it is produced and enacted in its many distributed forms, allows for human flourishing?

An important step toward addressing this question involves considering the ways in which those people and material products that are a part of our current learning systems have been changing in order to accommodate the knowledge practices that take place outside formal learning settings. How are existing parts of the contemporary learning system accommodating themselves to the situation of distributed cognition? Chapters in this section of the book investigate the ways that classrooms, textbooks, and teacher/student and student/student relations are changing given the introduction of digital technologies and increased access to the internet. In addition, they demonstrate how communities that have sought to temper the influence of these and other parts of the learning system are also changing.

To set the framework for the chapters in this section, this introductory chapter briefly reviews literature related to what has come to be known as *connected learning*: the kind of learning that occurs when young people are able to pursue their own passion with the support of educators, parents, and other adults and are able to link that learning and interest to academic achievement, career success, and civic engagement (Ito et al., 2013). Connected learning scholars aim to influence the design of educational environments by examining how young people traverse between formal and informal learning settings through the facilitating properties of technologically enhanced environments, thus offering important insights into the chapters that follow in this section. After this review and a brief overview of the chapters to come, this introductory chapter concludes with thoughts regarding how each chapter in this section suggests further questions regarding not only the learning that is currently occurring in designed to spontaneous environments but also how we might think about the learning that *ought* to be occurring. This chapter thus concludes with questions regarding the transformational mandate of education as it has been articulated by Freire (1968/1970) and others. In a time of societal upheaval, uncertainty, and disruption such as our own, such questions could not be more timely. We begin by exploring the ways others are thinking about how both educational systems and learners are accommodating themselves to new situations of distributed cognition.

From Designed to Spontaneous Learning: The Connected Learning Approach

The concept of distributed cognition recognizes that human cognition occurs in the dynamic relationships between individuals, groups, and the systems in which they participate, as noted earlier. "What evolves," Hutchins (2006) writes, "is not the brain alone, but the system of brains, bodies, and shared environments for action in interaction (p. 376)." Thus, an individual working alone with technological tools is a distributed cognitive system and so is an individual working alone *without* such tools, as Hoadley and Kali pointed out in their chapter. Distributed cognition is not a kind of cognition, then, but rather a framework for thinking about the processes of how, why, and when humans come to know.

Cognition is developed not in the singular mind but in the interrelations between minds, systems, and cultural artifacts. Some educational scholars who have considered the role of technology in learning have thus considered cognitive development in relation to media materials. For example, Darling-Hammond, Zielezinski, and Goldman (2014) found that at-risk US students performed better on standardized state exams when they had opportunities to learn with video-based activities and in environments where their specific needs were addressed. But a distributed approach to cognition also encourages us to consider technologies not merely as supporting the development of learning content but also as material expressions of cognition that, in turn, shape and are shaped by humans and their environments. For this reason, rather than focus on content acquisition, many in the educational community have been considering how digital and mobile media support peer and intergenerational learning that extends from formal to informal educational contexts (see, e.g., Larson & Marsh, 2014). With a foundation in sociocultural learning theory, scholars in what has come to be known as the *connected learning* approach have been interested in how society might foster environments that support learning as knowledge practices move back and forth between designed and spontaneous or "situated" learning (Lave & Wenger, 1991; Vygotsky, 1978).

One of the earliest and largest studies of this movement was undertaken by the Digital Youth Project, a multi-institution, multi-year qualitative and quantitative US research study funded by the MacArthur Foundation's Digital Media and Learning Initiative (Ito et al., 2009). This study affirmed the importance of friendships, families, and young people's own aspirations and interests in how, when, and where young people engaged in knowledge production practices both online and offline. Several other studies have elaborated on this work, delineating the different roles that parents play as they model independent learning and that young people themselves play in their own learning and in their siblings' and parents' learning as well (Barron, Martin, Takeuchi, & Fithian, 2009; Gee, Takeuchi, & Wartella, 2018; Jenkins, 2009; Plowman, McPake, & Stephen, 2008; Wartella, Rideout, Lauricella, & Connell, 2014). Research has affirmed that technology and media can be part of healthy family interactions and learning experiences, especially when parents harness media content for positive, family-defined purposes (Clark, 2013; Guernsey & Levine, 2015; Kamenetz, 2018).

Livingstone and Sefton-Green (2016) focused their efforts in the connected learning space on one particular classroom, examining the ways that young people learned as they moved from school to home and in both online and offline sites. They found that whereas many educational leaders are enthused about the possibilities for utilizing technologies to strengthen connections between home and school, few young people and their parents are able to take full advantage of the potential that such connections seem to hold. Works such as theirs as well as Gee et al. (2018)

advocate looking at how traditional educational structures are adapting and making space for the ways that informal learning can encourage cognitive development. They also note the importance of studying how our traditional educational systems are adapting to the opportunities that new media afford for the bridging of formal and informal educational settings, which is the starting point for the chapters that follow.

The Chapters to Come

The previous section in this book considered how spontaneous learning might be leveraged within traditional educational settings, following much of the insights of the connected learning approach outlined above. In the section to come, authors consider how those settings have already begun to adapt to the emergent situation, exploring the promises and the constraints that present themselves both to the existing educational institutions themselves and to the wider mission of learning within a model of distributed cognition.

Authors Kent, Rachavi, and Rafaeli focus on courses that have been designed for online platforms, with an interest in measuring how well such courses facilitate collaborative learning. They recognize that with the growth of MOOCs, a great deal of hope was placed in the capacity for online courses to revolutionize learning. Although some of the initial outsized enthusiasm for the democratizing potential of these courses has been tempered, such courses have found a permanent place in the offerings of universities and continuing education opportunities around the world. Yet we still know relatively little about how programs designed for the ease and convenience of individualized learning can best promote collaborative learning. Using network analysis techniques, this chapter explores how communities of learners construct knowledge together and how such processes and their results might best be assessed for quality.

Har-Carmel, Olsher, Elkin-Koren, and Yerushalmy share the general enthusiasm for the e-textbook movement that has enabled students to become coauthors of their own textbooks. They note, however, that because textbooks are part of a large system governed by legal and policy structures, new questions emerge. If publishers and textbooks are to remain important components of emergent learning systems, how will collaborative processes be both encouraged and monetized?

Hod, Aridor, Ben-Zvi, Pion, Weiss, and Zuckerman look at the ways that schools and related learning organizations have sought to reinvent themselves through a rethinking of the classroom. They look at several future learning spaces to consider the factors that seem to produce a positive return on the investment in such renovations, and why some such investments sometimes produce lackluster results.

Mishol Shauli, Shacham, and Golan consider the ways that a traditionally insular community with its own established norms for learning has grappled with the incursion of new media technologies into its formerly independent spaces. These authors are particularly interested in the role that parents, community journalists, and other socializing agents play in brokering access to information about informal educational realms. Their chapter suggests that even as aspects of existing educational systems such as classrooms, textbooks, and teacher/student experiences undergo change in the form of how and where knowledge production is to be encouraged, it is still the case that the closest ties of family and community shape how a larger learning system is to be understood and how one is to perform within and in relationship to it.

Conclusion

Systems shape the ways in which learning paths are scaffolded, and thus may both provide and constrain opportunities for the development of knowledge in contexts of practice. As we face the challenge of navigating an increasingly complex technological landscape, scholars in the LINKS project have sought throughout this book to develop frameworks that not only describe present-day learning activities but also question how learning can be transformational. Consistent with a neo-Marxist tradition that has embraced the importance of the dialectic, LINKS scholars are interested in a critical pedagogy: one that acknowledges the distance between *what is* and *what ought to be* and that creates spaces for learners to both envision this better world and to learn to leverage knowledge resources toward its aim. The fact that we have experienced an increased dissemination of information in a networked society is not the point, then, as these chapters have demonstrated. Rather, what arises are ethical challenges that relate to the aims of both education and knowledge.

Is education designed to reproduce existing social systems, viewing young people as workers-in-the-making who are primarily collectively being prepared for a changing workplace? Or is there a role in education that stretches beyond this? How can we think about designing for spontaneous learning that is not only effective in delivering desired content (or, in the case of the Haredi community, shielding young people from content considered undesirable) but that also encourages reflection on what ought to be? Such a question suggests that we must ask not only about content acquisition, informal workplace skills, collaboration and empowerment, economic benefit, and cultural preservation and innovation, but also about how people will attain the skills needed that will allow more people to flourish. Indeed, the section that follows explores this theme.

Bibliography

Barron, B., Martin, C. K., Takeuchi, L., & Fithian, R. (2009). Parents as learning partners in the development of technological fluency. *The International Journal of Learning and Media, 1*, 55–77.

Clark, A., & Chalmers, D. (1998). The extended mind. *Analysis, 58*(1), 7–19.

Clark, L. S. (2013). *The parent app: Understanding families in a digital age*. New York: Oxford University Press.

Darling-Hammond, L., Zielezinski, M. B., & Goldman, S. (2014). *Using technology to support at-risk students' learning*. Stanford, CA: Alliance for Excellent Education and Stanford Center for Opportunity Policy in Education.

Freire, P. (1968/1970). *The pedagogy of the oppressed*. New York: Continuum.

Gee, E., Takeuchi, L., & Wartella, E. (2018). *Children and families in the digital age: Learning together in a media saturated culture*. New York: Routledge.

Guernsey, L., & Levine, M. H. (2015). *Tap, click, read: Growing learners in a world of screens*. New Jersey: Wiley.

Hutchins, E. (1995). *Cognition in the wild*. Cambridge, MA: MIT Press.

Hutchins, E. (2006). The distributed cognition perspective on human interaction. In Enfield, N.J. and Levinson, S. *Roots of human sociality: Culture, cognition and interaction* (pp. 375–398). Oxford: Berg.

Ito, M., Gutierrez, K., Livingstone, S., Penuel, B., Rhodes, J., Salen, K., et al. (2013). *Connected learning: An agenda for research and design*. New Jersey: BookBaby.

Ito, M., Baumer, S., Bittani, M., boyd, d., Cody, R., Herr-Stephenson, B., Horst, H., Lange, P., Mahendran, D., Martinez, K., Pascoe, C.J., Perkel, D., Robinson, L., Sims, C., Tripp, L. (2009). Hanging out, messing around, and geeking out: Kids living and learning with new media. Cambridge, MA: MIT Press.

Jenkins, H. (2009). *Confronting the challenges of participatory culture: Media education for the 21st century*. Cambridge, MA: MIT Press.

Kamenetz, A. (2018). *The art of screen time: How your family can balance digital media and real life*. New York: PublicAffairs.

Larson, J., & Marsh, J. (2014). *Making literacy real: Theories and practices for learning and teaching*. London: Sage.

Lave, J., & Wenger, E. (1991). *Situated learning: Legitimate peripheral participation*. Cambridge, UK: Cambridge University Press.

Livingstone, S. & Sefton-Green, J. (2016). The class. New York: New York University Press.

Plowman, L., McPake, J., & Stephen, C. (2008). Just picking it up? Young children learning with technology at home. *Cambridge Journal of Education, 38*(3), 303–319.

Vygotsky, L. (1978). *Mind in society: The development of higher psychological processes*. Cambridge, MA: Harvard University Press.

Wartella, E., Rideout, V., Lauricella, A., & Connell, S. (2014). *Parenting in the age of digital technology*. Evanston, IL: Center on Media and Human Development, School of Communication, Northwestern University.

Chapter 9
Networked Learning Analytics: A Theoretically Informed Methodology for Analytics of Collaborative Learning

Carmel Kent, Amit Rechavi, and Sheizaf Rafaeli

Abstract Online social learning is a prevalent pedagogical tool, enabling learners across all ages and cultures to learn together. Educators, policy-makers, and international organizations such as the Organization for Economic Cooperation and Development (OECD) stress the need to assess collaborative learning systematically. However, the systematic assessment of large online groups' collaboration is still in its infancy. In this chapter, we suggest perceiving social learning through the lens of interaction networks between learners and content. Based on well-accepted learning theories, we demonstrate the harnessing of digital traces of online discussions to the assessment of social learning, at both the individual and the group levels. Practically, our contribution is to suggest a network analysis point of view for the assessment of the performance and design of learning communities. Our proposed methodology can be used by instructors to open-up the black box of collaborative learning, to be able to equip learners with twenty-first-century skill-set.

Keywords Learning analytics · Collaborative learning · Online social learning · Assessment · Interaction networks · Digital traces · Online discussions · Assessment of social learning · Network analysis · Assessment of learning communities

The ability to trace digital footprints easily and to extract analytics from social platforms provides socio-computational opportunities and challenges alike. Aside from ethical and privacy considerations (Pardo & Siemens, 2014), long-lasting dilemmas

C. Kent (✉)
Institute of Education, University College London, London, UK

A. Rechavi
Department of Business Administration, Ruppin Academic Center, Michmoret, Israel

S. Rafaeli
Samuel Neaman Institute, Technion, and Faculty of Management, University of Haifa, Haifa, Israel
e-mail: sheizaf@rafaeli.net

© Springer Nature Switzerland AG 2019
Y. Kali et al. (eds.), *Learning In a Networked Society*, Computer-Supported
Collaborative Learning Series 17, https://doi.org/10.1007/978-3-030-14610-8_9

surrounding any policy dependent on predefined performance indicators will accompany endeavors relating to learning assessment (Ellis, 2013), especially when based purely on online interactions. Despite these challenges, we perceive digital traces as a promising tool with which to access the rich world of online learning communities (Ferguson et al., 2014). Our aim is to join others who appended "analytics" to "social learning" and to suggest that quantifiable interactional patterns, based on well-accepted social learning theories, should be considered as tools for the assessment of collaborative online learning.

Online technologies have altered the way we conceive, deploy, and measure learning experiences significantly (Mickes et al., 2013). Students can access and interact with numerous learning resources and co-learners around the globe. Technical barriers such as size, fluidity, and diversity of datasets are manageable, and interactions can be recorded, traced, and analyzed easily (Pardo & Siemens, 2014). The potential of analytics and data mining methodologies for extraction of useful and actionable information from large datasets was discovered only recently, however, in the learning sciences community (Baker & Siemens, 2014; Ferguson, 2012). These techniques enable real-time informing of learners about optimal learning paths, shortening their feedback loops, guiding instructors within the variety of learning designs, conducting a fine-grained analysis of learning policies over time, and deepening scientists' understanding of behavioral learning patterns. Reviews of learning analytics literature may be found in Baker and Siemens (2014), Clow (2013), and Siemens (2015).

Social learning analytics focus on how communities of learners create knowledge together. MOOCs (massive open online courses) and other online learning endeavors are based on online conversations and enable rich logging data collection and data mining, based on learners' collaborative behavioral patterns (Sinha, 2014; Wu, Yao, Duan, Fan, & Qu, 2016). At the same time, the lack of face-to-face interactions in online learning calls for further analysis and research of online interactions. More on social learning analytics is offered by Shum and Ferguson (2012).

Specifically, our contribution is to suggest a network analysis point of view for assessment of the performance and design of learning communities. This chapter provides a brief review of our suggested methodology for social and collaborative learning analytics. We use social network analysis (SNA) techniques, demonstrating our methodology in a case study of a higher education learning community's online discussion. Our main research question is thus: How can collaborative learning be measured or assessed using network analysis techniques?

As suggested by educational research, *interaction* is among the most important means for learning (e.g., Barker, 1994; Vygotsky, 1978). Asynchronous online discussions provide learners with the opportunity to interact when reading and responding to peers' and teachers' postings. Consequently, interactivity (e.g., when learners are exposed or actively respond to each other's ideas) is an essential metric when evaluating learning communities' discussions. Conceptualizing interactivity as a process of relating to each other's postings by taking conversational turns (Rafaeli & Sudweeks, 1997) emphasizes the social foundations of knowledge construction (for an additional conceptualization of interactivity online, see Baram-Tsabari and

Schejter (Chap. 5) and Kidron, Tirosh, Kali, and Schejter (Chap. 7)). Modeling a collaborative learning process, however, must emphasize not only interactions among human community participants (Rechavi & Rafaeli, 2012) but also interactions between learners and content items, such as posts and other information resources (Siemens, 2005). Furthermore, we consider interactions among the content items themselves, often implemented as hyperlinks and actively curated by community participants (Kent & Rafaeli, 2016).

In view of the above observations, we suggest perceiving online discussions in learning communities as networks, in which both human agents and content posts are the nodes, while interactions among nodes are represented as edges. The collaborative learning process is thus regarded as the construction and growth of a network containing various types of interactions among learners and content items (AlDahdouh, Osório, & Caires, 2015).

As distant and blended learning play an increasingly central role in our lives, policies are required concerning the evaluation and assessment of individual and collective online learning. A data-driven, quantifiable framework for collaborative online learning can prove beneficial for cogent design and evaluation of mass learning. This chapter takes a step toward constructing such a framework. We propose a set of quantifiable learning indicators that we believe will complement traditional assessment tools, demonstrating this proposition based on a case study of a single higher education learning community that used online discussion in a blended mode during an entire academic semester.

We now briefly review the theoretical basis for social learning analytics as reflected in online discussions, laying the groundwork for our proposed units of analysis. We then raise a preliminary set of research hypotheses to demonstrate how our approach can shed more light on networked learning, showing how this can be done with an example of a particular case study. In the discussion, we use this example to propose preliminary insights regarding the validity of network analysis to the study and systematic assessment of collaborative online learning.

Learning Analytics in Online Discussions

Online discussions hold promise for collaborative knowledge construction: Online community members share ideas, learn from peers, and build knowledge collectively while reading and reflecting on each other's thoughts. The virtual settings enable less assertive participants to compose their thoughts (Hewitt, 2001) while allowing more time for all participants to reflect on and respond to others' contributions (Poole, 2000). Pedagogically, rationales for learning by online discourse typically make reference to the collaborative construction of meaning (Fried, 2016; Lander, 2015). Moreover, when learners build on the comments of others, a higher flow of communication and inference is achieved, compared with face-to-face, turn-taking discussion settings (Garrison, 2006).

Previous research involving learning analytics in online discussions has referred to content analysis methods (Kovanovic, Joksimovic, Gasevic, & Hatala, 2014), visualization of interactions (Wu et al., 2016), and social network analysis (Pedro et al., 2016; Reffay & Chanier, 2003), all designed primarily to provide managerial and instructional decision-making tools. In these contexts, learning analytics require combining data science methods with more established research methods (such as qualitative content analysis) to provide mechanisms for analyzing digital learning experiences with high-resolution and time-sensitive data (Gibson & de Freitas, 2015; Zhang, Scardamalia, Reeve, & Messina, 2009).

Online discussion differs from face-to-face discussion (Herring, 1999) and may also be informed by a different set of values (Shum & Ferguson, 2012). Thus, not only does it need different design criteria, but also an expanded conceptualization, followed by modified assessment frameworks (Deboer, Ho, Stump, & Breslow, 2014). The smooth transition of assessment approaches from the face-to-face learning world to the online world should not be taken for granted. A theory-grounded attempt should be made to reframe learning assessment in the collaborative online setting, as was accomplished, for example, by Swan and Ice (2010), who reviewed the use of the community of inquiry theoretical model to explain online educational experience.

Learning Analytics as a Theory-Based Research and Assessment Tool for Collaborative Learning

Can we use the structure and dynamics of interactions in online discussions to learn about online communities' collaborative learning processes? This chapter focuses on extracting quantitative analytics from the log-based structure of persistent conversations alone (Erickson & Herring, 2004), rather than on content analysis methods, such as categorizing demonstrated thinking skills (Bloom, 1974), or summative assessment, such as examination grading.

For decades, research in education has criticized instructivist approaches and has shown their limitation to support meaningful learning (see, e.g., the well-cited American National Research Council commissioned book on *How People Learn*, NRC, 2000). The conception of direct transfer of knowledge from the instructor into the mind of the learner is often used as a caricature of traditional instruction (e.g., Onyesolu, Nwasor, Ositanwosu, & Iwegbuna, 2013). The main flaw in this type of instruction, which might still be too prevalent, especially in higher education, is that it is based on a unidirectional tree of interactions. In social constructivism, on the other hand, implemented frequently using online discussions, the teacher is seen as a facilitator. The interactions formed are more "group-centered" than "authority-centered" (Garrison, 2006), and the flow of knowledge can be conceived as the formation of a complex network, consisting of back and forth interactions among the instructor, learners, and resources (either integral or extraneous to the learning environment).

We conceptualize an online discussion of a constructivist learning community as a network and analyze it accordingly with social network analysis (SNA) tools. While this chapter cannot elucidate all SNA concepts, we refer the reader to a canonical text about social network analysis in Wasserman and Faust (1994) and Easley and Kleinberg (2010). For the general note on the importance of SNA concepts, we refer the readers to Rafaeli (2017). SNA traditionally assumes that nodes in the network model are human agents, while edges represent human interactions among them, meaning that it is usually concerned with the role and relationships of individuals within the network. When considering a network derived from the set of interactions within a learning community, the learners themselves play a role of supporting other students' learning (e.g., when they comment on each other's insights).

Social constructivism (Vygotsky, 1978) emphasizes the central role played by co-learners and mediators in the construction of individual knowledge and views learning as the process by which learners are integrated into a knowledge community. Clearly, such a view supports the validity of the social network's traditional construction. Subsequent theories derived from the field of information sciences supported this view.

For example, interactivity theory (Rafaeli, 1988) focuses on interactions among community members to explain knowledge-forming processes. This theory, however, developed in light of the emergence of the Internet and distance learning and consequently refers to additional type of nodes beyond the scope of the human learning network, namely, the discussion's set of posts (text messages) through which human interactions take place (Rafaeli & Sudweeks, 1997). Accordingly, written posts and other information resources are another entity in the learning network, and human interactions can be modeled within the context of externalizing knowledge through them.

Modeling learning as a network of interactions among knowledge items, concepts, and ideas is not new. Cognitive learning theories have been based on this notion long before the advent of the Internet. Assimilation theory (Ausubel, 1968) emphasized relations among information items in the process of meaningful learning. Novak (1990) used concept maps as a learning tool, based on the principle of linking information items through semantic links into a network. The subsequent introduction of the Internet and its increasingly central role in collaborative learning led researchers such as Siemens (2005) to reframe the concept of learning within a digital ecosystem. Siemens introduced connectivism, with its notion of a hybrid network of learning, in which information items and devices, as well as human agents, act as nodes. The rise of online communities led social scientists to examine the interactivity of hybrid networks. Stromer-Galley (2000) pointed to the distinction between user-to-user and user-to-medium interactions. Many others also considered interactivity between users and text (Williams, Rice, & Rogers, 1988). Moore (1989) proposed three types of interactivity: learner-content, learner-instructor, and learner-learner.

Thus, when evaluating the process of interacting within an online discussion, both human and content agents need to be taken into account. Similarly, as interactions within a learning community involve such activities as knowledge exchange, questioning, associative learning, and learning by browsing, there is little point in the dichotomy of conceived interaction between two co-learners on the one hand and between a single learner and the content produced by another on the other. Accordingly, to evaluate learning within online communities, we model the learning network as composed of two types of nodes and three types of edges (interactions). Nodes represent (1) human agents (Haythornthwaite, 2008) and (2) information agents (posts or other media types contributed), while edges represent (1) interactions between human and information agents (such as view, vote, relate to, write), (2) interactions among human agents (such as user-follows-user), and (3) interactions among information agents (semantic links emphasizing relations among posts, such as "example of," "contrary to," or "makes me think of") (Novak, 2010).

Unit of Analysis: Collective Versus Individual Learning

Elsewhere (Kent & Rafaeli, 2016), we presented a framework for the quantitative analysis of interactivity in online learning discussions. Although these measures were extracted within a networked context (e.g., depth of threads, out-degree and in-degree of posts), the unit of analysis was the individual learner.

According to activity theory, learning is a collective participatory process of active knowledge construction emphasizing the interplay between individuals and cultural artifacts such as tools and symbols, while group cognition is conceptualized in terms of both context and interaction (Engeström, 2001). Consequently, in this chapter, we add the analysis of an entire community's learning (Haythornthwaite & De Laat, 2010).

Distributed cognition is defined as an extension of our internal cognition in the outside world through artifacts and other people (Hutchins, 1990). Stahl (2006) and Klimoski and Mohammed (1994) applied this understanding of an individual's sense-making to conceptualizing cognition as a shared (or collaborative) group-level phenomenon. Shared mental models refer to the overlapping mental representation of knowledge by team members (Bossche, Gijselaers, Segers, Woltjer, & Kirschner, 2010). Pena (2005) referred to collaboration as a coordinated synchronous activity that is the result of an ongoing attempt to construct and maintain a shared conception of a problem. Thus, collective learning in online communities may be viewed as an enabler of individual learning but should also be considered separately, analyzing the learning of the community as a learning unit in itself. As opportunities for conceptual coverage and enrichment (Stoyanova & Kommers, 2001) might lead to new and meaningful relations among bits of knowledge (Ausubel, 1968) at the individual level, similarly so – opportunities afforded to community participants to interact, reflect, and build on others' ideas (Rafaeli & Sudweeks, 1997; Vygotsky, 1978) can lead to social construction of knowledge, which makes a discussing community into a learning community.

Social Network Analysis

Social network analysis (SNA) is the process of investigating social structures through the use of graph theory to analyze large-scale relations between actors. These actors (called *nodes*) can be human actors or items within the network. The relations (or interactions) connecting the nodes are called *ties* (the literature uses also edges and links synonymously). Network analysis can supply topological features and process understanding (Barabâsi et al., 2002; Newman, 2004). Recently, there has been an increase in SNA research in cross-disciplinary fields such as social work (Gillieatt et al., 2015), psychology (Burt, Kilduff, & Tasselli, 2013), sociology (Cheadle & Schwadel, 2012), psychiatry (Wu & Duan, 2015), economics (Brown & Zimmermann, 2017), and information science (Otte & Rousseau, 2002). In Chap. 3 of this book, Raban and Geifman analyze the dynamics of cross-linking over time. Several studies have been carried out to investigate interactivity in online learning discussions using SNA, suggesting insights regarding group interaction patterns and individuals' roles and locations within networks (e.g., Reffay & Chanier, 2003 and Stewart & Abidi, 2012).

Static analysis of networks—statistical description of their topology on a particular date—is common in many academic fields. We suggest using dynamic analysis which opens up an opportunity to investigate the change in the network's parameters throughout a learning process. This approach is aligned with the dynamic nature of formative assessment and allows us to quantify the collective gain of learning, if any.

This chapter begins with investigating the correlation between individuals' network parameters and their learning outcomes, operationalized by using grades. Such a significant relationship allows us to infer that network analysis is relevant to learning, at least as far as the traditional assessment of learning gain is concerned. We then proceed to perform a network analysis of the entire community as the unit of analysis and demonstrate some topology parameters of the hybrid (i.e., containing both human and content nodes) learning network that are central to collaborative learning. The research hypotheses we suggest subsequently are by no means exhaustive. Instead, we seek to demonstrate the methodology of analyzing collaborative learning using a hybrid network of interactions.

Research Hypotheses

Online learning community members variously seek interaction, knowledge, or grades. In the process, they act within the social community and thus contribute to changing the online network structure (posts are added, links are created, etc.). These changes in the community's structure reflect the network's actual learning process and thus impact not only the single learner who has initiated them but the entire community.

Our main research question is: How can collaborative learning be measured or assessed using network analysis techniques? Learning interactions occur when a learner responds to or extends another learner's idea when she emphasizes the relation between two ideas posted by other classmates or even when she reads a post written by a learner to whom she had not been exposed earlier. Representing collaborative learning as the process of construction and growth of an interaction network, comprising all these interactions, allows us to evaluate the structure and dynamics of learning interactions among learners and resources.

Our primary unit of analysis is *individual learning*. We collect network topology parameters of learners and their associated learning outcome indicators (pre- and post-learning examination grades) and look for statistical correlations between them (see Appendix A for the list of SNA concepts). Our research builds on parameters used by:

- Russo and Koesten (2005), who used network prestige and centrality as robust predictors of cognitive learning outcomes
- Toikkanen and Lipponen (2011), who found the out-degree of replies and in-degree of reading to be most strongly correlated with the meaningfulness of the learning experience
- Romero and colleagues' (2013) finding that the number of messages sent and the number of words written, together with the degree of centrality and prestige, were the most important attributes for predicting final student performance
- Vaquero and Cebrian (2013) who found that more frequent and intensive social interactions generally implied higher student grades
- Joksimović and colleagues (2016) who studied centrality parameters and online learning

In this chapter, we explore further topological parameters (such as centrality parameters) to study the network's dynamics. We assume that the change in the student's knowledge is correlated with the topological parameters of her node. Therefore, our first hypothesis is:

H1a: At the individual level, positive correlations will be found between students' grades and their main topological parameters.

In an online community, learners can write new posts, comment, vote, etc., but they can also create new links between existing information resources (posts). When a learner contributes to the discussion, not by adding new content, but by merely relating between two existing posts of content (possibly contributed by two other learners), she is engaged in an activity we term *cross-referencing*. This goes beyond our earlier use of linking in the sense that cross-referencing is merely the technical implementation of the conceptual act of linking two concepts. Ausubel (1968) suggested that the act of curating new cross-references between existing content items is itself an indicator of learning. We thus hypothesize as follows:

H1b: Network centrality parameters are positively correlated with cross-referencing activity.

Individual and community collective knowledge are intertwined and mutually constructed (Scardamalia & Bereiter, 2003; Stahl, 2006). However, individual knowledge construction cannot be measured or conceptualized using the same assessment framework as the community's collective knowledge construction. In this chapter, we propose a quantitative method based on SNA to assess social learning at the community level. As learning and knowledge construction are formative processes, we use dynamic analysis to assess their characteristics.

In general, we look for changes in the community's network structure that can reflect the learning process and have potential to further support it. One topological parameter that depicts such structural change is *network distance*. The distance between nodes is the number of links that connect them (they can be connected by a common learner they both follow or by a common post with which they both interact). The average distance between nodes in a network often shrinks over time (Leskovec, Kleinberg, & Faloutsos, 2005). Specifically, in a learning community, we expect learners to interact with each other and with posts. This should result in a decrease of the average distance between nodes. Thus, new links are created and bring distant concepts closer, as part of learning. As the distance decreases, knowledge in the network moves between nodes more quickly and in shorter circuits. This means that learners can exchange new thoughts and ideas and thus learning can occur more effectively. Our next hypothesis is therefore:

H2: In the learning community as a whole, the average distance between nodes will decrease as the learning network evolves.

Effective learning occurs when groups are formed within networks and learners who share an interest in a certain topic work together to develop ideas. For learning to occur, collaborating learners should be close enough in terms of ideas or conceptual basis to start a discussion that can be productive for knowledge creation (Aviv, Erlich, Ravid, & Geva, 2003). At the same time, as learning progresses, they must retain a sufficient cognitive distance from each other for new insights to develop (Wuyts, Colombo, Dutta, & Nooteboom, 2005). This view of collaborative learning suggests that new knowledge appears as groups work closely together (Borgatti & Foster, 2003) but spreads among groups as knowledge begins to flow and make new inferences.

The *clique* is a commonly used group structure in studying networks. We define a *learning clique* as a subnetwork of nodes in which the number of interactions within the subnetwork is higher than the number of interactions between it and other nodes. Vaquero and Cebrian (2013) found that during the first weeks of a course, persistent interactions among high-performing students occur, while low-performing students fail to produce reciprocity in their interactions with these closed groups. Thus, we expect the formation of cliques within a community to accompany the process of knowledge creation within an effective learning process. On the other hand, Toikkanen and Lipponen (2011) found that meaningful learning was enabled only by reading and sharing with many community members (rather than settling for a few). Consequently, we posited that closed and small structures in a learning network (such as learning cliques) represent subnetworks that constrain social-constructivist learning and that the proportion of large cliques out of all cliques will decrease as learning evolves.

Transitive structures are another network form commonly used in such analyses. Transitive structures are created by directed links between three or more nodes, forming a closed shape, such as a circle. Due to its circular nature, the transitive structure is another closed structure that indicates closure and thus has a limiting effect on the entire network's flow (see Ravid, Erlich, and Aviv (2004) to learn more about transitivity).

To summarize, learning cliques are said to benefit the creation phase of new knowledge and, as a result, are expected to accompany a collaborative learning process. However, large cliques and transitive structures of interactions (such as views) are expected to limit the exposure of the entire community to the newly created knowledge, and their relative footprint is expected to decrease. Thus, we expect the manifestation of cliques to show two contradicting trends.

> H3: In the learning community as a whole, we expect the change in the general number of learning cliques to be aligned with the pace of the network's growth, while we expect the proportion of large learning cliques to decline and the number of transitive structures to become smaller as the network evolves.

Method

Data Source: A Case Study Exemplifying the Networked Analytics Approach

Twenty-eight graduate students used an online discussion platform, called Ligilo (described in the next section).[1] The online discussion accompanied an entire 8-week course on the subject of virtual communities, taught at the Information and Knowledge Management Department of the University of Haifa, Israel. Although the course consisted 8 weeks, the discussion extended beyond the course for another 2 weeks. The instructor served as the community moderator. Participation in the discussion was mandatory and accounted for 15% of the final grade. No minimum contribution was specified, and students were free to choose the extent and nature of their participation. The pedagogic goal of the discussion was to use online collaboration to enable conceptual coverage.

The discussion was seeded with nine initial posts about syllabus subjects. Students were asked to write their own posts about concepts raised in the course, relating them to relevant curriculum topics. In addition, they were advised to add and link reading materials and discuss them freely, along with the course topics in general. The instructor's moderation involved setting up the initial framing (the nine syllabus items) and including in the discussion some of the issues raised by the learners in classroom lessons.

---

[1] http://www.go-ligilo.com

Individual learning was assessed according to two multiple choice examinations, before and after the semester, that focused on conceptual coverage and inferences (Haladyna & Rodriguez, 2012). The assessment goal was to measure the change in knowledge and comprehension. Another aim was to assess high-order thinking skills (Bloom, 1974) gained and applied by each learner during the course, instead of just their final level of knowledge, that is, a summative assessment ignoring the learners' initial knowledge of the subject (Campbell & Stanley, 1963).

Ligilo

Ligilo is a hyperlinked discussion platform where each post is expressed as a node in a semantic network of posts. Using Ligilo, learning communities create collective concept maps while conducting online discussions. The *relations* among posts are semantically tagged by community members (examples of such tags are "reminds me of," "makes me ask," "for example," or "as opposed to"). In addition, Ligilo enables a zoomable map view of the emergent knowledge base, aiming at improvement of the participants' grasp of the constructed model's high-level context (see Appendix D for screenshots).

In terms of the collected data, Ligilo is implemented as a twofold network: A network of hyperlinked posts that underlies a social network of learners interacting based on the network of posts. In Ligilo, learners contribute to their community by posting, voting, and reading but also by relating to other learners' postings and by tagging these relations. The relating and tagging activities are based on the notion that meaningful learning is grounded in contexts and relationships rather than merely in the minds of individuals (Ausubel, 1968; Novak, 2010). Extracting data from Ligilo into a directed network dataset involves representing the learners and the posts as nodes, resulting in a two-mode network (Borgatti & Everett, 1997). The interactions among both types of nodes are represented by the network's links. This network formation dictates the existence of links between learners, between posts, and between learners and posts. Links between posts and learners cannot exist, however (as in this setting, a post is an entity that cannot initiate interactions). This exception implies that reciprocal relations cannot be formed between learner and post nodes, impacting negatively on the overall measured reciprocal ties (and other reciprocal parameters) in the network.

Topological Parameters

Two units of analysis were used to measure collaborative learning in this chapter: The learning process of an individual learner and the collective learning process of the entire community. We combined a set of network static and dynamic analyses (Reda, Tantipathananandh, Johnson, Leigh, & Berger-Wolf, 2011; Wei & Carley,

2015) to enable evaluation of the reciprocal structure of interactions in a specific temporal snapshot, as well as of the changes reflected by the interaction network throughout the learning process. In this subsection, we list the parameters used to reflect on their assessment as proxies of learning.

Learning parameters at the individual level Kent and Rafaeli (2016) presented an operationalization framework for measuring interactivity patterns in individual learning within online communities. The parameters were based on interactions and turn-taking, as well as on network analysis characteristics such as a post's level of relatedness to other posts in a discussion and out-degree (see Appendix A for definitions). Here, we add network parameters such as betweenness, Bonacich's centrality, Burt's effective network size and exclusivity to extend the individual learning's measurement (*H1a*) (see Appendix A for a brief explanation of each parameter). We also added an indicator for the number of cross-references a learner adds to the learning network when she posits a new relation between two existing posts (see Ligilo screenshot in Fig. 9.1), arguing that the tendency or ability to add relevant cross-references to the network is an indicator of individual learning. Such brokers can facilitate the coordination and alignment of meaning (Wenger, 1998) and enable knowledge flow and diffusion among different parts and cliques of a network (Aviv et al., 2003; Haythornthwaite, 2008).

Collective learning parameters Static analysis of the entire hybrid learning network as a snapshot at the end of the learning process can provide us with a descriptive structure. However, as we focus on the dynamic nature of the learning process, we measure topological parameters as they change on a week-by-week basis and cumulatively throughout the semester. The dynamics of the network's average path

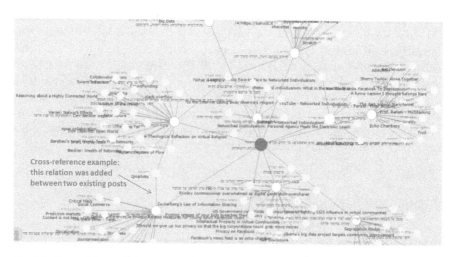

Fig. 9.1 Cross-reference link (a cross-reference is a link between two posts, added after both posts already existed. A learner who adds such a cross-reference contributes to the community not by adding new content but by restructuring the network and bringing posts closer together)

length (APL) indicates the change in the level of reach that learners and content posts have in relation to each other. Therefore, we measure the change in APL, assuming an effective learning process will eventually result in its decrease (*H2*). The presence of several learning cliques is indicative of knowledge and interaction diffusion in a learning network. There can be no directed link from a post to a learner (since a post cannot be reactive toward a learner). Therefore, a learning clique will, from this point on, refer to a *triad* in which there is a connection, which is not necessarily reciprocal, between all its members. We thus measure the change in the number of learning cliques, assuming their number will increase with the collaborative learning process, while the proportion of large cliques will decrease (*H3*).

Results

The network At the end of the semester, the network contained 512 nodes (learners and posts) sharing 4388 links. The platform constrains each post so that it is necessarily connected to at least one other post. The network is fully connected (no isolations). The APL (Average Path Length) is 5.73, meaning that it takes an average of slightly fewer than six links to connect any pair of random nodes. These results dovetail with the classical concept of 6 degrees of separation (Milgram, 1967), i.e., the network behaves as a small world network, including inner communities connected to one another.

The network has a very low reciprocal index (0.008) as (post) nodes cannot initiate links with learners. For the same reason, the average in- and out-degrees are relatively low (0.012 and 0.009, respectively). Figure 9.2 presents the hybrid learning network's final structure (after an 8-week semester). The network's terms are explained in brief in Appendix A, the visual topologies of the evolving network in Appendix B, and the daily changes of the diameter and the APL in Appendix C.

To gain a better understanding of structure, we move from the network level to the node level and analyze the main nodes in the network that are either posts (P) or learners (L). The most topologically significant post in the network is P1, the first and central post of the discussion, created by the community moderator. P1 has the highest in-degree, the highest total degree and the highest betweenness centrality, all of which point to the structural high centrality of the first post rooted by the instructor, outlining the entire aim and subject of the discussion.

The most central learner in the network is student L4. Its node has the highest closeness centrality, the highest hub centrality, and the highest out-degree centrality. This means that L4 is, on average, the closest node to all other nodes; it has the largest number of outbound links to other nodes and reaches the highest number of nodes in the network. This means that L4 was the most active and connected learner.

Next, we analyze the dynamics of the network. Figure 9.3 shows a daily graph of the change in the number of nodes and the number of links in the network.

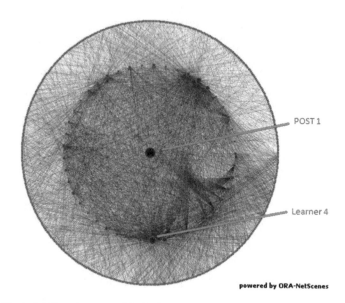

POST 1

Learner 4

powered by ORA-NetScenes

Fig. 9.2 The hybrid learning network's final structure (Nodes are learners and posts. Their size indicates the number of incoming and outgoing links to other nodes. The main nodes are Post 1 and Learner 4)

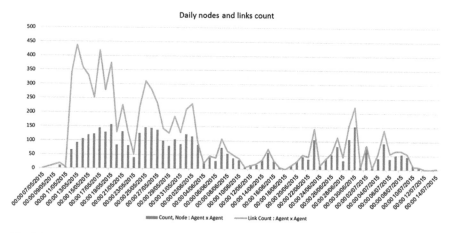

Fig. 9.3 Daily number of nodes and links

In the first month, the students were very active, and the number of links was much higher than the number of nodes (learners and posts). Early in the second month (June), however, the trend changed, and until the end of the semester, the daily number of nodes stabilized, while the number of links dropped sharply. This suggests that posts were still written and attached to existing posts (as is required), but the number of further actions concerning these posts—such as viewing or commenting—decreased.

We proceed to describe the results as associated with our four hypotheses.

H1a: At the Individual Level, Positive Correlations Will Be Found Between Students' Grades and Their Main Topological Parameters

When correlating learning—as operationalized by the improvement in individual learners' grades—with topological parameters, we found a medium positive correlation (0.39; $p < 0.05$) between a node's hub centrality index and the learner's grade improvement. In Ligilo, users can choose to either tag the relations between posts from a list of relations provided by the moderator or create their own semantic tagging (for screenshots, see Figs. 9.12 and 9.13 in Appendix D). We found a medium positive correlation (0.41; $p < 0.05$) between the relative number of originally tagged relations (out of all relations created by a learner) and the improvement in the respective grade.

H1b: At the Individual Level, Network Centrality Parameters Are Positively Correlated with Cross-Referencing Activity

Cross-referencing is the act of connecting two or more existing posts not previously connected. Community members engaged in cross-referencing contribute to the community's overall learning by paving logical paths between seemingly distant issues. Some significant positive correlations were found between the amount of cross-references curated by individual learners and their topological parameters, namely, high positive correlation with the betweenness centrality index of a node representing the learner (0.62; $p < 0.01$), the node's out-degree centrality index (0.55; $p < 0.01$), the exclusivity index (0.56; $p < 0.01$), Simmelian ties (0.48; $p < 0.05$), and the network's effective size (0.55; $p < 0.01$). These are not trivial relationships, since the activity of cross-referencing is an explicit interaction made by the user, while the out-degree, betweenness, and other parameters are a function of both explicit and implicit interactions (e.g., views). All other indicators suggest that the user is highly involved in connecting other nodes and bridging parts of the network.

Finally, we found significant positive correlations between the number of cross-references and several log-based (i.e., non-network) counts: high positive correlation (0.6; $p < 0.01$) with active behavior log counts of number of contributed posts and number of voting for posts and a medium positive correlation (0.36; $p < 0.05$) with passive behavior logs of viewing posts.

H2: In the Learning Community as a Whole, the Average Distance Between Nodes Will Decrease as the Learning Network Evolves

The APL (Average Path Length) of the entire hybrid network is the average number of connecting nodes among all nodes in the network. The graph in Fig. 9.4 presents the network's weekly APL and the accumulated APL. It displays a decline in the weekly distance from around four links between nodes at the beginning of the semester to a little more than two links at its end. The accumulated APL, however, shows a moderate decrease along the semester (from 6 to 5.5 links between nodes).

There is an initial rise in APL because many posts and learners joined the network in the first weeks and increased the average distance between nodes. As time

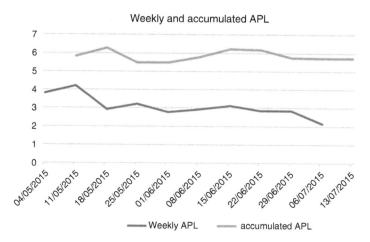

Fig. 9.4 The entire learning network APL on a weekly basis (blue) and accumulated (orange)

went by, all learners joined the network and began to interact, leading to a decline in diameter. From week 3 or 4, all learners were members of the network, and only posts were still joining. The entrance of new posts contributes to the slow rise in the APL in the middle of the course. In our network, however, each added post has to be linked by default to at least one existing post and to its creator (the learner). Hence these posts do not dramatically change the overall average distance. Toward the end of the semester, the accumulated APL stabilized at 5.5. The specific structure of Ligilo, that compels new posts to relate to a previously created post, enables connectivity and fosters learning in the network.

> *H3: In the Learning Community as a Whole, We Expect the Change in the General Number of Learning Cliques to Be Aligned with the Pace of the Network's Growth, While We Expect the Proportion of Large Learning Cliques to Decline and the Number of Transitive Structures to Become Smaller as the Network Evolves*

To map the evolution of cliques in the network from a cumulative point of view, we first present the evolution of all nodes, links, and cliques in the network. Although the number of links is not part of our hypothesis, we present it in the following graphs because it provides a broader context concerning the evolution of the network. The graph in Fig. 9.5b shows a rise in the numbers of nodes, links, and cliques. After week 3, the number of nodes stabilizes, while the number of links and cliques keeps rising. The cumulative number of cliques keeps growing gradually, and starting from the third week (see Fig. 9.6), the ratio of cliques per node stabilized around 5.5, and the ratio of nodes per clique evened out at around 5.7. This finding presents no change in the number of cliques per node, nor in the number of nodes per clique. These all suggest that the number of cliques increases in parallel to growth in the network.

Figure 9.7 presents the cumulative number of cliques. The small cliques (having three nodes, called *triads*) are in orange, while the large cliques (more than three nodes, called *non-triads*) are in gray.

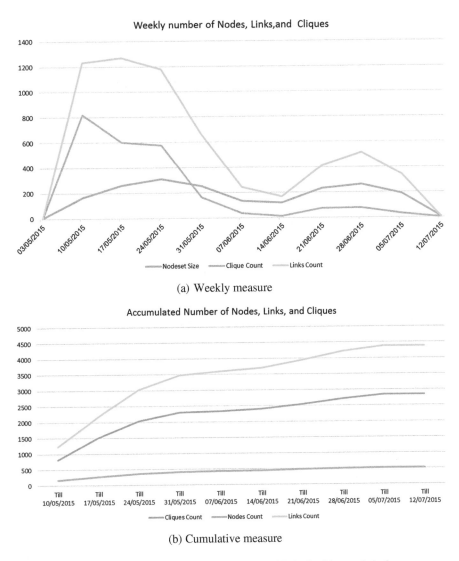

(a) Weekly measure

(b) Cumulative measure

Fig. 9.5 Number of nodes, links, and cliques (**a**) on a weekly basis; (**b**) cumulatively

Using absolute values, Fig. 9.7 shows a decrease in the number of large cliques and an increase in the number of the smallest cliques (three members). Table 9.1 shows how the relative portion of the large cliques decreases as the network evolves. This decrease is indicative of an opening of the network, enabling better information flow.

To improve our understanding of the network opening trend, Fig. 9.8 presents the cumulative transitivity of the network. Transitivity indicates the occurrence of strong, circular structures within the learning network. The decrease in transitivity suggests that the network opens its closed structures, thereby enabling a better flow of information.

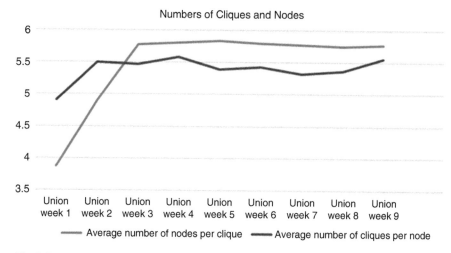

Fig. 9.6 Weekly average number of cliques per node during the semester

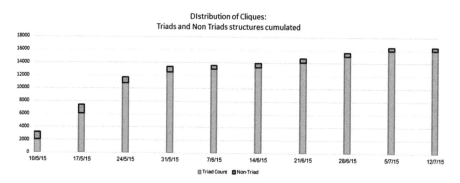

Fig. 9.7 Cumulative distribution among three-member or larger cliques

Table 9.1 Distribution of accumulated numbers of small and large cliques in the network

Week	10/05	17/05	24/05	31/05	07/06	14/06	21/06	28/06	05/07	12/07
Clique count	3172	7420	11,755	13,373	13,621	13,940	14,708	15,624	16,436	16,440
Triad count	2073	6085	10,835	12,591	13,068	13,310	14,101	15,050	15,943	15,951
% triad (small) cliques	65%	82%	92%	94%	96%	95%	96%	96%	97%	97%
Non-triad count	1099	1335	920	782	553	630	607	574	493	489
% non-triad (large) cliques	35%	18%	8%	6%	4%	5%	4%	4%	3%	3%

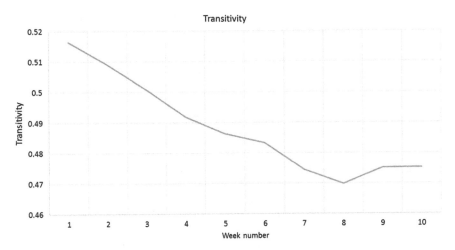

Fig. 9.8 Accumulated transitivity and Simmelian ties during the semester

Discussion and Main Conclusions

This chapter is about both the individual and collective levels of learning. As discussed by Hoadley and Kali in Chap. 1, learning involves situating one's knowledge within the collective knowledge. Online discussions are commonly considered effective tools for social learning, both formally and informally. They are believed to enable learning through the collective act of building persistent knowledge bases. Beyond serving as a stage for social interaction, sharing, and exchange of opinions, online discussions also document and preserve reflection and interaction with the learning resources themselves. The development of technological platforms, instruction designs, and learning materials accommodating online social learning for massive amounts and varieties of learners is not enough. The ability to measure quantitatively and then assess online collaborative learning from the perspective of an entire community as a learning unit in itself is critical for the process of deployment of online learning. The strengths and weaknesses of communities must be explored, in addition to the close tracking of individual learning. It is the power of collectives and the scaffolds of interactions that promote empowered individual learners.

In this chapter, we posited a suggestion for such a quantitative analysis methodology, informed by learning theories that view the learning community as a network of interactions among co-learners and learning resources. To demonstrate an empirical implementation of this approach, we explored a case study of a learning community's online discussion, analyzed by SNA techniques. Other techniques, both qualitative and quantitative (linguistics, discourse analysis, and others), are equally applicable and might be combined with SNA to achieve a more holistic understanding of learning.

H1a: At the Individual Level, Positive Correlations Will Be Found Between Students' Grades and Their Main Topological Parameters

Learning can be depicted in many ways: It is difficult to posit any universal rule for learning assessment. *H1a* was based on the notion that learning is a process of gaining knowledge; hence its effectiveness can be measured by improvement in learners' grades. In Kent, Laslo, and Rafaeli (2016), the average depth of a learner's posts that may indicate reading depth (before submitting a new post) was found to be positively correlated with grade improvement, specifically in the community discussion examined in this chapter.

The current chapter found that a high number of outgoing node links (hub centrality) and a high proportion of original relation tagging (as opposed to ready-made tagging) are positively correlated with improvement in grades. These results suggest that in the course of online learning, creating connections with surrounding resources and co-learners and being creative when doing so (proposing original tags for relations instead of choosing from a ready-made drop-down list) are correlated with improved grades.

H1b: Network Centrality Parameters Are Positively Correlated with Cross-Referencing Activity

Novak (1990) suggested that learning can be reflected in the activity of cross-referencing. We explored potential correlations between topological parameters and cross-referencing. Bridges are important in dealing with structural holes (Burt, 1992). In this context, cross-referencing characterizes learners who bridge otherwise disconnected subnetworks, contributing to overall connectivity and thus to community learning. Using SNA techniques, we found a significant positive correlation between the high level of cross-referencing and topological parameters such as out-degree centrality, betweenness centrality, exclusivity, and Burt's effective network. The positive correlation between cross-referencing and the above-noted parameters suggests that nodes involved in connecting detached information resources have special topological parameters and a high potential to contribute to community learning.

H2: In the Learning Community as a Whole, the Average Distance Between Nodes Will Decrease as the Learning Process Evolves

Looking at the network as a whole, at first, we detect an overt rise in accumulated APL (to about 6 degrees of separation between nodes) and then a decline to 5.5 during the semester. This dovetails with the social network community studies of Leskovec et al. (2005), Mislove, Marcon, Gummadi, Druschel, and Bhattacharjee (2007), Leskovec, Lang, Dasgupta, and Mahoney (2008), and Kumar, Novak, and Tomkins (2010) that demonstrated a decrease in both diameter and APL. In social networks, people become network-friends, represented by the decline in average distance between nodes. Our learning community, a hybrid social and content network, shows the expected decrease from 6 to 5.5, suggesting that by the end of the semester, students are better connected to each other (through social and content interactions) and to their created content. Unlike the accumulated APL, the weekly

APL snapshots focus on the subnetwork of interactions created only within a specific week. These weekly distances between nodes become closer as learning evolves, contributing to the communal sharing of ideas and knowledge.

H3: In the Learning Community as a Whole, We Expect the Change in the General Number of Learning Cliques to Be Aligned with the Pace of the Network's Growth, While We Expect the Proportion of the Large Learning Cliques to Decline and the Number of Transitive Structures to Become Smaller as the Network Evolves

Our findings suggest that the dynamics of the number of cliques, along with the ratio between small (triad) and large (non-triad) cliques, are essential to understanding the process of collaborative learning. The presence of cliques has been shown to affect the dynamics of groups and knowledge sharing (Borgatti & Foster, 2003; Toikkanen & Lipponen, 2011) in a way that might seem conflicting. Cliques have a crucial role in enabling knowledge creation in groups; at the same time, however, their presence might limit distribution of and exposure to information. Here, we suggest a delicate distinction between the role of cliques in general and that of large cliques, as well as other strong structures (such as transitive structures). Our findings show that, in general, the number of cliques grows concomitantly with the size of the network, buttressing the assumption that the presence of cliques supports the process of creating knowledge. Furthermore, we found evidence that the proportion of large cliques, as well as the transitivity index, decrease as the network evolves, pointing to the emergence of additional opportunities to interact.

Limitations Our empirical findings are based on a single case study—a preliminary step in an extensive methodological work that should connect social learning theories and learning analytics. The online discussion we examined was constructed for a specific pedagogical purpose, affected by the specific background and motivations of both learners and instructor and using a specific platform (Ligilo). There was no minimum number of contributions to the platform per user, and in general there were only minimal requirements regarding the nature and structure of contributions. Thus, our findings may not be generalized to other communities whose discussions were designed for other purposes, with different discussion structures and formal requirements. Nevertheless, the methodological aspects of this chapter are generalizable and may contribute to future work.

Kent et al. (2016) used the same community, along with other communities moderated in a more structured manner (e.g., building collaborative knowledge bases, Q&A bases, and more). This specific community showed a significantly lower number of correlations relative to the more structured discussions of our log-based measures with the outcome assessment, assumedly because of its freeform discussion structure. Indeed, other studies based on content analysis suggested that a structured discussion involves substantial participation in the first phases of knowledge construction, while unstructured discussion became stalled (Fried, 2016). Hence correlations with grades, as well as the level or quality of interactions, may well be higher in the more structured discussions. A further drawback of the present chapter is its use of SNA techniques without analyzing the posts' content.

Summary and Future Research

Qualitative and traditional assessment methods, along with contemporary pedagogy and theories of learning, are the basis for learning analytic methodologies. In this chapter, we harnessed social network analysis to advance collaborative online learning assessment. Learning interaction networks are shaped and developed by creating links between ideas and participants and interacting as learning instruments. A single learner's motivation to learn leads to the creation of digital footprints. By doing so, it changes the topological parameters of the entire learning network.

Analysis of additional online communities and their network dynamics is required for full comprehension of the network topology implications of learning attributes such as group size, instruction and moderation style, as well as the discussion's structure. Furthermore, we need to take another step forward and establish a correlation between topological properties and changes discussed, as well as with qualitative evaluations of the community's collaboration efficacy, should such methods become a common standard.

However, we believe that capturing the collective formation of knowledge can be informed by analyzing networks of learning interactions. We think that assessing those collective processes can, in return, feed back into the learning process of the individual and, by extension, that of the entire community. Consequently, in this chapter, we have shown how analysis of network parameters such as distance, transitivity, and centrality can lead to evidence related to the dynamics of collaborative learning. We have also demonstrated that the presence and size distribution of inner structures, such as cliques, can serve as an indicator for the dynamics of social constructivist processes. Practically, this framework can be used to assess online social learning using online discussions and to compare the collaborative essence of learning among different learning designs, subjects, and populations.

Methodologically, conceptualizing the learning community as a two-mode network of learners and knowledge resources paves the way to additional research questions. It is clear that network parameters used in unimodal networks (social networks as a classic example) make sense in a different manner and establish different semantics with regard to describing the evolution process of the networks. For example, filtering out only the content nodes and the semantic relations between them creates a knowledge map of the online community. Similarly, exploring only human nodes and their social interactions results in charting the online community's social network. Switching the focus to specific network structures, such as star shapes, circles, and dyads in a two-mode conceptualization of learning, is challenging, as it requires rethinking of the weighting scheme for links, an examination of reciprocity, and other core concepts.

It is important to note the special structure of this two-mode network of interactions presented in this chapter, especially in light of its effect on the network parameters. As nonhuman objects interact only with other nonhuman objects (i.e., posts connect via semantic links) and do not actively interact with humans (but rather are acted on by humans), the network does not contain any directional links going from posts to learners. This is a major distinction that sets two-mode networks apart from traditional social networks. Network parameters based on mutuality are very limited in their semantics. Learners can maintain mutual relations with other learners, and posts can have mutual relations with other posts, but they cannot establish mutual relations with learners. It should be interesting to see how these specific characteristics of learning interaction networks change as the technology develops and its deployment and use grow. To summarize, online collaborative discussions over platforms like Ligilo illustrate how the affordances of measuring network interactions structures, both at the individual and collective levels, can contribute to both cognitive gains and to assessment practices in learning contexts of networked societies.

Appendix A: Topological Parameters—Brief Index

While this chapter cannot elucidate all SNA concepts, we bring here the necessary SNA definitions. We refer the reader to a canonical text about networks and their topological parameters in Wasserman and Faust (1994) and Easley and Kleinberg (2010). For the general note on the importance of SNA concepts, we refer the readers to Rafaeli (2017).

- Authority and Hub Degree: Authority and hub values are defined in terms of one another in a mutual recursion. An authority degree of a node is computed as the sum of the scaled hub values that point to that node. A hub value is the sum of the scaled authority values of the nodes to which it points. A node has a high authority degree if numerous hubs point to it and a high hub degree if it points to numerous authorities. As Kleinberg (1999) puts it: "…, a review paper may refer to other authoritative sources: it is important because it tells us where to find trustworthy information. Thus, there are … two types of central nodes: authorities, that contain reliable information on the topic of interest, and hubs, that tell us where to find authoritative information."
- Betweenness Centrality: For each node, the betweenness centrality is the number of shortest paths between any two nodes that pass through this node. High betweenness means that a node is connecting many pairs of nodes that would not be connected without it.
- Clustering Coefficient: The network's clustering coefficient measures the degree to which nodes in a network cluster together. In social networks, in which nodes (people) tend to create groups with a relatively high density of links within them, a high clustering coefficient is expected. For a single node, it is the ratio of network links connecting a node's neighbors to each other to achieve the maximum (potential) number of links.
- Burt's Effective Network: The number of nodes a given node can reach in the network. It measures the overall reach of a node in a network.

- Clique: A group of nodes in which each individual node is directly linked with every other individual. For example, Alice follows Bob and Charlie, Bob follows Charlie, and Charlie follows Alice. In this chapter, cliques need not be reciprocally connected.
- Eigenvector Centrality: The connections of a node to high-scoring nodes are assumed to contribute more to the score of the node in question than would an equal number of connections to low-scoring nodes. The rationale behind this centrality score is that if Alice is a friend of Bob and Bob knows everybody, Alice can benefit from Bob's connections. Eigenvector centrality assigns relative scores to all nodes in the network to measure the influence of each.
- Exclusivity: The degree to which the node is the only node that connects to other (less popular) nodes. Exclusivity indicates that the node in question has access to unique nodes (people or resources).
- In-Degree: The number of incoming links a particular node receives.
- Out-Degree: The number of outgoing links of one node to other nodes.
- Total Degree: The sum of in- and out-degrees.

Appendix B: Topological Change in the Network (Fig. 9.9)

From right to left: first week, fourth week, and eighth week. The brown nodes are posts, and the central one is Post 1, the root of the discussion (including its title). The brown nodes in the second tier are Posts 2 to 10 that constitute the skeletal nodes, including the course's subject. The green nodes depict the learners. Nodes with the highest betweenness centrality appear in the center of the network

Appendix C: Daily Changes in Diameter and APL (Fig. 9.10)

Appendix D: Ligilo Screenshots (Fig. 9.11)

Posts at the left side of the screen are connected by blue tagged relations to posts on the right.

Fig. 9.9 Network evolution

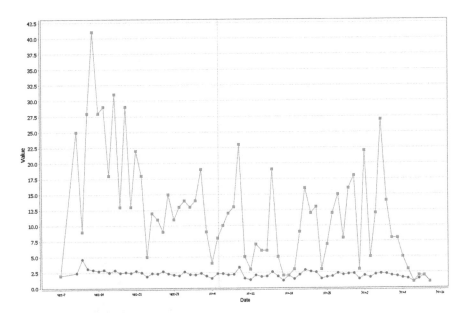

Fig. 9.10 Daily changes in the network's diameter (red) and APL (blue)

Fig. 9.11 A basic view of Ligilo

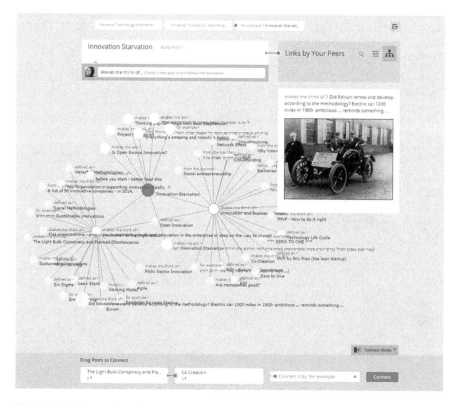

Fig. 9.12 Bird's eye view of Ligilo posts

Fig. 9.13   Tagging relations in Ligilo

Bibliography

AlDahdouh, A. A., Osório, A. J., & Caires, S. (2015). Understanding knowledge network, learning and connectivism. *International Journal of Instructional Technology and Distance Learning, 12*(10), 3–21.

Ausubel, D. P. (1968). *Educational psychology: A cognitive view*. New York: Holt, Rinehart and Winston.

Aviv, R., Erlich, Z., Ravid, G., & Geva, A. (2003). Network analysis of knowledge construction in asynchronous learning networks. *Journal of Asynchronous Learning Networks, 7*(3), 1–23.

Baker, R., Siemens, G. (2014) Educational data mining and learning analytics. In Sawyer, K. (Ed.) Cambridge handbook of the learning sciences: 2nd, 253–274.

Barabâsi, A. L., Jeong, H., Néda, Z., Ravasz, E., Schubert, A., & Vicsek, T. (2002). Evolution of the social network of scientific collaborations. *Physica A: Statistical Mechanics and its Applications, 311*(3), 590–614.

Barker, P. (1994). Designing interactive learning. In T. de Jong & L. Sarti (Eds.), *Design and production of multimedia and simulation-based learning material* (pp. 1–30). Dordrecht, Netherlands: Springer.

Bloom, B. S. (1974). *Taxonomy of educational objectives: The classification of educational goals. Handbook 1–2*. New York: Longman.

Borgatti, S., & Foster, P. (2003). The network paradigm in organizational research: A review and typology. *Journal of Management, 29*, 991–1013.

Borgatti, S. P., & Everett, M. G. (1997). Network analysis of 2-mode data. *Social Networks, 19*(3), 243–269.

Bossche, P., Gijselaers, W., Segers, M., Woltjer, G., & Kirschner, P. (2010). Team learning: Building shared mental models. *Instructional Science, 39*(3), 283–301. https://doi.org/10.1007/s11251-010-9128-3

Brown, A. J., & Zimmermann, K. F. (2017). Three decades of publishing research in population economics. *Journal of Population Economics, 30*(1), 11–27.

Burt, R. S. (1992). *Structural holes: The social structure of competition*. Cambridge, MA: Harvard University Press.

Burt, R. S., Kilduff, M., & Tasselli, S. (2013). Social network analysis: Foundations and frontiers on advantage. *Annual Review of Psychology, 64*, 527–547.

Campbell, D. T., & Stanley, J. C. (1963). *Experimental and quasi-experimental designs for research. NIDA Research Monograph.* Boston: Houghton Mifflin. https://doi.org/10.1016/0306-4573(84)90053-0

Cheadle, J. E., & Schwadel, P. (2012). The 'friendship dynamics of religion,' or the 'religious dynamics of friendship'? A social network analysis of adolescents who attend small schools. *Social Science Research, 41*(5), 1198–1212.

Clow, D. (2013). An overview of learning analytics. *Teaching in Higher Education, 18*(6), 683–695. https://doi.org/10.1080/13562517.2013.827653

Deboer, J., Ho, A. D., Stump, G. S., & Breslow, L. (2014). Changing "course": Reconceptualizing educational variables for massive open online courses. *Educational Researcher, 43*, 74–84. https://doi.org/10.3102/0013189X14523038

Easley, D., & Kleinberg, J. (2010). *Networks, crowds, and markets: Reasoning about a highly connected world.* Cambridge, UK: Cambridge University Press.

Ellis, C. (2013). Broadening the scope and increasing the usefulness of learning analytics: The case for assessment analytics. *British Journal of Educational Technology, 44*(4), 662–664.

Engeström, Y. (2001). Expansive learning at work: Toward an activity theoretical reconceptualization. *Journal of Education and Work, 14*, 133–156. https://doi.org/10.1080/13639080020028747

Erickson, T., & Herring, S. (2004, January). Persistent conversation: A dialog between research and design. In *System sciences, 2004. Proceedings of the 37th annual Hawaii international conference.* IEEE.

Ferguson, R. (2012). Learning analytics: Drivers, developments and challenges. *International Journal of Technology Enhanced Learning, 4*(5–6), 304–317. https://doi.org/10.1504/IJTEL.2012.051816

Ferguson, R., Macfadyen, L. P., Clow, D., Tynan, B., Alexander, S., & Dawson, S. (2014). Setting learning analytics in context: Overcoming the barriers to large-scale adoption. *Journal of Learning Analytics, 1*(3), 120–144. https://doi.org/10.1145/2567574.2567592

Fried, A. (2016). *Social network analysis of asynchronous discussion in online learning.* Doctoral dissertation, University of Toronto, Canada.

Garrison, D. R. (2006). Online collaboration principles. *Journal of Asynchronous Learning Networks, 10*(1), 25–34. Retrieved from http://citeseerx.ist.psu.edu/viewdoc/download?doi=1 0.1.1.96.4536&rep=rep1&type=pdf

Gibson, D., & de Freitas, S. (2015). Exploratory analysis in learning analytics. *Technology, Knowledge and Learning, 21*(1), 5–19. https://doi.org/10.1007/s10758-015-9249-5

Gillieatt, S., Fernandes, C., Fielding, A., Hendrick, A., Martin, R., & Matthews, S. (2015). Social network analysis and social work inquiry. *Australian Social Work, 68*(3), 338–351.

Haladyna, T. M., & Rodriguez, T. M. (2012). *Developing and validating multiple-choice test items.* New York/Abingdon, UK: Routledge.

Haythornthwaite, C. (2008). Learning relations and networks in web-based communities. *International Journal of Web Based Communities, 4*(2), 140. https://doi.org/10.1504/IJWBC.2008.017669

Haythornthwaite, C., & De Laat, M. (2010). Social networks and learning networks: Using social network perspectives to understand social learning. In *7th international conference on networked learning* (pp. 183–190). Aalborg, Denmark.

Herring, S. (1999). Interactional Coherence in CMC. *Journal of Computer-Mediated Communication, 4*(4), 0. https://doi.org/10.1111/j.1083

Hewitt, J. (2001). Beyond threaded discourse. *International Journal of Educational Telecommunications, 7*(3), 207–221.

Hutchins, E. (1990). The social organisation of distributed cognition. In L. Resnik & J. Levine (Eds.), *Perspectives on socially shared cognition.* Washington, DC: APA Press.

Joksimović, S., Manataki, A., Gašević, D., Dawson, S., Kovanović, V., & De Kereki, I. F. (2016). Translating network position into performance: Importance of centrality in different network configurations. In *Proceedings of the sixth international conference on learning analytics & knowledge* (pp. 314–323). Edinburgh, UK: ACM.

Kent, C., Laslo, E., & Rafaeli, S. (2016). Interactivity in online discussions and learning outcomes. *Computers and Education, 97*(C), 116–128. https://doi.org/10.1016/j.compedu.2016.03.002

Kent, C., & Rafaeli, S. (2016). How interactive is a semantic network? Concept maps and discourse in knowledge communities. In *HICSS*. Kauai, Hawaii.

Kleinberg, J. M. (1999). Authoritative sources in a hyperlinked environment. *Journal of the ACM (JACM), 46*(5), 604–632.

Klimoski, R., & Mohammed, S. (1994). Team mental model: Construct or metaphor? *Journal of Management, 20*(2), 403–437.

Kovanovic, V., Joksimovic, S., Gasevic, D., & Hatala, M. (2014). Automated cognitive presence detection in online discussion transcripts. In *Proceedings of the fourth international conference on learning analytics and knowledge*. Indianapolis, IN: LAK Workshops.

Kumar, R., Novak, J., & Tomkins, A. (2010). Structure and evolution of online social networks. In P. S. Yu, J. Han, & C. Faloutsos (Eds.), *Link mining: Models, algorithms, and applications* (pp. 337–357). New York: Springer.

Lander, J. (2015). Building community in online discussion: A case study of moderator strategies. *Linguistics and Education, 29*, 107–120. https://doi.org/10.1016/j.linged.2014.08.007

Leskovec, J., Kleinberg, J., & Faloutsos, C. (2005). Graphs over time: Densification laws, shrinking diameters and possible explanations. In *Proceedings of the eleventh ACM SIGKDD international conference on knowledge discovery in data mining* (pp. 177–187). Chicago.

Leskovec, J., Lang, K. J., Dasgupta, A., & Mahoney, M. W. (2008). Statistical properties of community structure in large social and information networks. In *Proceedings of the 17th international conference on World Wide Web* (pp. 695–704). Beijing, China: ACM.

Mickes, L., Darby, R. S., Hwe, V., Bajic, D., Warker, J. A., Harris, C. R., et al. (2013). Major memory for microblogs. *Memory & Cognition, 41*(4), 481–489.

Milgram, S. (1967). The small world problem. *Psychology Today, 2*(1), 60–67.

Mislove, A., Marcon, M., Gummadi, K. P., Druschel, P., & Bhattacharjee, B. (2007). Measurement and analysis of online social networks. In *Proceedings of the 7th ACM SIGCOMM conference on internet measurement* (pp. 29–42). San Diego, CA: ACM.

Moore, M. G. (1989). Editorial: Three types of interaction. *American Journal of Distance Education, 3*(2), 1–6.

National Research Council (NRC). (2000). *How people learn: Brain, mind, experience, and school: Expanded edition*. National Academies Press.

Newman, M. E. (2004). Who is the best connected scientist? A study of scientific coauthorship networks. In R. Menezes, A. Evsukoff, & M. C. González (Eds.), *Complex networks* (pp. 337–370). Berlin/Heidelberg, Germany: Springer.

Novak, J. D. (1990). Concept maps and Vee diagrams: Two metacognitive tools to facilitate meaningful learning. *Instructional Science, 19*(1), 29–52.

Novak, J. (2010). *Learning, creating, and using knowledge. Concept Maps as facilitative tools in schools and corporations* (2nd ed.). Abingdon, UK: Taylor & Francis.

Onyesolu, M. O., Nwasor, V. C., Ositanwosu, O. E., & Iwegbuna, O. N. (2013). Pedagogy: Instructivism to socio-constructivism through virtual reality. *International Journal of Advanced Computer Science and Applications, 4*(9), 40–47. Retrieved from http://ijacsa.thesai.org/

Otte, E., & Rousseau, R. (2002). Social network analysis: A powerful strategy, also for the information sciences. *Journal of Information Science, 28*, 441–453.

Pardo, A., & Siemens, G. (2014). Ethical and privacy principles for learning analytics. *British Journal of Educational Technology, 45*(3), 438–450. https://doi.org/10.1111/bjet.12152

Pedro, L., Santos, C., Batista, J., Cabral, G., Pais, F., & Costa, C. (2016). Social network analysis and digital learning environments: A framework for research and practice using the Sapo Campus Platform. In *INTED2016 proceedings* (pp. 061–1070). Valencia, Spain.

Pena, A. (2005). Collaborative student modeling by cognitive maps. In *International conference DFMA'05 distributed frameworks for multimedia applications* (pp. 6–9). Besançon, France: IEEE Computer Society.

Poole, D. M. (2000). Student participation in a discussion-oriented online course: A case study. *Journal of Research on Computing in Education, 33*(2), 162–177.

Rafaeli, S. (1988). Interactivity: From new media to communication. In R. P. Hawkins, J. M. Wieman, & S. Pingree (Eds.), *Advancing communication science: Merging mass and interpersonal processes* (pp. 110–134). Newbury Park, CA: Sage.

Rafaeli, S. (2017). Networks. In *What scientific term or concept ought to be more widely known? Edge.* Available at https://www.edge.org/response-detail/27036

Rafaeli, S., & Sudweeks, F. (1997). Networked interactivity. *Journal of Computer-Mediated Communication, 2*(4). https://doi.org/10.1111/j.1083-6101.1997.tb00201.x

Ravid, G., Erlich, Z., & Aviv, R. (2004), Mechanisms and architectures of online learning communities. *Advanced learning technologies, IEEE International Conference on(ICALT)*, Joensuu, Finland, pp. 400–404.

Rechavi, A., & Rafaeli, S. (2012). Knowledge and social networks in Yahoo! Answers. In *System science (HICSS), 2012 45th Hawaii international conference on* (pp. 781–789). IEEE.

Reda, K., Tantipathananandh, C., Johnson, A., Leigh, J., & Berger-Wolf, T. (2011). Visualizing the evolution of community structures in dynamic social networks In: Computer graphics forum 30(3), 1061–1070. Hoboken, NJ: Blackwell.

Reffay, C., & Chanier, T. (2003). How social network analysis can help to measure cohesion in collaborative distance-learning. In B. Wasson, S. Ludvigsen, & U. Hoppe (Eds.), *Designing for change in networked learning environments* (pp. 343–352). Dordrecht, Netherlands: Springer.

Russo, T. C., & Koesten, J. (2005). Prestige, centrality, and learning: A social network analysis of an online class. *Communication Education, 54*(3), 254–261.

Romero, C., López, M. I., Luna, J. M., & Ventura, S. (2013). Predicting students' final performance from participation in on-line discussion forums. *Computers & Education, 68*, 458–472.

Scardamalia, M., & Bereiter, C. (2003). Knowledge building. In J. W. Guthrie (Ed.), *Encyclopedia of education* (pp. 1370–1373). New York: Routledge.

Shum, S. B., & Ferguson, R. (2012). Social learning analytics. *Educational Technology & Society, 15*(3), 3–26. https://doi.org/10.1145/2330601.2330616

Siemens, G. (2005). A learning theory for the digital age. *Instructional Technology and Distance Education, 2*(1), 3–10.

Siemens, G. (2015). Learning analytics: The emergence of a discipline. *American Behavioral Scientist, 57*(10), 1380–1400. https://doi.org/10.1177/0002764213498851

Sinha, T. (2014). *Supporting MOOC instruction with social network analysis. Arxiv preprint.* Ithaca, NY: Cornell University Library.

Stahl, G. (2006). *Group cognition: Computer support for building collaborative knowledge (acting with technology).* Cambridge, MA: MIT Press.

Stewart, S. A., & Abidi, S. S. R. (2012). Applying social network analysis to understand the knowledge sharing behaviour of practitioners in a clinical online discussion forum. *Journal of Medical Internet Research, 14*(6), 170.

Stoyanova, N., & Kommers, P. (2001). Learning effectiveness of concept mapping in a computer supported collaborative problem solving design. In *First European International Conference on Computer-Supported Collaborative Learning (13)*. Maastricht, Netherlands: Euro-CSC. https://doi.org/10.1145/1015579.810983

Stromer-Galley, J. (2000). On-line interaction and why candidates avoid it. *Journal of Communication, 50*(4), 111–132. https://doi.org/10.1093/joc/50.4.111

Swan, K., & Ice, P. (2010). The community of inquiry framework ten years later: Introduction to the special issue. *The Internet and Higher Education, 13*(1–2), 1–4. https://doi.org/10.1016/j.iheduc.2009.11.003

Toikkanen, T., & Lipponen, L. (2011). The applicability of social network analysis to the study of networked learning. *Interactive Learning Environments, 19*(4), 365–379.

Vaquero, L. M., & Cebrian, M. (2013). The rich club phenomenon in the classroom. *Scientific Reports, 3*, 1174.

Vygotsky, L. S. (1978). *Mind in society: The development of higher psychological process.* Cambridge, MA: Harvard University Press.

Wasserman, S., & Faust, K. (1994). *Social network analysis: Methods and applications* (Vol. 8). Cambridge university press.

Wei, W., & Carley, K. M. (2015). Measuring temporal patterns in dynamic social networks. *ACM Transactions on Knowledge Discovery from Data, 10*(1), 1–27. https://doi.org/10.1145/2749465

Wenger, E. (1998). *Communities of practice: Learning, meaning, and identity.* Cambridge, UK: Cambridge University Press.

Williams, F., Rice, R., & Rogers, E. (1988). *Research methods and the new media.* New York: Free Press.

Wu, T., Yao, Y., Duan, Y., Fan, X., & Qu, H. (2016). NetworkSeer : Visual analysis for social network in MOOCs. In *2016 IEEE Pacific visualization symposium* (pp. 194–198). Taipei, Taiwan.

Wu, Y., & Duan, Z. (2015). Social network analysis of international scientific collaboration on psychiatry research. *International Journal of Mental Health Systems, 9*(1), 2.

Wuyts, S., Colombo, M. G., Dutta, S., & Nooteboom, B. (2005). Empirical tests of optimal cognitive distance. *Journal of Economic Behavior & Organization, 58*(2), 277–302.

Zhang, J., Scardamalia, M., Reeve, R., & Messina, R. (2009). Designs for collective cognitive responsibility in knowledge-building communities. *Journal of the Learning Sciences, 18*(1), 7–44. https://doi.org/10.1080/10508400802581676

Chapter 10
eTextbooks: Challenges to Pedagogy, Law, and Policy

Yoni Har Carmel, Shai Olsher, Niva Elkin-Koren, and Michal Yerushalmy

Abstract In the world of print, textbooks were the most important tools for dictating what and how student learn in schools. The introduction of Information and Communication Technology (ICT), however, gave rise to eTextbooks – a multi-modal, hardware mediated, and connectable, curriculum material. Indeed, the emergence of eTextbook creates fascinating opportunities for teaching and learning, but at the same time, it poses new challenges for both educational practices and policy making by revolutionizing the traditional pedagogical practices, classroom culture and the textbook publishing industry. These new challenges require rethinking and reexamining the appropriateness of the institutional and legal norms which govern the use and authorship of textbooks. This paper identifies the new challenges introduced by eTextbooks, and offers some insights on the policy and legal implications.

Keywords eTextbooks · ICT · Curriculum materials · Publishing industry · Authorship · Interactive environment · Quality assurance · Learning in a monitored environment · Surveillance · Collaborative writing

"Books are the most essential tool of education since they contain the resources of knowledge which the educational process is designed to exploit," stated the US Supreme Court almost half a century ago (*Board of Education v. Allen*, 1968, p.252). Indeed, the central role of textbooks in modern schools is universally acknowledged. In Hebrew, for example, the word for "school" (*beit sefer*) literally means "house of the book."

Y. H. Carmel (✉)
University of Haifa, Haifa Center for Law & Technology, Haifa, Israel

S. Olsher · M. Yerushalmy
University of Haifa, Faculty of Education, Haifa, Israel
e-mail: olshers@edu.haifa.ac.il; michalyr@edu.haifa.ac.il

N. Elkin-Koren
University of Haifa, Faculty of Law, Haifa, Israel
e-mail: koren@univ.haifa.ac.il

177

© Springer Nature Switzerland AG 2019
Y. Kali et al. (eds.), *Learning In a Networked Society*, Computer-Supported Collaborative Learning Series 17, https://doi.org/10.1007/978-3-030-14610-8_10

Since the early days of the modern educational system, nothing has defined *what* should be learned and *how* it should be taught more than textbooks (Friesen, 2013). "[T]extbooks are the bearers of messages that are multiply-coded. In them the coded meanings of a field of knowledge (what is to be taught) are combined with those of pedagogy (how anything is to be taught and learned)" (Stray, 1994, p.2).

Even in today's technology-driven age, where other sources of information compete for students' attention, the textbook prevails as the most commonly used instructional material at schools (Williams & Agosto, 2012). Nevertheless, the textbook has begun to undergo an unprecedented evolution since the beginning of the second decade of the twenty-first century. As part of the intensive and extensive penetration of ICTs into schools, educators increasingly acknowledge the outstanding advantages of eTextbooks that combine the traditional concept of textbooks with components of ICTs.

The Israel Ministry of Education (IMOE) launched The National Program for Adapting the Israeli Education System to the Twenty-First Century (NPIES) in April 2010. This multi-year program is a process that strives to promote implementation of innovative pedagogy at schools, while providing twenty-first century skills and incorporating ICTs in school routines as an integral part (IMOE, 2012).

One major objective of the NPIES is the systematic adoption of eTextbooks in lieu of the traditional textbooks that have prevailed in schools for generations (IMOE, 2011). The IMOE is striving to achieve this target by allocating budgets, amending regulations, and encouraging schools to adopt eTextbooks.

With ICTs becoming pivotal in school systems, the transition from paper textbooks to eTextbooks is proceeding at full speed. It is only a matter of time before eTextbooks become the key vehicle for facilitating students' access to knowledge and skills. But the technological evolution of the textbook is by no means solely a matter of media transformation. It is, in fact, a paradigmatic change that can potentially revolutionize traditional pedagogical practices, classroom culture and the textbook publishing industry. The emergence of the eTextbook creates fascinating opportunities, but at the same time, poses new challenges for both educational practices and policy making. This tension, between opportunities and challenges, such as the notion of new media as a "double-edged sword" is presented by Baram-Tsabari and Schejter (Chap. 5), and the search for innovative educational responses for contemporary challenges is presented by Barzilai and Chinn (Chap. 4). Here we focus on the tensions between authority and autonomy, centralized and ubiquitous quality assurance, privacy and economic dependence, and intellectual property and ownership, brought about by the new educational technology.

What Is an eTextbook?

eTextbooks are characterized by the following:

(a) Multimodal—eTextbook content can be presented in various media (text, audio, video, and any combination thereof). Digital content can be relatively easily copied, edited, published, and stored.

(b) Hardware-mediated—use of eTextbooks is mediated by an end device that may have an enormous storage capacity, allowing for the addition of nearly unlimited amounts of information. End devices may also include hardware components that enrich users' experience with eTextbooks, such as speakers, microphones, touch screens, tilt sensors, velocity meters, compasses, etc.

(c) Connectable—mediated by digital end devices, the eTextbook can be connected to the internet for file transfers, access to databases, and online applications (Marczak, 2013).

There is no common definition, however, for the term "eTextbook" in the literature.

The definition of eTextbooks is still evolving. The new definitions that emerge in contemporary educational discourse pertain less to the properties of the object and more to the way it is being created. Three models of eTextbooks can illustrate this development by emphasizing the central dimensions and uses of eTextbooks by teachers and students. While these models do not differ substantially from one another, this categorization may help clarify the debate surrounding the appropriate definition, as each one reflects a key rationale or aspect of functionality.

The *interactive eTextbook* model is based on a set of learning objects, i.e., tasks and interactives (diagrams and tools) that can be linked and combined. The interactive tasks are an integral part of the textbook (rather than add-on tools). As the interactive tools require input from students and provide feedback, the eTextbook also functions as an eWorkbook; it is often difficult to separate the two.

The *integrative eTextbook* is an *add-on model* in which a digital version of a (traditional) textbook is connected to other learning objects that were not previously considered part of textbooks, such as learning management, course management, authoring tools to add or edit activities (controlled by teachers), and more.

The *evolving eTextbook* refers to a digital textbook that is *constantly developing* through ongoing input received from practicing teachers or even from students. Both *integrative* and *interactive* eTextbooks can continue to *evolve* thanks to the contributions of external users.

The IMOE refers to the eTextbook in its textbook regulations, as a "textbook that contains content, skills and values conforming with an annual curriculum for a specific grade level, that can be accessed via a learner's computerized end device" (IMOE, 2015). Unlike print technology that did not develop extensively over the years, digital technology is advancing rapidly, and eTextbooks may thus be produced at different levels of technological complexity. The IMOE defined two technological levels of eTextbooks that schools are at liberty to adopt:

(a) *Basic*—a digital version of print textbooks that can be activated offline. The digital documents contain fixed content and support limited interactive activities such as searching, navigating, annotating, and creating web links.

(b) *Advanced*—an eTextbook compliant with basic level demands that integrates media resources into the learning trajectory, including video/audio files, animations, simulations, interactive activities, games, 3D models, etc.

Challenges and Opportunities for Law and Education

Challenge 1: From Authority to Autonomy in an Interactive Environment

Textbooks are the mediating link between the *intended curriculum* (what students are supposed to learn) and the *implemented curriculum* (what students are actually taught), as they possess the capacity to translate a curricular policy (contents, topic, terms, skills, teaching approaches, time frames, etc.) into a planned pedagogical trajectory. Consequently, textbooks are often referred to as a "potentially implemented curriculum."

The fulfillment of the textbook's "curricular potential" is largely dependent on the teachers who use it and on their beliefs, philosophies, and knowledge (Pepin & Haggarty, 2001). Nevertheless, the teachers' ability to exercise their freedom and professional discretion is limited by the authoritative presence of the textbook in the classroom. According to Herbel-Eisenmann (2009), traditional classroom culture perceives the textbook as an authority that dictates what and how teachers teach and learners learn. In most cases, teachers rely on the textbook as their prime source of information and ensure that the students have learned the content of the textbook in a particular order (Herbel-Eisenmann, 2009). Students deem the information in textbooks to be legitimate and unquestionable.

Moreover, the textbook is perceived as a didactic-pedagogic authority that instructs the teacher how to teach the curricular knowledge. Indeed, as Yerushalmy (2012) notes, the authority of the textbook is the chief characteristic of traditional classroom culture, the "textbook culture" in which teaching is *by* and not *with* the textbook.

Combining ICT components with the traditional textbook is changing the nature of textbooks, learning environments, and pedagogical approaches toward using textbooks. These developments are undermining the balance of power in traditional classroom culture. On the one hand, this combination reduces the authoritative presence of the textbook, while on the other, it increases the autonomy of both teachers and learners to control teaching and learning processes (see a related discussion regarding technology-mediated democratization of twenty-first century education by Kidron et al., in Chap. 7).

The flexibility of the eTextbook affords teachers the power to adjust and modify the textbooks they use according to their professional discretion, so that all students will have the opportunity to learn with a textbook that is adapted to their personal learning style, aptitudes, and pace. Moreover, technology offers tools that teachers and learners can use for designing, creating, and sharing textbooks, thereby blurring the distinction between authors and users.

Although there is no shortage of examples of eTextbooks, only a few studies discuss the design rationales and analyze the use of non-ordered textbooks. In a description of the design rationale for an undergraduate textbook on filming, Kuhn (2011) uses academic arguments to discuss the work in the context of research about the changing ways in which knowledge is produced. Kuhn applies the *recursive approach* to characterize a filming textbook, in which digital pages are perceived as stand-alone nodes that can be traversed by different themes. Although it is true that the pages of a conventional textbook may be accessed in any order at the reader's discretion, it is expected that the order of the text is deliberate, usually hierarchical and always dictated by the author. As emphasized, the linearity of text creates an internal temporal ordering and a logical sequence of development. This logical development, in which every concept or idea uniquely builds on the previous page, has been challenged in Kuhn's textbook, as the pages of this text must be able to stand alone to a certain extent. Another model, the *role play model* for designing and learning with a non-ordered multimodal textbook, is described by Spielvogel and Spielvogel (2010). According to Spielvogel and Spielvogel, digital pages are structured as stand-alone nodes, whereas tools and avatars are designed to immerse the reader in the plot (concerning Japanese culture and history) and to support the simultaneity of voices.

Adding to the new affordances of the eTextbook, technology-enhanced digital environments allow teachers and learners to control the times, locations, and participatory circles in which the pedagogical process will take place. Thus, the use of eTextbooks can be emancipated from the institutional norms that typically dictate a hierarchical textbook-teacher-learner relationship.

The pedagogical approaches that can be applied when using an eTextbook emphasize the shift from knowledge delivery to knowledge construction, which in turn changes the power center of teachers and learners, learning activity, and the role of technology in pedagogy (Har Carmel, 2016, p.3). eTextbooks serve as a laboratory for students and teachers. The eTextbook is no longer a structured, stable, and unified source of content but rather a construct and a framework that can motivate generation of knowledge, supporting this process with tools and feedback.

Governments have long recognized the "curricular potential" of the textbook and consequently have aspired to regulate its content and design to achieve statewide curriculum uniformity. Presumably, underlying this observed objective of "textbook regulation" is the assumption that the textbook acts as an authority that dictates what is to be taught and learned at schools and how it will be accomplished. The transition from paper textbooks to eTextbooks, as described above, challenges such assumptions.

The eTextbook, as opposed to its paper-based predecessor, is not a coercive authority. It is a tool of potential empowerment for internal teacher-learner autonomy, rendering it the pivot of the pedagogical process. As it becomes less authoritative in the classroom, it decreases the likelihood of producing a correlation between the state-determined curriculum (intended curriculum) and what is actually being taught in schools (implemented curriculum). Theoretically speaking, the textbooks of the digital age may thus no longer serve as "curricular agents" in the classroom for educational policymakers. This, in turn, has driven policymakers to seek alternative methods of applying their statutory authority to achieve statewide curricular uniformity.

While eTextbooks are empowering teachers to contribute more input and participate in shaping the textbooks that they use, the rise of eTextbooks may also weaken the power of teachers and learners in other ways, as discussed in the next section.

Challenge 2: From Centralized to Ubiquitous Quality Assurance

Another significant challenge facing policy makers as they attempt to facilitate access to eTextbooks is quality assurance. One prominent measure applied by a state to guarantee access to quality textbooks is application of centralized regulation that controls their content and design (Tulley, 1985). Many countries—including India, Taiwan, Pakistan, and certain states in the United States (California and Texas)—have had strong centralized systems for many decades, in which textbooks must undergo some kind of quality assurance before being offered to schools (Ho & Hsu, 2011; India Ministry of Human Resource Development, 2005; Mahmood, 2006; Watt, 2009).

In Israel, since the 1950s, the IMOE Textbook Approval Department (TAD) has conducted a rigorous multilevel textbook approval process. Throughout the pedagogical and academic evaluation phase, the textbook is scrutinized and evaluated rigorously for conformity with the statewide curriculum and alignment with the IMOE's official pedagogic, scientific, graphic, linguistic, and other standards. Institutes are strictly prohibited from using unapproved textbooks (State Education Law, 1953s).

This policy is clearly based on the traditional concept of the textbook: a fixed, static, and linear object that does not evolve with time. On selection of a certain textbook from the TAD's approved list, teachers and students are limited in what they can contribute or in how they can generally affect the books they use in the classroom.

The eTextbook, on the other hand, is a dynamic, evolving, and flexible techno-pedagogic application that users can adjust and change with relative ease and at minimal cost (Fletcher, 2012). Teachers may update the eTextbooks, add to or erase some of its content. They can also incorporate or embed hyperlinks to various learning objects (i.e., "any digital resource that can be reused to support learning") (Wiley, 2009, p. 8) and multimedia productions such as interactive games, videos, audio files, texts, animations, surveys, interactive activities, and so forth. For example, if a student is struggling with a topic, the teacher can link his or her eTextbook to an online tutorial that can provide additional explanations, interactive activities, and assessment tools (Sharples et al., 2012). As such, the eTextbook may continuously evolve at the teacher's professional discretion. For this reason, the adopted approved version of the eTextbook is not necessarily the one used in the classroom. It is merely a starting point.

The dynamic, flexible, and evolving nature of eTextbooks may leave educators in limbo. Most educators lack the necessary time and training for ongoing assessment of the quality of educational resources available on the Web. Consequently, to ensure that educators can take advantage of the new opportunities provided by eTextbooks, we should offer efficient measures to guarantee that resources adhere to quality criteria or meet the curriculum requirements. Centralized governmental quality assurance processes are limited in their capacity to provide teachers with the information needed to make informed decisions regarding resources that can be integrated into eTextbooks.

Challenge 3: The Limitations of Quality Assurance Systems

We consider the Israeli case to demonstrate the weaknesses of applying a centralized quality assurance process designed for print textbooks as a quality assurance measure for eTextbooks. First, the IMOE evaluates only resources that have been submitted for approval. eTextbooks can be integrated with resources from different sources. Learning objects originate in various sources, including professional organizations and policymakers such as the Mathematics Teachers' Centers operated under the supervision of the IMOE or teachers' unions such as the National Council of Teachers of Mathematics (NCTM). Both organizations publish online resources for teachers to use in their classrooms. Naturally, these materials go through a review process before being published. Publishers and commercial entities are another interest group that produces online learning resources subjected to IMOE approval. A third type of repository is generated by a Content Development Community (CDC), comprised of a group of people who use a content-generating tool (e.g., Geogebra, Wikipedia) and have common interests (e.g., mathematics education). These communities are not necessarily online communities and are not restricted to professionals working in the defined area of interest, nor are they subjected to any central standardization or regulation for the materials that they produce (e.g., Geogebratube, Wikibooks). While traditional publishers have incentives to comply with IMOE standards, CDC authors are not required to adhere to any standard and need no governmental approval to publish. Consequently, their work is unevaluated.

The second limitation on quality control regulation of eTextbooks is the duration of the approval process that can extend over several months. Clearly, this timetable does not correspond with the dynamics of using eTextbooks, wherein a teacher integrates learning objects spontaneously to match students' needs during class. Moreover, although eTextbooks evolve by nature, the IMOE does not reevaluate them during the term of approval. Evaluation of a single version only is insufficient for practice of ICT-supported instruction, as digital curricular materials may evolve at any given time (Vargo, Nesbit, Belfer, & Archambault, 2003).

Finally, evaluation is not based on the evaluator's experience using the eTextbook in real time (in class) and therefore does not address its utility within the classroom. As the primary characteristic of learning objects is their reuse in various contexts (Brickell, Kanuth, Freeman, Latshaw, & Larson, 2006), evaluating eTextbooks under laboratory conditions does not guarantee that teachers will know how to use them optimally throughout the dynamic ICT-supported instruction process (Wiley & Gurrell, 2009), nor does it ensure selection of the highest quality resource.

The principal conclusion to be drawn from the above analysis is that centralized quality assurance mechanisms are limited in their capacity to assure that the eTextbooks offered to schools are indeed of optimum quality. Achieving a one eTextbook per studentstatus (1:1) with respect to quality eTextbooks is critical because they are becoming the pathway to knowledge and skills in this new era. It is not merely a matter of bringing about a marked improvement in the quality of education but rather an indispensable means of carrying out children's educational opportunity rights. The potential of eTextbooks for facilitating access to knowledge creates new challenges for policymakers to ensure both the affordability and quality of textbooks.

The limited capacity of traditional legal mechanisms to achieve these goals should not imply that state intervention is unnecessary to facilitate access. On the contrary, the state should adopt legal instruments that reflect the paradigm of the digital age and thereby enrich the supply of affordable quality eTextbooks.

Challenge 4: Learning in a Monitored Environment

A new business environment The introduction of the eTextbook has constituted a game changer in the educational ecosystem, introducing new players into the production and dissemination of educational materials and potentially transforming their roles. Unlike traditional textbooks, an eTextbook is not simply a stack of printed papers bound by publishers but rather a virtual environment that continuously engages students and teachers on a platform that is often owned by a private publishing company.[1] As textbooks are transformed from a commodity to a service, the relationship between textbook publishers and the teachers and students who use them is reshaped.

Learners become increasingly dependent on eTextbook publishers. For example, when systems are stored in the cloud, teaching resources (software, books, academic articles, music, and videos) are placed beyond the learners' control. Remotely stored content is subject to central management that can determine what becomes available, what will be removed, and which restrictions apply to each resource. Decisions on what to upload and download, what to watch, and what to share and how are increasingly governed by publishers and online intermediaries. Teachers and students may not have the perpetual access to eTextbook content that they would have when using physical textbooks, as their access to the content may expire at any time.

The rise of eTextbooks may also introduce new book publishing business models that may entail radical consequences for teachers and students. While textbook publishers in the print business have no direct relationship with buyers, eTextbook publishers may develop direct interactions with system users and gain ongoing access

---

[1] This shift from selling commodities (books, records, CDs, DVDs) to services takes place in other sectors too, such as in music (e.g., Spotify) and movies (e.g., Netflix and YouTube).

to the personal data that is generated through use. While traditional publishers benefit once from selling copies of their books, today's data and data-related services have become an independent and recurring source of revenue. Publishers have adjusted their business models to suit the digital environment. In fact, they have adopted and adapted business models that resemble those of online intermediaries who are able to track users through a variety of online services (e.g., search, display, Internet access) offered free of charge or via the content-rendering device (e.g., iPhone, Kindle).

Collecting data on users' interests and online behavior creates a stream of revenue from targeted advertising. For example, Elsevier recently purchased SSRN, a platform used by academics in the social sciences, humanities, and law for sharing works in progress. One major motivation for this acquisition was the potential use of data and analytics. Elsevier has also begun to purchase technologies and startups, such as Mendeley, that may threaten its dominance. Mendeley is a social network for academic papers that uses reference management software to generate valuable data such as scholars' research agendas and topics, determining what can be licensed and at what price. These emerging business models that generate revenues from data analytics redefine the role of publishers in the educational environment.

Learning under surveillance eTextbooks offer built-in opportunities for ongoing surveillance. When an eBook is downloaded to an eReader such as Kindle, rights holders may collect and retain detailed information about users, their reading habits, and their intellectual preferences. This may turn the reading experience, once intimate and private, into public knowledge. One example of built-in surveillance is Adobe Spyware that allegedly tracks and reports the reading habits of users of Digital Editions, Adobe's eBook software. This example illustrates growing concerns for readers' privacy and security (McSherry, 2014). The ability to track and monitor every small move in a digitally mediated environment (browsing time, reading space, and even typing speed) renders eTextbooks a medium radically different from printed books.

Students' everyday use of eTextbooks can generate vast amounts of granular learning-related data that open up a new world of potential evidence on how students learn. "Student data" may include information about students' learning processes such as mistake rates, session times where a student has clicked or touched while pondering a problem and even physical indicators, such as eye pupil movement while performing academic work (White House, 2014). Nowadays, every keystroke made by every student can be recorded in log files and remain potentially available for analysis. Every word entered during student online interaction and work can be recorded and analyzed.[2]

---

[2] Moodle, for example, is a popular open source LMS that can be used, inter alia, for task assignments, quizzes, content delivery, etc. The system contains detailed logs of user actions available through teacher or administrator user interfaces. Moodle is capable of logging user information and access time and view and upload actions, information about user submission, start and end time, order of questions, question time, and correctness.

Using new technologies or services to improve learning processes is certainly not new to the education domain (Polonetsky & Jerome, 2014). Yet the concept of tracking data in eTextbooks should be understood within the framework of the emerging economic structure known as *surveillance capitalism* (Zuboff, 2015). The data economy is based on production and sale of data as an independent asset. This industry is governed by "a logic of accumulation," mandating that all possible data should be tracked, recorded, and analyzed to optimize the system's operation and refine its outcomes (Zuboff, 2015). Data collected by any teaching system, however, is not used only to improve the skills and abilities of the student using the system. It is also often detached from the particular student to become part of a data flow that is traded by the data industry. Aggregated data of this kind can enhance the functionality of systems across the board. Data collected by eTextbooks could be linked to other data sources and become invaluable for designing marketing strategies and developing new teaching resources. Consequently, all possible data should be collected, recorded, and aggregated to render the data flow more useful and beneficial. Data analytics enable evaluation and prediction based on big data analysis.

The shift to data collection as a business model is raising an entirely new set of policy challenges. The emergence of textbooks that can be monitored constantly poses the unprecedented educational and legal challenge of preserving students' privacy within the learning process.

Strong emotions and high stakes have given rise to a polarized debate surrounding the use of student data in the United States that subsequently led to a deluge of state and federal regulatory reforms aimed at protecting students and allaying the public's deep concerns.[3] Parents, education and privacy advocates, and other critics have been concerned that extensive dissemination of student data to private vendors might risk students' privacy by disclosing sensitive information such as learning disabilities, disciplinary problems, or family trauma (Singer, 2014). Of particular concern is the likelihood that vendors will improperly mine or sell student data, or otherwise monetize student information by building advertising profiles or conducting marketing activities (Herold, 2014). These issues are obviously relevant to any use of technological applications that collect data, whether for educational purposes or otherwise.[4]

---

[3] Growing student data-related concerns have garnered attention from US legislators on alert who passed laws to protect student privacy from the potential harm that student data use may cause. By October 2015, 46 states had introduced 186 bills addressing use of student data, of which 28, in 15 states, became law. Several federal bills are currently pending as well. Many of these bills focus on who can access student information and mandate that private entities may only use student data for educational purposes. They often stipulate substantive restrictions on the use of student data for creating advertising profiles and for marketing purposes. A considerable number of these rules focus on providing more opportunities for notice and choice for parents to consent to particular uses or collection. Indeed, some of the key challenges posed by the media transformation are student privacy, the need to obtain consent (of either the students or their parents) for its invasion and mandatory respect for their (potentially diverse) individual preferences regarding use thereof (see Data Quality Campaign, 2015).

[4] In 2014, Google admitted that it mines student data from its Google Apps for Education for targeted advertising purposes.

Systems capable of aggregating data collected from various sources and linking it to other data would entail a competitive edge. For example, the logic of accumulation and the challenges it raises are demonstrated by Google's collection of data on students in the educational sector. Google was accused of collecting personal information from children who use Google educational products that were provided to their schools free of charge.[5] In these cases, Google tracked students who signed into their Google Apps for Education account but used other related Google services such as Search, YouTube, Blogger, and Maps that are not considered Google core educational applications. The commercial value of data generated during educational processes for the data industry suggests that the eTextbook market is likely to be dominated by several players, large conglomerates, or online intermediaries that govern the data. This is likely to further weaken the autonomy of teachers and increase pressure to extract data.

Surveillance and the educational process Surveillance of learning processes raises additional issues as well that extend far beyond the need for "appropriate" flow of information (Nissenbaum, 2009, p.155)[6] within and outside the educational institution. These issues are related to the implications of collecting data for learning purposes and for achieving the goals of the educational process. One such issue is the freedom to learn and explore without surveillance.

Surveillance may have a chilling effect on readers, potentially causing people to refrain from seeking specific information and reading particular material for fear that their interests might be monitored and recorded. A learning environment should encourage exploration and experimentation and therefore should offer the freedom to explore material of any type, without the knowledge of others.[7] Freedom from ongoing monitoring might be necessary to protect the intimacy and private nature of the educational experience that is essential for meaningful learning.

Intellectual privacy, i.e., "the ability, whether protected by law or social circumstances, to develop ideas and beliefs away from the unwanted gaze or interference of others" (Richards, 2008, p.389),[8] is also important for maintaining academic freedom and for guaranteeing the freedom of users as active participants in creating culture (Richards, 2008).

---

[5] In a complaint filed in December 2015 with the Federal Trade Commission (FTC), the Electronic Frontier Foundation (EFF) claimed that Google was collecting data about students while they were signed into their school-based Google accounts.

[6] Privacy, according to Nissenbaum, is "a function of several variables, including the nature of the situation or context; the nature of information in relation to that context; the roles of agents receiving information, their relationships to information subjects; on what terms the information is shared by the subject and the terms of further dissemination."

[7] Surveillance may affect the virtues of reading adversely. Reading a novel, for example, involves intimate interaction, wherein readers are asked to rely on their own cognitive insights and emotional experiences to make sense of the text. Readers are given the opportunity to engage in intimate dialogue through the text. Consequently, the ability to read in private could be important for constituting one's identity and for developing empathy toward others. These processes are essential to the development of an empowered and accountable citizenry.

[8] Richards offers a normative theory of intellectual privacy that begins with freedom of thought and radiates outward to justify protection for spatial privacy, the right to read, and the confidentiality of communications.

It may be deemed necessary to monitor the teaching process as well. Accurate and complete data might be essential to facilitate teaching, optimize the system, and enable teachers to respond to the specific needs of individual students. Consequently, continuous monitoring is often necessary—and might indeed be inevitable—in learning environments that seek to provide teachers with efficient tools for tracking specific capabilities, progress, and needs of each student. The logic of big data is based on ongoing surveillance. Collection practices involve an uncompromising demand for full transparency on the part of users without reciprocal transparency from data processors and owners.

Another concern regarding mass surveillance in eTextbooks is its potential impact on conformism and compliance. The power of eTextbook publishers to shape the learning environment exceeds selection of content. In the print industry, publishers determine the content itself and can possibly impact its meaning through the order and context in which it is presented. In an interactive digital environment, it is possible to shape meaning and nudge behavior (Thaler and Sunstein, 2009)[9] in far more subtle ways (Yeung, 2016). For example, Facebook conducted experiments on contagious moods to demonstrate its ability to regulate individual behavior using the social graph (Coviello et al., 2014). Tracking and monitoring eTextbooks should not be viewed as a passive, neutral observation, but rather as a possible alternative to regulating behavior. Surveillance may shape behavior to conform with certain norms. The availability of data on a particular learner and the ability to apply predictive insights based on that data by processing it together with data on other subjects give eTextbook publishers powers that can shape the behavior of both students and teachers who use the system (Pentland, 2014). This ambition was reflected in a statement by James Fowler, a co-author of the Facebook study, claiming that "we should be doing everything we can to measure the effects of social networks and to learn how to magnify them so that we can create an epidemic of wellbeing" (Kiderra, 2014).

This aspect of eTextbooks may shift power back from the teacher to the commercial entity that governs the data and may have interests that can conflict with the particular needs of teachers and students in a given setting. The opacity of the algorithm is likely to render it more difficult to oversee such instances.

One vital regulatory measure would have policymakers secure students' freedom to use eTextbooks "[...] away from the unwanted gaze or interference of others" (Richards, 2008, p. 389). Broadly speaking, they should set boundaries between private and public spaces within digital learning environments that will safeguard students' freedom of thought and belief, their right to read and to engage in intellectual exploration, and the confidentiality of communications among participants (Richards, 2015).

It is presumed, however, that the law alone cannot construct an intellectual sanctuary for students. If we care about guaranteeing all aspects of student privacy, we

---

[9] "Nudging," according to Thaler and Sunstein, is "any aspect of choice architecture that alters people's behavior in a predictable way without forbidding any options or significantly changing their economic incentives."

must offer protection beyond the legal system as part of the culture and norms of a contemporary data-infused educational landscape, including pedagogical norms, technological design, and professional ethics.

Writing eTextbooks: The Many Faces of Authorship and Collaborative Writing

One challenge presented by eTextbooks is the concept of authorship. Copyright law, which regulates relationships between the author who owns the copyrighted materials and its users (non-owners), assumes a single author. This particular concept of a "romantic author" was developed during the eighteenth century and was tailored to the world of print, but the interactive nature of the digital format facilitates a wide range of new forms of authorship and different levels of contribution of users to the original creative work (e.g., remixing music and video clips, using a filter on Snapchat, editing Wikipedia). This applies to eTextbooks as well, for which different systems enable various levels of participation in generating the text, its meaning and its functions. Below we provide a brief discussion of collaborative and other emerging forms of authorship by users of eTextbooks. We then discuss the ramifications of these developments for authority, licensing and liability, ownership, the right to exploit the work commercially and receive remuneration, and the right to attribution.

Before the introduction of ICTs into the realm of education, the costs of textbook production and distribution were relatively high, and subsequently the likelihood of a return on investment was relatively low. Consequently, textbooks were most commonly published by authorities or by a handful of private enterprises (Siminoff, 2013). Despite their central role in delivering the curriculum, teachers did not generally take an active part in developing and producing the textbooks they used (Chazan & Yerushalmy, 2014). eTextbooks open up new opportunities for co-authorship and collaborative writing. There are many different ways of contributing to the authorship of open books.

A rough categorization reveals three formats of interactive reading that demand the readers' engagement. The first applies to books that call on the reader to participate in portions of authoring. These are known as *hypertext books*. Their chief feature is a *nonlinear, multiple path* through the content that the reader can create using different links associated with key characters or topics. The flexible trails formed can be followed from beginning to end. Although this idea had been explored with regard to printed books in the past, digital media are much better suited to this type of book than to print editions.

The second format involves readers serving as writers in networked, socially developed, evolving books. This presents a more dramatic change that introduces a different aspect of interactivity in which the reader becomes the writer. Despite numerous attempts at producing socially evolving books, however, most of the interactions consist of reading a version of the content and reflecting on it rather than becoming actively involved in contributing to it.

A third option requires thinking about a book in an entirely new set of terms. Young (2007) suggests thinking analogically about how media changes altered the perception of music and photography. If books no longer represent the idea of ownership and authority of the external expert (the author), then digital books are no longer members of the class of objects that we refer to as "books." Instead, they are something else that serves a similar external function without bearing the same key notion of authority.

Collaborative Authorship in Textbooks

Contemporary technology offers teachers various digital platforms that facilitate self-production and distribution of eTextbooks—or parts thereof—and enables them to share their materials online. Digital networks lower the cost of coordinating joint efforts, thus enabling a massive number of users to join forces in creating new collaborative works. Collaborative initiatives have become highly prominent. Classic examples are programmers contributing to code and fixing security bugs in free software, users editing entries on Wikipedia, and collaborative tagging and ranking generated by users of YouTube and Digg. Technology also enables teachers to collaborate in eTextbook development with many other collaborators while overcoming geographical barriers. Teachers may opt to contribute to open textbooks for several reasons: self-expression, creative satisfaction, a desire to establish their online reputation or strengthen their self-esteem, or simply to engage with, influence, and contribute to their community of teachers and students. Social motivation, however, does not rule out a desire for monetary recompense. Teachers may be socially motivated to contribute to collaborative teaching materials, but this does not mean that they will never seek to profit from their creativity. Indeed, teachers may attempt to sell some of their teaching materials or use them to develop new independent works.

In an analysis of major trends in teachers' digital resource use, Remillard (2015) reminds us that "for any type of curriculum resource and for any teacher, using a resource is never a matter of simply taking it up and following it. When teachers 'use' curriculum resources, they are interpreting, authoring, appropriating, adapting, framing and reframing the content" (p.138). Authoring now takes place frequently using open educational resources (OER), such as "digitized materials offered freely and openly for educators, students and self-learners to use and reuse for teaching, learning and research" (Hylén, 2007, p.336). From a dual-lens point of view, this implies assuming authority for the creation of teaching materials. Alternatively, it may mean simply composing or using resources but is limited to what appears to be sporadic picking from the web. Teachers rarely author—or even substantially edit—eTextbooks that will serve as the core source of their teaching. This is certainly not expected of them in their capacity as teachers (Chazan & Yerushalmy, 2014), although there are some examples of sustained projects of community-authored resources.

Sésamath, a French online association of mathematics teachers, started with approximately 20 mathematics teachers who shared their personal websites and subsequently designed a drill-and-practice software program called *Mathenpoche*. Many teachers (approximately one hundred, for each textbook) contributed to the design in a collaborative and iterative way, as "authors of content," or "designers of didactical scenarios," or "testers," or "experimenters" in classes (a single teacher may have several roles, or change roles at different times). The textbooks produced in this manner became highly successful within a short period of time and were used by many teachers and students. Since 2005, Sésamath has designed textbooks for grades 6–10 that are now among the most popular textbooks in France. The possibilities and opportunities for organizing collaborative work, offering a set of flexible resources and tools and enabling questioning of its structure and development (e.g., through discussions with researchers), led Sésamath to become a major reference in the French educational landscape (Trouche, Drijvers, Gueudet, & Sacristan, 2012). According to Gueudet, Pepin, Sabra, and Trouche (2016), Sésamath's textbooks are "living" objects that evolve frequently.

VisualMath (VM) began as a web 1.0 authored eTextbook that was then redesigned as a collaborative platform that supports re-sourcing by teachers (Yerushalmy et al., 2014). VM is an example of a textbook that functions as a workbook, so that learning requires active participation using multimodal interactive activities. The collaborative authoring platform, still in the pilot stage, supports convenient editing of tasks and flexible restructuring of units and sequences. Editing or replacing interactive tools and diagrams, however, is not a structured feature of the platform. The design attempts to deliver a message that these tools and diagrams are the major building blocks of the "language" that VM speaks. They can be reused, repositioned, and reordered, but not replaced. The design of external and collaborative authoring in another platform—STEP (Olsher, Yerushalmy, & Chazan, 2016)—does support authoring of new tasks and external interactive diagrams, provided that the task is structured according to output that allows evaluation using the mathematical definitions that serve as the basic data for assessment.

Collaborations like Sésamath and collaborative platforms such as VM and STEP are still relatively rare. There are clearly many challenges posed by peer production of eTextbooks that are aligned with an annual curriculum, including requirements for coherence, quality assurance, and sustainability of the collaborative process (Yerushalmy, 2012). Nevertheless, we cannot ignore the textbook's technological evolution that can potentially shift the power to publish from centralized bodies to natural users, such as teachers. Every tool's design carries a message, and every collaborative design is based on the tools or resources provided. Consequently, new centralized bodies may begin to contribute to designing or otherwise controlling the tools that support these collaborations (Yerushalmy, 1999).

Ownership of eTextbooks

Use and exploitation of materials generated through large-scale collaborations are likely to raise many questions. One set of challenges relates to managing the rights of the different contributors. For example, who has the right to edit and transform a work created by many? How should the output of collaborative production be managed and subsequently governed? What rights should the respective participants have to their individual contributions or to the outcome as a whole? Should users be free to use their contributions to a collaborative endeavor as they please? What if editing the content or implementing a particular business model affects the endeavor as a whole, or at least the micro-contributions made by others?

Another set of issues concerns attribution. Copyright law often accords authors the moral right of attribution, entitling them to associate their names with their work in a manner suiting the specific circumstances. Collaborative textbooks have yet to develop any conventions regarding the assigning of credit. How should contributors to a collaborative work be listed? Is it sufficient to list each contribution next to its contributor's name, or should credit be given for the work as a whole? When every participant might have the power to modify the collaborative outcome, is it fair to grant credit for the work as a whole? Should other contributors have the right to opt out and remove their names if they wish to disassociate themselves from the final outcome?

These questions are not addressed by current legislation. Copyright law that governs exploitation of creative works does not provide an adequate framework for meeting these challenges. It confers power on each of the contributing individuals to decide how to exploit his or her contribution. When their contributions are inseparable, the law forms a legal partnership among them. Copyright law defines rights that protect authors from strangers—rights of owners against non-owners. It entitles owners to prohibit unlicensed use of their work by potential exploiters. The law, however, fails to provide an organizational structure for social production in large-scale collaboration. It lacks a framework for addressing the rights and duties of collaborators toward one another regarding their respective contributions and the exploitation of their joint effort. The law does not sufficiently address the appropriate mechanisms for governing the output of social production and resolving conflicts and disagreements related to it. This deficiency is particularly crucial in the case of large-scale collaborations between a large number of users who are not organized by any formal legal structure.

Even if some collaborative works may fall under the strict definition of *joint authorship* and would consequently confer joint ownership on all participating authors, this legal tool does not offer a useful means of governing the output of large-scale collaboration. Joint owners equally share copyright ownership, unless agreed otherwise. The rules related to co-ownership in copyright are derived from co-ownership of tangible property. Each owner can act unilaterally and independently of the other co-owners. This does not mean that each contribution should be copyrighted to the individual user. Social production reflects a joint effort, but in this case, value is created by the cumulative efforts of a massive number of participants. Viewing the output of online collaboration as a single coherent work often fails to address the special nature of such collaboration as a dynamic and interactive process. The collaborative nature of such creative projects may weaken the claim of each individual user for exclusivity over the bits and pieces contributed by each to the collaborative endeavor. The output of such collaboration is actually more a reflection of an ongoing social process than of a commodity that can be owned and transferred.

If the contribution of each user is considered copyrighted, participating users and social media platforms must take precautions to avoid any unauthorized use of other users' contributions. Any user who wishes to make use of a preexisting work must first acquire an appropriate and often costly license. The user must determine which license is needed, identify the specific copyright holder, negotiate a license to use the work, and pay the license fee. The high cost of licensing erects barriers that often make it difficult for users to participate in generating content, especially in collaborative initiatives by volunteers that lack the fee structure and the organizational infrastructure necessary to maintain a licensing system. Copyright law does not leave sufficient space for users to base their work on preexisting materials. Fair use privileges, which protect some unlicensed transformative uses, are rather vague and indeterminate, exerting a chilling effect even in cases in which use is legitimate.

Copyright law treats content as a commodity; use of content in a copyright regime is framed as a business transaction. The law focuses on the author as the center of the creation process and emphasizes the author's authority over the fate of his or her work. Social production, on the other hand, is often generated as a type of communicative act, reflecting engagement in a conversation or an interaction with a community that is ultimately merged into an information flow. Communicative acts reflect the social norms of sharing, participating, and collaborating. Users who upload voiceovers of famous movies may be trying to communicate a message using the available cultural language shared by their peers. These authors/users do not purchase the work, nor do they sell their added value. They simply interact and communicate with others. Shaping relationships among users as transactions and not as conversations may undermine social motivation that depends on a sense of belonging to a community and on reciprocity. Exclusive rights over individual contributions may disrupt social cohesion and a sense of community, both of which are byproducts of social production and the mechanism that keeps it alive.

In summary, individualistic focus on the sovereignty of owners regarding use of their work—and the legal power to exclude others that is the essence of the proprietary approach to copyright—may conflict with the fundamentals of social production. Proprietary emphasis on the sovereignty of owners further weakens social cohesion by emphasizing differences and disparities of interests rather than shared values and goals. This emphasis on the rights of each owner over their respective contributions creates impediments to large-scale collaboration, as it gives each contributor the power to decide how his/her contribution will be used.

The deficiencies of copyright in governing relationships among contributors to collaborative creative efforts might be partly addressed through private arrangements within communities of users/authors. Licenses, contracts, and terms of use (ToU) enable online communities to opt out of the standardized rights and duties applied by copyright and to establish a legal regime that suits their needs. Classic examples are the General Public License (GPL) of the Free Software Foundation (FSF) that secures the freedom to operate, edit, and share software, as well as

Creative Commons licenses that govern contributions to Wikipedia. Such self-governing, private ordering has an important advantage, as it allows communities to tailor the governance of their content to the nature of their collaboration, the group identity, and the values shared by its members. At the same time, however, private ordering provides only a limited remedy to some of the deficiencies of copyright discussed above, as it suffers from several disadvantages. A major shortcoming of private ordering is that obtaining the consent of thousands of collaborators to a contract and to any revision thereof might prove a highly formidable (and costly) task. This process of collective action is much more difficult to achieve than simply coordinating the work of collaborators in creating new content. Collective action requires a procedure that would enable the group to reach decisions that bind the entire group of collaborators regarding exploitation of their work. It is hard to reach such agreements in large-scale collaborations where the parties are not bound by any formal legal structure.

Alternatively, rules governing ownership and rights of contributors to collaborative authorship initiatives could be defined by a contract provided by the facilitating platform. Such terms of use, however, may sometimes be abusive, taking advantage of participants and not paying tribute to their rights.

Facilitating Access to eTextbooks

Textbooks are seminal to a student's learning experience because they serve as the primary tool for accessing the knowledge and skills necessary to become productive citizens and employees (Oakes & Saunders, 2002). Consequently, it is no surprise that a large body of studies elucidates the importance of access to quality textbooks to a student's educational opportunities, particularly with respect to low-income students (Fuller & Clarke, 1994). The Organization of Economic Cooperation and Development (OECD) stipulates that textbooks are an important international indicator of educational quality. Its standard for an adequate supply of textbooks is one textbook for each student in every subject. This 1:1 textbook standard has also been used by the United Nations Educational, Scientific, and Cultural Organization (UNESCO) as it works toward the goal of universal education articulated in its World Declaration on Education for All (UNESCO, n.d.). Accessing textbooks, however, is also a matter of cost. In Israel, for example, the issue of textbook prices has been at the core of recent public discourse regarding the country's socioeconomic problems (Trajtenberg, 2012).

eTextbooks are often presented as a sustainable solution for skyrocketing textbook prices, as an effective vehicle for facilitating access for underserved communities, and as a means for reducing structural inequalities in education (Kim & Jung, 2010). Central authorities in developing economies, such as India and African countries, view the eTextbook as a unique opportunity to supply curricular materials to remote rural areas.

The potential of eTextbooks as a means for reducing expenditure and promoting access stems from the relatively low costs of publishing and distributing digital media (assuming that end devices are available). On the other hand, the shift from print to digital media that has created new models for publishing has also created new opportunities for publishers to govern proprietary rights. Consequently, publishing a textbook via digital media enhances the publishers' control of the textbook market and enables them to impose additional charges, thus limiting access to textbooks.

In most jurisdictions, creative works (including eTextbooks) are automatically endowed with all-rights-reserved copyrights under the presumption that such protection serves the interests of the copyright holder (Israel Copyright Act, 2007; Berne Convention, 1886 [rev. 1971]). Publishers of digital content often contract directly with end users through end-user license agreements (EULA). These commonly used standard contracts often expand the scope of rights granted under copyright law by further limiting the rights of users. For example, licenses may seek to limit the alienability of eTextbooks by contractually restricting resale or transfer of used copies, notwithstanding the rights of users under the copyright first-sale doctrine. EULAs may further stipulate a prohibition on lending the eTextbook to others or may limit access to specific devices or to a limited number of workstations.

eTextbooks further facilitate self-help measures that were not effectively available for governing access to printed textbooks. By employing digital rights management (DRM) systems, eTextbook publishers can technically control the actual use of the work. DRM systems allow publishers to define the terms of access in the digital package that contains the content. Publishers can define a maximum number of users and limit resale but can also block uses that copyright law would have permitted. For example, DRM can block use by teachers and students that might have been considered non-infringing fair use. The fair use doctrine may permit limited use of copyrighted works for purposes such as research, self-study, teaching, and assessment by an educational institute.

By design, the availability of contracts and restrictions dramatically enhances the control exercised by publishers over access to eTextbooks (Elkin-Koren, 2002). The power of publishers to control use of eTextbooks after they have been purchased enables them to increase the cost to consumers without raising the original price of the book.

First, publishers may charge extra for uses that are not restricted under copyright law and are otherwise available in print books, such as marking the text or copying certain sections for self-study, teaching, or assessment. Second, publishers may charge extra for any change in ownership or otherwise sharing the eTextbook with a fellow student or a younger sibling (Elkin-Koren, 2006). This could further impede the development of a secondary market for eTextbooks that would reduce the effective price of a new copy, as consumers can resell their purchases. Moreover, a secondary market competes with the primary market and consequently contributes to price reductions (Elkin-Koren, 2006). Taking these observations into consideration, it is argued that the potential of eTextbooks for enhancing access to knowledge and skills creates new challenges for policy makers to ensure their affordability.

Conclusion

Traditional textbooks and their use are rapidly disappearing, as eTextbooks are becoming part of the general push toward integration of ICTs into the educational landscape. eTextbooks offer unprecedented opportunities for teachers and learners (pedagogic, professional, economic), but at the same time, these new curricular materials are posing challenges for the entire educational ecosystem. This chapter sought to examine multiple aspects of these challenges, in order to help learners, teachers, and policymakers better address this transmission. This chapter illustrated the different definitions of eTextbooks, encapsulating their unique characteristics with ramifications for learning, authority, autonomy, and power.

We further highlighted the opportunities and risks introduced by eTextbooks: With the introduction of the eTextbook, educators have to reexamine the authoritative presence of their instructional tools in the classroom and consequently to adjust their pedagogical practices. Teachers also must safeguard their own privacy and that of their students, as the flow of information from classroom to third parties increases on an unprecedented scale. With the new capabilities to author eTextbooks dynamically and interactively, educators must establish efficient mechanisms and develop a novel scheme for authorship, whether collective or individual. They must also develop new measures to assure the quality of such eTextbooks. Finally, this medium of delivery introduces innovative measures for restricting access to educational materials, requiring a new approach to securing access to knowledge and making sure that eTextbooks remain affordable for all students.

This chapter argues that the challenges raised by eTextbooks are relevant to educators, lawyers, and policymakers alike. Policy should aim at facilitating positive externalities of the emergence of the eTextbook, while reining in its potential negative consequences. While regulations should provide means to monitor the production and use of eTextbooks, other stakeholders, such as educational design experts and ICT solutions providers, should also adopt a multidimensional approach that could benefit from cooperation among educators, lawyers, and technology experts.

Looking into the future, it appears inevitable that the combination of digital learning resources, along with corresponding data on their use, will serve as a basis for assessment of users (students) according to their use of this data, possibly leading to personally tailored learning trajectories designed by algorithms. While these practices require substantial research in the domains of learning analytics and their use in education (see, e.g., Kent et al.'s chapter on Networked Learning Analytics, Chap. 9), they could potentially change the roles of schools, teachers, and peers. These implications emphasize the need for interdisciplinary research methods for analysis, as well as novel theoretical frameworks that encompass the complexity of multiple disciplinary research, such as those afforded by the LINKS center (see Tabak, Ben-Zvi, & Kali, Chap. 2), exemplified in the current chapter by the conceptual experiment performed by our teams of researchers from the domains of law and education.

Bibliography

Berne Convention for the Protection of Literary and Artistic Works, Sep. 9, 1886, as last revised at Paris on Jul. 24, 1971, 1161 U.N.T.S. 30.

Brickell, J., Kanuth, M., Freeman, V., Latshaw, S., & Larson, C. (2006). Learning objects: Resources for instruction. *Clinical Laboratory Science, 19*(3), 184–187.

Board of Education v. Allen, 392 U.S. 236 (1968).

Chazan, D., & Yerushalmy, M. (2014). The future of mathematics textbooks: Ramifications of technological change. In M. Stocchetti (Ed.), *Media and education in the digital age: Concepts, assessments, subversions* (pp. 63–76). Frankfurt: PL Academic Research.

Cohen, J. E. (2012). *Configuring the networked self: Law, code, and the play of everyday practice.* New Haven, CT: Yale University Press.

Committee of the Central Advisory Board of Education Ministry of Human Resource Development Government of India, Regulatory mechanisms for textbooks and parallel textbooks taught in schools outside the government system. (2005). Available at http://www.teindia.nic.in/Files/Reports/CCR/cabe/Rmtbptb.pdf

Coviello, L., et al. (2014). Detecting emotional contagion in massive social networks. *PLoS One, 9*(3), e90315. https://doi.org/10.1371/journal.pone.0090315

Data Quality Campaign. (2015). Student data privacy legislation: What happened in 2015, and what is next? Available at: http://dataqualitycampaign.org/wpcontent/uploads/2015/09/DQC-Student-Data-Laws-2015-Sept23.pdf

Education Week. (2014). http://blogs.edweek.org/edweek/DigitalEducation/2014/01/american_worried_uninformed_student_data_privacy.html

Elkin-Koren, N. (2002). Self-copyright in the information age. *Alei Mishpat* [Pages of Law], *2*, 319–323; 332-end. [Hebrew]

Elkin-Koren, N. (2006). Copyright and competition—from a copy market to a licensing regime. *Din Udevarim* [English Title: *Haifa Law Review*], *9*(2): 485–549. [Hebrew]

Fletcher, G. (2012). Out of print: Reimagining the K-12 textbook in a digital age. State Educational Technology Directors Association (SETDA). files.eric.ed.gov/fulltext/ED536747.pdf.

Friesen, N. (2013). The past and likely future of an educational form: A textbook case. *Educational Researcher, 42*(9), 498–508.

Gueudet, G., Pepin, B., Sabra, H., & Trouche, L. (2016). Collective design of an e-textbook: Teachers' collective documentation. *Journal of Mathematics Teacher Education, 19*(2–3), 187–203. https://doi.org/10.1007/s10857-015-9331-x

Fuller, B., & Clarke, P. (1994). Raising school effects while ignoring culture? Local conditions and the influence of classroom tools, rules, and pedagogy. *Review of Educational Research, 64*(1), 119–157.

Har Carmel, Y. (2016). Regulating "big data education" in Europe: Lessons learned from the US. *Internet Policy Review, 5*(1). https://doi.org/10.14763/2016.1.402

Herbel-Eisenmann, B. A. (2009). Negotiating the "presence *of* the text": How might teachers' language choices influence the positioning of the textbook? In J. T. Remillard, B. A. Herbel-Eisenmann, & G. M. Lloyd (Eds.), *Mathematics teachers at work* (pp. 134–151). New York, NY\Abingdon, UK: Routledge.

Herold, B. (2014). Americans worried, uninformed about student data privacy, survey finds, *Education Week* (January 22).

Ho, J., & Hsu, Y. (2011). Improving the textbook adoption process in Taiwan. *International Educational Studies, 4*(4), 92–98.

Hylén, J. (2007). *Giving knowledge for free: The emergence of open educational resources.* Paris: OECD Publishing—Center for Educational Research and Innovation (CERI).

Israel Copyright Act. (2007). L.S.I. 34; Berne Convention for the Protection of Literary and Artistic Works, Sep. 9, 1886, as last revised at Paris on Jul. 24, 1971, 1161 U.N.T.S. 30.

Israel Ministry of Education. (2015). Procedure and processes for instructional material and textbook approval [Hebrew]. Available at: http://cms.education.gov.il/EducationCMS/Applications/Mankal/EtsMedorim/6/6-3/HoraotKeva/K-2015-9-3-6-3-16.htm

Israel State Education Law, 1953s § 4(d).

Israeli Ministry of Education. (2011). Digital Textbooks [in Hebrew]. Available at: http://sites.education.gov.il/cloud/home/S_D/Pages/sfarim_digitaliim_1.aspx.

Israeli Ministry of Education. (2012). Adapting the educational system to the 21st-century [in Hebrew]. Available at: http://cms.education.gov.il/NR/rdonlyres/79B5A8CF-F812-4A63-89BE-3BEFEB887EC5/142454/12.pdf.

Kiderra, I. (2014). *Facebook feelings are contagious, study shows*. San Diego, CA: UC San Diego News Center (March 12). Available at http://ucsdnews.ucsd.edu/pressrelease/facebook_feelings_are_contagious_study_shows

Kim, J. H., & Jung, H. (2010). South Korean digital textbook project. *Computers in the Schools, 27*(3–4), 247–265.

Kuhn, M. (2011). *Filmnarratologie: Ein erzähltheoretisches Analysemodell* [Film Narratology. An Analysis Model of Narrative Theory]. Berlin: De Gruyter. [German].

Love, E., & Pimm, D. (1996). "This is so": A text on texts. In A. J. Bishop, K. Clements, C. Keitel, J. Kilpatrick, & C. Laborde (Eds.), *International handbook of mathematics education* (Vol. 4, pp. 371–410). Dordrecht: Springer.

Mahmood, K. (2006). The process of textbook approval: A critical analysis. *Bulletin of Education & Research, 28*(1), 1–22.

Marczak, M. (2013). Selecting an E-(text)book: Evaluation criteria. *Teaching English with Technology, 13*(1), 29–41.

McSherry, C. (2014). Adobe spyware reveals (again) the price of DRM: Your privacy and security (October 7). Available at: https://www.eff.org/deeplinks/2014/10/adobe-spyware-reveals-again-price-your-privacy-and-security

Nissenbaum, H. (2009). *Privacy in context: Technology, policy, and the integrity of social life*. Stanford, CA: Stanford University Press.

Oakes, J., & Saunders, M. (2002). Access to textbooks, instructional materials, equipment, and technology: Inadequacy and inequality in California's public schools. Available at http://www.schoolfunding.info/resource_center/legal_docs/California/Williams_Experts_Reports/Williams_Oakes_report_2_InstructMaterials.pdf

Olsher, S., Yerushalmy, M., & Chazan, D. (2016). How might the use of technology in formative assessment support changes in mathematics teaching? *For the Learning of Mathematics, 36*(3), 11–18.

Pentland, A. (2014). *Social physics: How social networks can make us smarter*. New York: Penguin.

Pepin, B., & Haggarty, L. (2001). Mathematics textbooks and their use in English, French and German classrooms: A way to understand teaching and learning cultures. *ZDM (Zentralblatt für Didaktik der Mathematik)—International Journal of Mathematics Education, 33*(5), 158–175.

Polonetsky, J., & Jerome, J. (2014). Student data: Trust, transparency, and the role of consent. Available at http://papers.ssrn.com/sol3/papers.cfm?abstract_id=2628877

Remillard, J. T. (2015). Keeping an eye on the teacher in the digital curriculum race. In M. Bates & Z. Usiskin (Eds.), *Digital curricula in school mathematics* (pp. 195–204). Greenwich, CT: Information Age Publishing.

Richards, N. (2008). Intellectual privacy. *Texas Law Review, 87*, 387–445.

Richards, N. (2015). *Intellectual privacy: Rethinking civil liberties in the digital age*. New York: Oxford University Press.

Sharples, M., et al. (2012). Innovating pedagogy. Open University Innovation Report, 8. Available at http://www.open.ac.uk/personalpages/mike.sharples/Reports/Innovating_Pedagogy_report_July_2012.pdf

Siminoff, D. (2013). The Etext revolution: Rewriting the textbook model. *Internet@Schools* (May 1). Available at http://www.internetatschools.com/Articles/Editorial/Features/The-Etext-Revolution-Rewriting-the-Textbook-Model-89288.aspx

Singer, N. (2014). With tech taking over in schools, worries rise. *The New York Times* (September 14). Available at http://www.nytimes.com/2014/09/15/technology/with-tech-taking-over-in-schools-worries-rise.html

Spielvogel, C., & Spielvogel, L. (2010). Speaking the language of digital natives: Role-playing simulations in the communication classroom. *Electronic Journal of Communication, 20*(1–2). Available at: http://www.cios.org/EJCPUBLIC/020/1/020123.html

Stray, C. (1994). Paradigms regained: Towards a historical sociology of the textbook. *Journal of Curriculum Studies, 26*(1), 1–29.

Thaler, R. H., & Sunstein, C. R. (2009). *Nudge: Improving decisions about health, wealth, and happiness.* Penguin.

Trajtenberg, M. (2012). *Trajtenberg report: Creating a more just Israeli society* (p. 40). Jerusalem: Israel Prime Minister's Office.

Trouche, L., Drijvers, P., Gueudet, G., & Sacristan, A. I. (2012). In M. A. Clements, A. J. Bishop, C. Keitel, J. Kilpatrick, & F. J. S. Leung (Eds.),. Third international handbook of mathematics education *Technology-driven developments and policy implications for mathematics education* (pp. 753–789). New York: Springer.

Tulley, M. A. (1985). A descriptive study of the intents of state-level textbook adoption processes. *Educational Evaluation & Policy Analysis, 7*, 289–308.

United Nations Educational, Scientific and Cultural Organization (UNESCO). (n.d.). *Basic learning materials initiative.* Available at http://www.unesco.org/education/blm/chap1_en.php

Vargo, J., Nesbit, J. C., Belfer, K., & Archambault, A. (2003). Learning object evaluation: Computer-mediated collaboration and inter-rater reliability. *International Journal of Computers & Applications, 25*(3), 1–7.

Watt, M. G. (2009). Research on the textbook selection process in the United States of America. *IARTEM e-Journal, 2*(1). Available at files.eric.ed.gov/fulltext/ED506523.pdf

White House. (2014). Big data: Seizing opportunities, preserving values. Available at https://www.whitehouse.gov/sites/default/files/docs/big_data_privacy_report_5.1.14_final_printpdf

Wiley, D. (2009). Impediments to learning object reuse and openness as a potential solution. *Revista Brasileira de Informática na Educação* [Brazilian Journal of Information on Education], *17*(3). Available at: https://doi.org/10.5753/rbie.2009.17.03.08

Wiley, D., & Gurrell, S. (2009). A decade of development. *Open Learning: The Journal of Open, Distance & e-Learning, 24*(1), 11–21.

Williams, R., & Agosto, V. (2012). Missing and shrinking voices: A critical analysis of the Florida textbook adoption policy. In H. Hickman & B. J. Porfilio (Eds.), *Politics of the textbook: Critical analysis of the core content areas* (pp. 17–40). Rotterdam: Sense Publishers.

Yerushalmy, M. (1999). Guest Editor. Special issue on Learning big ideas: Curriculum reform and the use of technology. *International Journal of Computers for Mathematical Learning, 4*(2–3).

Yerushalmy, M. (2012). Will everyone be writing textbooks? (November 9). Available at: http://cloudworks.ac.uk/cloud/view/6609

Yerushalmy, M., Shternberg, B., & Katriel, H. (2014). *VisualMath: Functions & algebra.* The University of Haifa. http://visualmath.haifa.ac.il/

Yeung, K. (2016). 'Hypernudge': Big data as a mode of regulation by design. *Information, Communication & Society, 20*(1), 118–136.

Young, S. (2007). *The book is dead: Long live the book.* Sydney: University of New South Wales Press.

Zuboff, S. (2015). Big other: Surveillance capitalism and the prospects of an information civilization. *Journal of Information Technology, 30*(1), 75–89.

Chapter 11
Future Learning Spaces: Exploring Perspectives from LINKS Research

Yotam Hod, Keren Aridor, Dani Ben-Zvi, Carmit Pion, Patrice L. Weiss, and Oren Zuckerman

Abstract Future learning spaces (FLSs) have become a topic of immense interest as educational researchers and practitioners have reconceptualized learning in the networked society. This dual interest is vital as the scientific field has been fragmented across disciplines on this topic while in practice billions of dollars are being spent but often fail to achieve their desired goals. This chapter advances both theoretical and practical issues related to FLSs with a novel definition of the term, by explaining its relevance to LINKS, and through the examination of three different categories of FLSs. Specifically, the chapter takes a careful look at FLSs in classroom learning communities, in informal settings, and in professional settings as a basis to identify strengths, opportunities, limitations, and challenges of FLSs. We end with three specific recommendations to help bridge the research-practice gap and advance our understand of this vital facet of LINKS.

Keywords Future learning spaces · Physical locations · Online locations · Learning communities · Informal settings · Professional settings

The networked society has introduced dramatic changes in the way people learn. A major issue of interest has been learning spaces, which have attracted particularly intense interest as a topic of discussion in public media (e.g., *future learning spaces*: The New York Times, 2013; Hod et al., 2016), popular educational discourse (e.g., *the flipped classroom*: Bishop & Verleger, 2013), and large-scale school reforms

Y. Hod (✉) · K. Aridor · D. Ben-Zvi · C. Pion
University of Haifa, Faculty of Education, Haifa, Israel
e-mail: yhod@edu.haifa.ac.il; dbenzvi@univ.haifa.ac.il

P. L. Weiss
University of Haifa, Faculty of Social Welfare and Health Sciences, Haifa, Israel
e-mail: plweiss@research.haifa.ac.il

O. Zuckerman
Interdisciplinary Center (IDC) Herzliya, School of Communication, Herzliya, Israel
e-mail: oren.zukerman@milab.idc.ac.il

© Springer Nature Switzerland AG 2019
Y. Kali et al. (eds.), *Learning In a Networked Society*, Computer-Supported Collaborative Learning Series 17, https://doi.org/10.1007/978-3-030-14610-8_11

(e.g., *the small school movement*: Semel & Sadovnik, 2008). The 2016 *Horizon Report*, a highly comprehensive international report on educational innovation, views the redesign of learning spaces as a key driver of educational change in the years to come (Adams Becker, Freeman, Giesinger Hall, Cummins, & Yuhnke, 2016). Nevertheless, the billions of dollars that have been allocated in recent years to implement large and expensive renovations to learning spaces at all levels of education, in both formal and informal settings, have by no means brought about the desired outcomes. The resulting challenge calls for rigorous scholarship to further explore, understand, and guide this sphere of development (Ellis & Goodyear, 2016). To advance achievement of the desired goal, this chapter refines the relatively new notion of *future learning spaces* (FLS) (Hod, 2017; Sutherland & Fischer, 2014) via the unique prism of learning in the networked society (LINKS). Synthesizing what is known about FLSs with the aim of sharing new insights about this generative and timely concept, we elucidate in this chapter a conceptual framework for FLSs and analyze several examples using it, which are related to the LINKS project.

Motivation of Research on Learning Spaces in the Networked Society

Recent changes in the structural underpinning of modern civilization—what we refer to as the *networked society* (see Chap. 1)—have added new challenges to scholarship on learning (see Chaps. 2 and 3). The rapid creation of new spaces in both the physical and digital realms (e.g., *Minecraft*), dynamic transitions among these spaces (e.g., mobile technologies), and the new ways that people engage in these spaces (e.g., interactivity) increasingly blur the lines between where and what is learned. Collins and Halverson (2009) pointed out the pressure imposed on the traditional schooling system, increasingly challenged because people are able to learn meaningfully through participation in web communities and distance education, at the workplace and even at home. Along these lines, the networked society has seen a proliferation of newly designed spaces that discard traditional educational paradigms in favor of those with an eye toward the future (Oblinger & Lippincott, 2006). Early examples include the student-centered activities for large enrollment undergraduate programs (SCALE-UP) and technology-enabled active learning (TEAL), which have spread profusely (Dori & Belcher, 2005). More recent examples include active learning classrooms (Charles & Whittaker, 2015), immersive simulations such as EvoRoom (Slotta, Tissenbaum, & Lui, 2013), innovation studios (Rook, Choi, & McDonald, 2015), and efforts at connecting distant knowledge-building communities (Zhang et al., 2015). Together with surges such as makerspaces (Halverson & Sheridan, 2014) and other smart, connected learning communities (CSSC, 2015), the FLS concept adds a newly unexplored layer of learning space research.

Investigating FLSs is both a practical and a theoretical challenge. In the world of practice, initiatives to design learning spaces have often failed to impact learning in the desired manner. This is similar to the effort to integrate computers in classrooms in the 1980s and 1990s, which were largely *oversold* and *underused* (Cuban, 2001). While there is often a great deal of hype about fanciful or futurist visions of educational architectures, efforts frequently overvalue the role of space without according sufficient consideration to its purpose, its facilitation of learning, the integration of educational technologies and online spaces, the subject matter, and the process by which the spaces are designed and implemented (Hod, 2017). Coherent research-derived frameworks are thus needed to guide the (re)design and construction of spaces and thus to ensure beneficial returns on investments, as demonstrated by meaningful progress in learning (Peters & Slotta, 2010; Sawyer, 2014).

Research on learning spaces (without specific focus on the future) has been conducted in several disciplines, including architecture, environmental psychology, human-computer interaction, computer-supported collaborative learning, and the learning sciences. In general, studies have fallen into two broad domains, according to their foci: (1) physical places, with some spillover into online worlds, and (2) digital tools and artifacts, with some incursion into physical worlds (Ellis & Goodyear, 2016). Two relatively recent reviews of learning spaces research concluded that what is known is dispersed and fragmented (Ellis & Goodyear, 2016; Temple, 2008). Moreover, learning space research does not yet have a strong history of empirical evidence. A large majority of the literature makes claims that are either unsupported or anecdotal regarding the manner in which spaces may benefit learning, creating a serious challenge for this line of inquiry (Temple, 2007). Following Kurt Lewin's (1952) maxim that "there is nothing more practical than a theory," we proceed to clarify the theoretical notions of FLSs.

A Framework for Future Learning Spaces

As a key LINKS concept and research embodiment, FLSs are more than the sum of their parts (*future, learning,* and *spaces*). Much the same way as the advent of word processing programs drastically changed the content and process of writing in comparison to classical methods like handwriting and typewriting, the three parts of FLSs are intertwined and form a unique synergy. Still, in our effort to add clarity to the meaning of FLSs, it is useful to consider the parts separately. This is akin to the way an organ within the body can be focused on without losing sight of its interdependence with the entire human body system. In this section, we offer a framework based on the three parts of FLSs to create a set of operational conditions that can be used to qualify if and in what ways or extent a particular context should be considered an FLS.

In referring to *future*, we must consider the fact that society is in the midst of a digital revolution that shows no signs of decelerating. It would be hard to consider a space as an FLS if it had no digitized component. Likewise, the immediacy of innovative technologies minimizes the distinctions between "what is" and "what will be," allowing us to relate to a "future that is already here" (Isaacson, 2011). The rapid saturation of the smartphone and tablet market exemplifies the unprecedented pace of change and the rapid realization of enormous potential. It is consequently appropriate to focus on emerging or existing (but developing) technologies as a condition to apply the term "future."

Regarding *learning*, a distinction can be made by excluding "institutionalized public basic schooling" (Cole & Packer, 2016, p. 506), *classroom-as-container* metaphors (Leander, Phillips, & Taylor, 2010), or instructivist pedagogies that emphasize knowledge transmission and acquisition. Rather, FLSs are predicated on pedagogies that are based on advancements in the way people learn. The learning sciences offer a foundational set of principles that can be applied as general criteria. These include whether the learning environment is learner-, knowledge-, assessment-, or community-centered (Bransford, Brown, & Cocking, 2000). To be learner-centered, students must be active constructors of their own knowledge, first eliciting what they already think and know and building from there. To be knowledge-centered, ideas should be organized around central concepts that can be explored in depth (over breadth). Assessment-centered refers to the focus on formative tools like feedback and self-reflection that aim to scaffold personal growth instead of evaluation. Finally, being community-centered entails engaging in authentic activities where students typically build knowledge collaboratively. While there are endless ways to design learning environments based on different combinations of these principles, all varieties offer a radical and empirically based departure from the type of passive learning and rote memorization learning practices that were often emphasized in the past.

Finally, *spaces* can be a highly ambiguous and loosely defined term which does not help in the effort to set a clear definition for FLSs. Ellis and Goodyear (2016) note the frequent confusion with *places* and *learning environments*, to which we add here the overlap with *digital learning tools*. Similar to their conception, we focus on material spaces and their virtual or digital counterparts that share some equivalent features. We contend that it is the opportunities given to lived experiences or identity expression that most notably distinguishes a space from the other similar conceptions. This is why most people would consider a virtual world as a clear example of a space, while a tool or platform, like Wikipedia, would be a more contentious choice. Furthering this point, some have used wikis in their classrooms as a way to build community, having students build personal pages and group norms pages as ways to connect between the members (Hod & Ben-Zvi, 2018). When used in this way, the lived experiences of the participants much more closely resemble the characteristics of physical spaces, and the same wiki now feels more like a lived-in space. Following this reasoning, when material and digital worlds become integrated, in a trend that has been growing (Ellis & Goodyear, 2016), it becomes much easier to classify a particular context, tool, or learning environment as a space.

Altogether, we view FLSs as a framework that underscores several nuanced ideas that have become relevant for the conceptions of LINKS. Building on the theoretical and practical challenge of bridging together fragmented research on

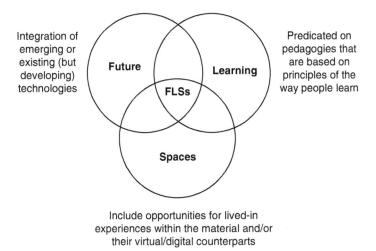

Fig. 11.1 Future learning space criteria

learning spaces and using it as a foundation to examine the new FLS phenomenon, Fig. 11.1 summarizes these three criteria. These can be used to distinguish FLSs from general (non-futuristic) learning spaces, learning tools, places, and the like. This is a vital goal toward establishing FLSs as a research niche, so that rules of inclusion and exclusion are clear, allowing for comparison and contrast of even the most distant and diverse examples. The intertwining of these three conditions with the way teaching and learning are conceived makes it clear why FLSs are associated with broader reconceptualizations of traditional schooling. It is no coincidence that along with calling for the redesign of spaces, the *Horizon Report* suggests rethinking "how schools work" together with it (Adams Becker et al., 2016, p. 2).

As an attempt to demonstrate how our conceptualization of FLSs can be operationalized, we explore three different settings in which FLSs have been implemented in LINKS-related research. Specifically, our examples focus on learning communities, makerspaces, and simulations as FLSs. Within each of the examples, we characterize the FLSs based on our notions of (a) future, (b) learning, and (c) spaces, with special emphasis on the manner in which all three are interwoven. We conclude with a discussion that draws on these examples to advance the overall FLS research agenda.

Learning Communities as FLSs

Classroom learning communities (LCs) have been among the most significant reconceptualizations of schooling over the past few decades (Bielaczyc, Kapur, & Collins, 2013). In the early 1990s, significant developments in socio-constructivist and sociocultural ideas of learning led to the introduction of many new LC models worldwide (e.g., Brown & Campione, 1994; Rogoff, Turkanis, & Bartlett, 2001; Scardamalia & Bereiter, 1994). The innovations have continued ever since, often beyond the scope of the classroom and into informal or web communities (Hod, Bielaczyc, & Ben-Zvi, 2018). Because LCs necessitate a variety of participation structures and activities, they provide an ideal context for FLSs as they can benefit from dynamic and flexible use of one or more spaces. As a result, in recent years many LC models have paid a great deal of attention to creating digital or physical learning spaces in which they take place (e.g., Charles & Whittaker, 2015; Rook et al., 2015; Slotta et al., 2013).

There are several examples of LINKS-related FLS research in the context of LCs, such as students learning about learning in a wiki-based environment (Hod & Ben-Zvi, 2014, 2015, 2018), reconfiguring lecture halls into small inquiry-based communities (Kali, McKenney, & Sagy, 2015), or students learning to think in interdisciplinary ways (Kidron & Kali, 2015; Kidron, Tirosh, Kali, & Schejter, 2019). In this section, we describe two examples that have emphasized how learning spaces support LC goals: (1) the *Connections* project that aims at developing and studying students' statistical reasoning as they learn in inquiry-based environments and (2) the *Knowledge Community and Inquiry in Smart Classrooms* (KCI-SC) project, in which students create a collective knowledge base through collaborative knowledge inquiry activities (Slotta & Najafi, 2012).

The Connections Project

In the Connections project, elementary or middle school students learn to reason with, analyze, represent, evaluate, and present authentic data-based situations while informally inferring and modeling the populations investigated (e.g., Makar, Bakker, & Ben-Zvi, 2011; Manor & Ben-Zvi, 2015). The goal of students' statistical investigations is to gain insights from data about a realistic and authentic phenomenon (Makar et al., 2011; Wild & Pfannkuch, 1999). As a result, a statistical investigation requires knowledge of the statistical investigation's context (such as beliefs, theories, and dispositions) (Gal, 2002).

The physical environment of Connections is a primary school classroom equipped with laptops that combines both peer collaborations and whole-class discussions (Fig. 11.2). At times, students leave the classroom to engage in various data-gathering activities that they submit for analysis using innovative data software called TinkerPlots (Konold & Miller, 2011). The project's online environment consists of a formal and an informal space. In the formal space, students are asked to share the outcomes of their investigations (i.e., graphs, TinkerPlots files, and textual inferences), while in the informal one, students reflect on and discuss their learning processes and outcomes. Students' freedom to manage the way they participate in both the physical and the online learning environments adds an aspect of informal learning. At the end of the Connections project, students present their primary results to a broader community comprising of peers, parents, and teachers.

Fig. 11.2 Connections participants gather data that they then bring back to the classroom for analysis and sharing using digital tools

The interactions between the knowledge arising from the data and from the students' statistical models are key components of space-mediated learning in the Connections project. Both the physical and online spaces provide opportunities to negotiate between them. In the physical spaces, students are involved in data investigations, class presentations, and discussions, guided by the need to relate to both data and context, to bridge between them in models, and to evaluate the level of certainty in the ability to infer and model them. In the online spaces, students examine their certainty as they evaluate and share their products while reflecting on and discussing their learning process and its connection to their real-life experience on the project website. Both of these spaces support participation in the personal and shared learning experiences that emerge from these activities.

The KCI-SC Project

The second example of an FLS in the context of LCs is Knowledge Community and Inquiry in Smart Classrooms (KCI-SC: Slotta & Najafi, 2012). Collaborative knowledge inquiry activities are central to the KCI-SC project, designed to engage students with an emergent knowledge base as a resource to which new ideas and elements can be added (Lui & Slotta, 2014). A technological architecture called SAIL plays an essential role in aggregating the knowledge base, visualizing the collective product, promoting student contributions, and connecting the base to inquiry activities (Najafi & Slotta, 2010).

KCI-SC fuses the physical environment (e.g., walls, furniture) with designed digital tools and materials to support student interactions across multiple social planes and to encourage dynamic collaboration. This enhances face-to-face interactions while capturing and advancing the collective wisdom of the entire class (Slotta, 2010). Figure 11.3 shows an example of a typical classroom setup; the interaction between the physical and digital spaces may be viewed at https://vimeo.com/88915070.

Fig. 11.3 KCI smart
classroom setup

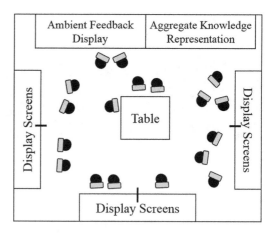

One theoretical idea of FLS research is *classroom orchestration* (Ellis & Goodyear, 2016). KCI-SC helps orchestrate complex inquiry designs, presenting aggregate visualizations and responding to student interactions in real time (Lui & Slotta, 2014). Teachers play an orchestrational role scaffolded by the technological environment specifically designed for this purpose (see Fig. 11.3). The teachers are responsible for moving the inquiry forward through a progression of predesigned activities at physical and virtual learning stations. They orchestrate the flow of inquiry activities based on the content of student interactions and artifacts and engage in specific scripted interactions with students. Furthermore, they may refer to representations of aggregated community knowledge to inform reflective discussions (Acosta & Slotta, 2013). In summary, KCI-SC orchestrates a learning space, both virtual and physical, in which the teacher, technology, and the physical environment all play key roles (Slotta et al., 2013).

The Connections project and KCI-SC share many characteristics, but differ in the way the FLSs orchestrate the advancement of community knowledge. In KCI-SC, FLSs are a vital component of the design, expressed by the centrality of the shared knowledge. Technology plays an essential role in aggregating the knowledge base, visualizing the collective knowledge, promoting student contributions, and connecting the knowledge base to inquiry activities (Najafi & Slotta, 2010). Connections, by contrast, does not rely on the space to orchestrate and advance the knowledge base. The spaces—particularly the TinkerPlots software, online collaborative environment, and the physical places where students collect data (e.g., outside)—are all mutually supportive but depend on the agency of the students to traverse them. Knowledge advancement is not collected and advanced *through* the spaces but rather with the *support* of the spaces. Consequently, the learning spaces are a fundamental conceptual component of the KCI-SC project and a supportive design component of the Connections project.

Overall, the interrelated aspects of future, learning, and spaces can be seen throughout both projects. They both use emerging and/or developing technologies, they challenge traditional educational paradigms through LC activities, and they provide rich, lived-in experiences for their students between material and digital spaces. The two different examples illustrate different ways that LCs can be ideal contexts for FLSs.

Makerspaces as FLSs

Over the past 5 years, what have come to be known as makerspaces have emerged as part of a movement involving a "growing number of people who are engaged in the creative production of artifacts in their daily lives and who find physical and digital forums to share their processes and products with others" (Halverson & Sheridan, 2014, p. 496). These makerspaces, found in a variety of formal and informal educational settings, enable learners to develop expertise in different areas and learn from each other in generally open learning configurations (Iversen, Smith, Blikstein, Katterfeldt, & Read, 2015; Peppler, Halverson, & Kafai, 2016). The interrelated aspects of future, learning, and spaces, which serve as the building blocks to conceptualize FLSs, are evident within makerspaces. These include new and emerging technologies like 3D printers and electronics kits (future), informal pedagogies that allow students to customize their own learning trajectories (learning), and an integration of physical and digital spaces that students can experience and actively explore (spaces). In this section, we describe Maketec, a small makerspace at a public library in Tel Aviv that was created by the LINKS Innovation Lab team at the Interdisciplinary Center to demonstrate how makerspaces can be FLSs.

The Maketec is both a social and research project, empowering children to create and interact with technology, as well as to examine learning through the process of their "making." The space layout was designed to provide functionality for the making process and to encourage social interaction, as well as active and peer learning.

Children typically arrive at the Maketec in the afternoon. Attendance is not mandatory, and participants need not join any structured courses or workshops, nor is there any direct teaching. Mentors are present at all times in the Maketec (volunteer high school students), and children are encouraged to work on projects using the various technologies and tools available. Children can use support materials (in the form of project cards) and request help from mentors or other participating children.

A common work table is set at the center of Maketec, providing space for individual work but also encouraging informal social interaction and peer learning (Fig. 11.4). On one wall is a floor-to-ceiling whiteboard, providing sketching and planning functionality but also conducive to doodling and informal discussion. The 3D printer area is visible and accessible, welcoming curious observation, as well as informal discussion and a deeper understanding of the fabrication process. There is a visible storage unit for craft materials and electronic components, providing access for users to explore new techniques. One shelf serves as an informal showcase of past creations, providing idea generation for new projects and also encouraging self-efficacy, as the examples are not made by professionals but by children (Fig. 11.4). Another shelf holds transparent plastic cases for long-term storage of

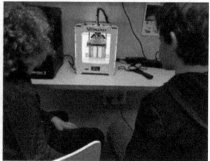

Fig. 11.4 Maketec space (left) and 3D printers' area (right)

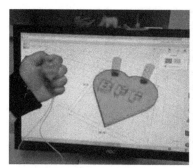

Fig. 11.5 The 3D model and 3D object of a personal artifact created by a 10-year-old girl (left) and a few examples from an informal showcase of children's creations (right)

work in progress, providing functional storage but also encouraging a sense of belonging to a local community, as each stored project has a visible label with the learner's name. The Maketec layout, as a whole, provides functionality for the do-it-yourself fabrication revolution by encouraging informal social interaction, a sense of belonging, and a culture of learning by doing (Fig. 11.5).

The Maketec model is designed in accordance with the low floor/wide walls principle originally suggested by Seymour Papert in *Mindstorms* (Papert, 1980). Papert defined low floor in the form of access, meaning that the new technology is accessible to a wide variety of people, including novices and children, requiring no specialized knowledge or skills to start exploring/using it. The wide walls principle extends this concept: Resnick (2006) describe wide walls as technologies that enable a wide variety of creation, rather than limiting or directing the user toward a certain type thereof. Wide variety in the context of children's interests and learning styles encourages and supports mathematics and science projects, as well as dance and music creations.

The technologies used in Maketec support low floor/wide walls principles. They require no prior knowledge in programming, mathematics, or science and support the creation of a wide variety of projects. For example, the *Makey Makey* (Resnick

& Rosenbaum, 2013) is an electronics kit that encourages playful extension of video games with custom-created input devices that replace the keyboard and mouse. Another example consists of paper-based electronic circuit-making kits (Qi & Buechley, 2014) that lend themselves to spirited production of electronic circuits using paper, conductive tape, LEDs, and craft materials. Other selected software tools following the same principles include Tinkercad by Autodesk—a 3D modeling tool for kids and novices—and Scratch, a programming environment for children (Resnick et al., 2009).

Learning at Maketec is conceptualized as balancing between mentoring and scaffolding, removing impediments for children so they can create and invent. Striking the right balance between student autonomy and support is a design challenge. Some children are intimidated by open-ended activities, while others thrive without explicit instructions. To meet this challenge, various mentoring and scaffolding techniques are designed. Scaffolding is provided by mentors or project cards—basic instructions for a few sample projects that serve three goals: helping children familiarize themselves with new technologies, introducing them to design processes comprising several key steps, and providing them with concrete artifacts they can take home after creating them themselves. The mentors are teenagers who chose to be makerspace mentors as part of the 60 hours of volunteer social activity required of all high school students in the country. They are always present when the Maketec is open, providing technical and design support, helping children tackle challenges and encouraging them to explore new technologies and innovative types of projects.

The interrelated aspects of future, learning, and spaces can be seen throughout Maketec. The future is built in as a Maketec design principle is conducive to a variety of new technologies and to providing students with low floors and wide walls to realize their innovative conceptions. Learning, along the lines of spontaneous-designed learning environments (Tabak, Ben-Zvi, & Kali, 2019), is embodied in Maketec's structure as a repurposed library, bringing together a wide range of participants who can explore their own interests on a voluntary, interest-driven basis. Finally, the physical and online spaces are integrated so that they use physical technologies to help children develop digital skills. The physical is thus also digital (3D printers, electronics kits), and acquired digital skills translate into physical abilities (e.g., construction projects using craft materials) as well as into strictly digital knowhow (designing personal objects using software tools). Overall, Maketec illustrates how the specialized conditions of makerspaces can render them as FLSs.

Simulations as FLSs

One challenge entailed in teaching health-care students is the provision of opportunities to attain practical clinical skills in interviewing, physical examination, and critical thinking (Cohen, Kitai, David, & Ziv, 2014; Weller, 2004). It is easier to assess and teach factual knowledge (by testing it for validity and reliability) than to impart interpersonal skills, data collection techniques, and clinical reasoning. Nevertheless, the latter skills have a decisive influence on medical outcomes and on patient satisfaction. Consequently, it is of utmost importance to assess their acquisition meticulously (Lane, Ziv, & Boulet, 1999). Such skills may be attained through extensive interaction with a variety of clients that proves difficult technically, ethically, and in terms of patient cooperation.

This section describes an FLS that uses a range of simulation tools for medical education, referred to as medical simulation centers (MSCs). MSCs are designed to enable students to develop their theoretical knowledge and hone their clinical practice skills via experiential methods in ecologically valid situations. MSCs have been pioneers in developing simulation-based training programs that enable a participatory, structured, and safe learning experience that is recorded on video to facilitate whole-class debriefing following individual or group learning, providing immediate feedback of one's own performance, as well as that of others. Such facilities have been shown to be highly effective learning paradigms (Barrows, 1993; Brock, Cohen, Sourkes, Good, & Halamek, 2017; Lee Gordon et al., 2005).

In 2001, an MSC was established at the Chaim Sheba Medical Center in Ramat Gan, Israel (https://eng.msr.org.il/about_Msr), with diverse learning activities aimed at fulfilling a broad range of objectives. For example, improving patient communication and assessment skills may be accomplished in a physical mockup of a clinician's office equipped with a plinth (examination table), basic medical assessment equipment (e.g., plethysmometer), office furniture, a sink, and medical supplies. Actors are trained to simulate medical conditions ranging from physical paralysis to extreme pre-exam anxiety (Fig. 11.6, right panel). Each student plays the role of a clinician performing an intake history and assessment and then round-robins through a series of mockup clinical rooms while being observed by fellow students (Fig. 11.6, left panel) and recorded by closed-circuit video cameras. A technician at an on-site studio edits the various sessions that are then used by the instructor to debrief the student group, providing opportunities for learning from both positive and negative feedback. According to Colliver and Williams (1993), a patient's performance remains largely unchanged in real cases and simulations, supporting criterion validity. Furthermore, most people who witnessed simulation with

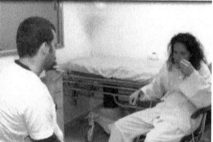

Fig. 11.6 Students in MSC simulations

virtual patients reported that the session appeared very real (Ladyshewsky, 1999). Woodward and Gliva-McConvey (1995) found that only two to three sessions were required to achieve more than 90% agreement between simulated patients and observers. Shahabudin, Almashoor, Edariah, and Khairuddin (1994) found that the ratings did not exceed 5% among different simulated patients in the same case or the same actor in two different observations within the space of 1 week.

A second example related to the objective of learning and practicing skills concerning procedures such as patient anesthesia (intubation) and vital sign monitoring. Students enter simulated physical mockups of fully equipped hospital operating rooms with medical supplies and life-support monitors. Computer-driven physiological mannequins are programmed to respond in real time to maneuvers conducted by the students as they learn the designated procedures (Chen, Kelly, Hayes, van Reyk, & Herok, 2016). A third example assesses the principles and practice of first responder skills via a physical mockup of an emergency triage (casualty) ward in which virtual reality simulations are used to provide training in skills that would otherwise have to be performed on real patients (e.g., inserting an epidural anesthetic) (Everett-Thomas et al., 2016; Lerant et al., 2017) (Fig. 11.7).

MSCs can be considered FLSs as they address the conditions of future, learning, and spaces from the framework we have outlined. The ongoing development of technologies that provide students with substantially greater opportunities to understand and implement new clinical materials suggests that these are futuristic environments. For example, low-tech simulated patients, high-tech physical robots (mannequins), or virtual environments make use of the latest video and sensor technologies to respond in real time to what students/apprentices are learning to do.

Relating to learning, MSCs train students to acquire skills that are required of physicians in contemporary medical practice. For example, students learn how to communicate with patients in real settings. Debriefing sessions involve individual and group reflection that enhances their ability to take advantage of apprenticeship situations. The use of MSCs has become a worldwide phenomenon (Qayumi et al., 2014), wherein people who have created established instances interact with medical education centers throughout the world to implement MSCs customized to local conditions (Brock et al., 2017). Thus, medical and other health-care training is

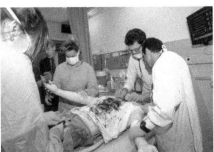

Fig. 11.7 Physical simulation via a robotic mannequin (left panel) and virtual simulation (right panel) in an MSC

available to students in third-world countries or to those who have no physical access to such facilities. Conversely, people in highly industrialized cultures can become aware of different health challenges, such as epidemics, in technology-impoverished areas or in places in which certain cultural norms and taboos may affect patient-provider dynamics. Such cultural interaction is especially relevant in this era of globalization.

Finally, MSCs display seamless integration of physical and online spaces in which real-world mockups (physical and/or virtual) of challenging health-care situations are implemented in ecologically valid settings. Students, in pairs and small groups, learn to respond in real time to realistic medical problems that occur in both local and unfamiliar contexts (Chen et al., 2016; Ziv, Ben-David, & Ziv, 2005). Space, technology, and pedagogy thus combine to provide unique learning opportunities.

MSCs appear to promote the student's consistent exposure to a variety of clinical presentations and procedures, including irregular behaviors, rare diseases, and unusual incidents. The process and structure of medical education thereby become a series of progressive possibilities provided by educators and not a response to a lack of clinical accessibility. Students are more able to practice clinical skills at their own pace, repeating any process required to achieve an adequate level of security and expertise Ziv et al., 2005). The use of simulation may help get the educational and ethical message across to all those connected to the health professions: patients must be protected as much as possible and are not commodities to be used for convenience and practice. When considered based on our framework, MSCs are clear examples of FLSs.

Consideration for Future FLSs

The preceding sections sought to conceptualize and define FLSs using a new framework with operational definitions for future, learning, and spaces. We explored three types of FLSs in the context of ongoing LINKS research. In the following sections, we look beyond these examples to evaluate the strengths and opportunities of FLSs, as well as describe their limitations and outline challenges to advance the FLS agenda.

Strengths and Opportunities

FLSs offer an array of strengths and exciting opportunities, justifying their relevance to learning in the networked society. Their particular strengths are related to a broad application of pedagogies and technologies in various content areas, as part of an inherently embedded innovation mindset. These strengths provide new opportunities for experimentation, cross-fertilization of ideas, and growth in novel teaching methods.

As the LINKS examples demonstrate, FLSs allow many types of sophisticated pedagogies to be implemented, whether by supporting free-flowing activities (e.g., Connections and Maketec) or in more orchestrated and scripted designs (e.g., KCI-SC and MSC). In this way, they represent the full spectrum from spontaneous to designed technology-enhanced learning that characterizes learning in a networked society (Tabak et al., 2019). Similarly, the learning process can be supported by different technologies, such as online spaces for gathering community data (e.g., SAIL architecture), with digital tools that facilitate the development of reasoning skills (e.g., TinkerPlots), physical devices that encourage creation (e.g., Makey Makey), or video equipment used for self-reflection of acquired skills (e.g., structured feedback on interactions with virtual patients), ranging from low- to high-tech solutions. Together with content areas that span statistical learning in elementary and middle schools, medical education during undergraduate and residency programs, and interdisciplinary topics in public spaces, there is a broad range of diverse FLS designs, all of which share several core characteristics.

The diversity of FLS pedagogies and technologies provides exciting opportunities for application of innovation mindsets toward the design of learning environments in a continuously expanding endeavor. FLSs are a cornucopia of innovation—testbeds in which a wide range of pedagogies and technologies can be combined and remixed, with few restrictions. For example, an established innovative infrastructure, such as an MSC, could be leveraged to support the use of online spaces in Connections so that medical students can collaboratively share their advances in practices. FLSs thus provide a way forward for the design of educational environments. They are at the forefront of an exciting age of development and warrant all the attention they receive.

Limitations and Challenges

The excitement around FLSs is also accompanied by certain limitations and challenges. Like any innovation, they entail a learning curve whose initial stages require one to overcome major impediments. Furthermore, they often necessitate expensive infrastructure and may thus encounter various types of resistance. Creative thinking to identify solutions to these constraints and challenges is vital for FLSs to progress both efficiently and effectively.

The initial (re)design, construction, and implementation of FLSs are typically the first hurdles faced by forward-looking educators. Because creating or redesigning a learning space requires making relatively permanent changes to facilities, as well as significant financial investments, the key stakeholders need to discuss and agree on the expected outcomes. This requires the support of a community with a culture of innovation (Hod, 2017). Resistance may originate in a variety of sources, such as community members who are not convinced of the need to change, those who prefer to invest elsewhere, or even logistical problems such as lack of a feasible, dedicated space. Similarly, new learning spaces often have to coexist with more traditional ones in the same facility or building, adding complexities and challenges to the process.

Once community support and funding are obtained, however, the process of designing and constructing an FLS remains time-consuming and expensive and requires extensive planning from the earliest stages, with the involvement of numerous stakeholders, including architects, managers, and experts in construction, computer programming, and/or technology. Ideally, the learning specialists (e.g., learning scientists, teachers) and the eventual users (e.g., students) should be involved and even lead the design process; otherwise, the space has the potential to inhibit its intended purpose. The important act of bringing learning specialists to the table is not standard practice and requires a considerable amount of coordination and collaboration (Rook et al., 2015).

Even if FLSs are planned thoughtfully, broadening their usage within a community is an ongoing challenge. When plans become reality, concrete needs arise, such as designing activities that suit each target audience, solving unforeseen technological problems and allocating space use fairly. Immense efforts will have to be invested into the development of FLS professionals—an expensive and extended process often inadvertently omitted from budgets. Finally, there is no guarantee that the space will be used in the way it was intended. The complexity of FLSs entails the risk of service users with different techno- or space-centric perspectives, overly emphasizing the material features of a space and undervaluing the subtle learning process opportunities that FLSs provide. Thus, the FLSs approach must be kept alive through discussion, advancing community knowledge and continued experimentation and refinement with an eye on things to come.

All these limitations and challenges point to the need for accumulating interdisciplinary research-based insights on this topic. Unfortunately, current knowledge about future learning spaces is only beginning to take shape, as theoretical frameworks and methods are discussed at international levels (Hod & Eberle, 2017). The field can benefit from partnerships that span research and practice, particularly as technological advances develop rapidly hand-in-hand with appropriate pedagogies.

In summary, the limitations and challenges of FLSs are dynamic—evident from the outset, even before any groundwork is laid, yet extending long after the FLS is up and running. The dynamic nature of FLSs strengthens the notion that a central concept is needed to carry on the discussion of a given space's purpose, rendering it coherent and focused enough to bear a central message yet broad enough to support a wide range of activities.

Conclusions

In this chapter, we advanced the conceptualization of FLSs by discussing them within the context of three companion examples that illustrate the diversity and strength of this approach to learning. Recent research in the area has moved the discussion forward significantly (Ellis & Goodyear, 2016; Hod, 2017). Moreover, reports such as *Horizon* (Adams Becker et al., 2016) show that this is only the beginning of much more engaged and intense efforts to bring these ideas together in the international arena. Our hope is that this chapter serves to sharpen our thinking about these timely issues and that our collective efforts can set up the fertile ground for the types of empirical studies needed to advance knowledge on this emerging concept.

References

Acosta, A., & Slotta, J. D. (2013). Evaluating knowledge community curricula in secondary science using model-based design research. *Paper presented at the 17th Annual Knowledge Building Summer Institute* (pp. 1–11). Puebla, Mexico: Knowledge Society Network.

Adams Becker, S., Freeman, A., Giesinger Hall, C., Cummins, M., & Yuhnke, B. (2016). *NMC/CoSN horizon report: 2016 K-12 edition*. Austin, TX: New Media Consortium.

Barrows, H. S. (1993). An overview of the uses of standardized patients for teaching and evaluating clinical skills. AAMC. *Academic Medicine, 68*(6), 443–451.

Bielaczyc, K., Kapur, M., & Collins, A. (2013). Cultivating a community of learners in K-12 classrooms. In C. E. Hmelo-Silver, C. A. Zhang, C. K. Chan, & A. M. O'Donnell (Eds.), *International handbook of collaborative learning* (pp. 233–249). New York: Routledge.

Bishop, J. L., & Verleger, M. A. (2013). The flipped classroom: A survey of the research. *ASEE National Conference Proceedings, 30*(9), 1–18.

Brock, K. E., Cohen, H. J., Sourkes, B. M., Good, J. J., & Halamek, L. P. (2017, April 24). Training pediatric fellows in palliative care: A pilot comparison of simulation training and didactic education. *Journal of Palliative Medicine, 20*, 1074–1084. https://doi.org/10.1089/jpm.2016.0556

Brown, A. L., & Campione, J. C. (1994). Guided discovery in a community of learners. In K. McGilly (Ed.), *Classroom lessons: Integrating cognitive theory and classroom practice* (pp. 229–272). Cambridge, UK: The MIT Press.

Bransford, J. D., Brown, A. L., & Cocking, R. R. (2000). How people learn: brain, mind, experience, and school (Expanded ed.). Washington, DC: National Academy Press.

Charles, E. S., & Whittaker, C. (2015). Active learning spaces: Blending technology and orchestration. In O. Lindwall, P. Hakkinen, T. Koschmann, T. Tchounikine, & S. Ludvigsen (Eds.), *Exploring the material conditions of learning: The CSCL conference* (Vol. I, pp. 225–226). Gothenburg, Sweden: ISLS.

Chen, H., Kelly, M., Hayes, C., van Reyk, D., & Herok, G. (2016). The use of simulation as a novel experiential learning module in undergraduate science pathophysiology education. *Advances in Physiology Education, 40*(3), 335–341.

Cohen, A. G., Kitai, E., David, S. B., & Ziv, A. (2014). Standardized patient-based simulation training as a tool to improve the management of chronic disease. *Simulation in Healthcare, 9*(1), 40–47.

Cole, M., & Packer, M. (2016). Design-based intervention research as the science of the doubly artificial. *Journal of the Learning Sciences, 25*(4), 503–530.

Collins, A., & Halverson, R. (2009). *Rethinking education in the age of technology: The digital revolution and schooling in America*. New York: Teachers College Press.

Colliver, J. A., & Williams, R. G. (1993). Technical issues: Test application. AAMC. *Academic Medicine, 68*(6), 454–460.

CSSC. (2015, September 14). Cultivating smart and connected communities. Retrieved from: https://nsf.gov/news/news_summ.jsp?cntn_id=136253

Cuban, L. (2001). *Oversold and underused: Computers in the classroom*. Cambridge, MA: Harvard University Press.

Dori, Y. J., & Belcher, J. (2005). How does technology-enabled active learning affect undergraduate students' understanding of electromagnetism concepts? *Journal of the Learning Sciences, 14*(2), 243–279.

Ellis, R. A., & Goodyear, P. (2016). Models of learning space: Integrating research on space, place and learning in higher education. *Review of Education, 4*(2), 149–191.

Everett-Thomas, R., Turnbull-Horton, V., Valdes, B., Valdes, G. R., Rosen, L. F., & Birnbach, D. J. (2016). The influence of high fidelity simulation on first responders' retention of CPR knowledge. *Applied Nursing Research, 30*, 94–97.

Gal, I. (2002). Adults' statistical literacy: Meaning, components, responsibilities. *The International Statistical Review, 70*(1), 1–25.

Halverson, E. R., & Sheridan, K. (2014). The maker movement in education. *Harvard Educational Review, 84*(4), 495–504.

Hod, Y. (2017). Future learning spaces in schools: Concepts and designs from the learning sciences. *Journal of Formative Design in Learning, 1*(2), 99–109.

Hod, Y., & Ben-Zvi, D. (2014). A group psychotherapeutic perspective on transforming participation in a learning community. *Instructional Science, 42*(6), 949–970.

Hod, Y., & Ben-Zvi, D. (2015). Students negotiating and designing their collaborative learning norms: A group developmental perspective in learning communities. *Interactive Learning Environments, 23*(5), 578–594.

Hod, Y., & Ben-Zvi, D. (2018). Co-development patterns of knowledge, experience, and self in humanistic knowledge building communities. *Instructional Science, 46*(4), 593–619.

Hod, Y., Bielaczyc, K., & Ben-Zvi, D. (2018). Revisiting learning communities: Innovations in theory and practice. *Instructional Science, 46*, 489. https://doi.org/10.1007/s11251-018-9467-z

Hod, Y., Charles, E., Bielaczyc, K., Kapur, M., Acosta, A., Ben-Zvi, D., et al. (2016). Future learning spaces for learning communities: New directions and conceptual frameworks. In C. K. Looi, J. L. Polman, U. Cress, & P. Reimann (Eds.), *Transforming learning, empowering learners: The International Conference of the Learning Sciences (ICLS)* (Vol. 2, pp. 1063–1070). Singapore: International Society of the Learning Sciences.

Hod, Y., & Eberle, J. (2017). Synthesizing CSCL perspectives on the theory, methods, design, and implementation of future learning spaces. In B. K. Smith, M. Borge, E. Mercier, & K. Y. Lim (Eds.), *Making a difference: Prioritizing equity and access in CSCL, 12th international conference on Computer Supported Collaborative Learning (CSCL)* (Vol. 1, pp. 897–900). Philadelphia, PA: International Society of the Learning Sciences.

Isaacson, W. (2011). *The man in the machine*. New York: Simon & Schuster.

Iversen, O. S., Smith, R. C., Blikstein, P., Katterfeldt, E. S., & Read, J. C. (2015). Digital fabrication in education. *International Journal of Child-Computer Interaction, 5*(C), 1–2.

Kali, Y., McKenney, S., & Sagy, O. (2015). Teachers as designers of technology enhanced learning. *Instructional Science, 43*(2), 173–179.

Kidron, A., & Kali, Y. (2015). Boundary breaking for interdisciplinary learning. *Research in Learning Technology, 23*(1), 26496. https://doi.org/10.3402/rlt.v23.26496

Kidron, A., Tirosh, N., Kali, Y., & Schejter, A. (2019). Democracy, communication, and education in the twenty-first century (Chap. 7). In Y. Kali, A. Baram-Tsabari, & A. M. Schejter (Eds.), *Learning in a networked society: Spontaneous and designed technology enhanced learning communities*. Cham: Springer.

Konold, C., & Miller, C. (2011). *TinkerPlots* (Version 2.0) [Computer software]. Oakland, CA: Key Curriculum Press. http://www.keypress.com/tinkerplots

Ladyshewsky, R. (1999). Simulated patients and assessment. *Medical Teacher, 21*(3), 266–269.

Lane, J. L., Ziv, A., & Boulet, J. R. (1999). A pediatric clinical skills assessment using children as standardized patients. *Archives of Pediatrics & Adolescent Medicine, 153*(6), 637–644.

Leander, K. M., Phillips, N. C., & Taylor, K. H. (2010). The changing social spaces of learning: Mapping new mobilities. *Review of Research in Education, 34*(1), 329–394.

Lee Gordon, D., Issenberg, S. B., Gordon, M. S., LaCombe, D., McGaghie, W. C., & Petrusa, E. R. (2005). Stroke training of prehospital providers: An example of simulation-enhanced blended learning and evaluation. *Medical Teacher, 27*(2), 114–121.

Lerant, A., Bates, O. J., Holder, M. G., Orledge, J. D., Rockhold, R. W., Kyle, R., et al. (2017). Medical simulation as an instructional tool in health education: A worked example for clinical training. In J. Stefaniak (Ed.), *Advancing medical education through strategic instructional design* (pp. 101–132). Hershey, PA: IGI Global.

Lewin, K. (1952). *Field theory in social science: Selected theoretical papers by Kurt Lewin.* London: Tavistock.

Lui, M., & Slotta, J. D. (2014). Immersive simulations for smart classrooms: Exploring evolutionary concepts in secondary science. *Technology, Pedagogy and Education, 23*(1), 57–80.

Makar, K., Bakker, A., & Ben-Zvi, D. (2011). The reasoning behind informal statistical inference. *Mathematical Thinking and Learning, 13*(1), 152–173.

Manor, H., & Ben-Zvi, D. (2015). Students' articulations of uncertainty in informally exploring sampling distributions. In A. Zieffler & E. Fry (Eds.), *Reasoning about uncertainty: Learning and teaching informal inferential reasoning* (pp. 57–94). Minneapolis, MN: Catalyst Press.

Najafi, H., & Slotta, J. D. (2010). Analyzing equality of participation in collaborative inquiry: Toward a knowledge community. In K. Gomez, L. Lyons, & J. Radinsky (Eds.), *Learning in the disciplines: Proceedings of the 9th International Conference of the Learning Sciences (ICLS 2010)* (Vol. 1, pp. 960–967). Chicago: International Society of the Learning Sciences.

New York Times Magazine. (2013, September 15). *The education issue: The all-out, all-ages overhaul of school is happening now.* New York: New York Times Magazine.

Oblinger, D., & Lippincott, J. K. (2006). *Learning Spaces.* Brockport Bookshelf. http://digitalcommons.brockport.edu/bookshelf/78. Retrieved 17 July 2016.

Papert, S. (1980). *Mindstorms: Children, computers, and powerful ideas.* New York: Basic Books.

Peppler, K., Halverson, E., & Kafai, Y. B. (Eds.). (2016). *Makeology: Makerspaces as learning environments* (Vol. 1). New York: Routledge.

Peters, V. L., & Slotta, J. D. (2010). Scaffolding knowledge communities in the classroom: New opportunities in the Web 2.0 era. In M. J. Jacobson & P. Reimann (Eds.), *Designs for learning environments of the future: International perspectives from the learning sciences* (pp. 205–232). Secaucus, NJ: Springer.

Qayumi, K., Pachev, G., Zheng, B., Ziv, A., Koval, V., Badiei, S., et al. (2014). Status of simulation in health care education: An international survey. *Advances in Medical Education and Practice, 28*(5), 457–467.

Qi, J., & Buechley, L. (2014). Sketching in circuits: Designing and building electronics on paper. In *Proceedings of the SIGCHI conference on human factors in computing systems* (pp. 1713–1722). Toronto: ACM.

Resnick, M. (2006). Computer as paintbrush: Technology, play, and the creative society. In D. Singer, R. Golikoff, & K. Hirsh-Pasek (Eds.), *Play = learning: How play motivates and enhances children's cognitive and social-emotional growth.* Oxford: Oxford University Press.

Resnick, M., Maloney, J., Monroy-Hernandez, A., Rusk, N., Eastmond, E., Brennan, K., et al. (2009). Scratch: Programming for all. *Communications of the ACM, 52*(11), 60–67.

Resnick, M., & Rosenbaum, E. (2013). Designing for tinkerability. In M. Honey & D. E. Kanter (Eds.), *Design, make, play: Growing the next generation of STEM innovators* (pp. 163–181). New York/Abingdon (UK): Routledge.

Rogoff, B., Turkanis, C. G., & Bartlett, L. (2001). *Learning together: Children and adults in a school community.* London: Oxford University Press.

Rook, M. M., Choi, K., & McDonald, S. P. (2015). Learning theory expertise in the design of learning spaces: Who needs a seat at the table? *Journal of Learning Spaces, 4*(1), 1–13.

Sawyer, R. K. (2014). The future of learning: Grounding educational innovation in the learning sciences. In K. R. Sawyer (Ed.), *The Cambridge handbook of the learning sciences* (2nd ed., pp. 726–746). New York: Cambridge University Press.

Scardamalia, M., & Bereiter, C. (1994). Computer support for knowledge-building communities. *Journal of the Learning Sciences, 3*(3), 265–283.

Semel, S. F., & Sadovnik, A. R. (2008). The contemporary small-school movement: Lessons from the history of progressive education. *Teachers College Record, 110*(9), 1744–1771.

Shahabudin, S. H., Almashoor, S. H., Edariah, A. B., & Khairuddin, Y. (1994). Assessing the competence of general practitioners in diagnosing generalized anxiety disorder using standardized patients. *Medical Education, 28*(5), 432–440.

Slotta, J. D. (2010). Evolving the classrooms of the future: The interplay of pedagogy, technology and community. In K. Mäkitalo-Siegl, F. Kaplan, J. Zottmann, & F. Fischer (Eds.), *Classroom of the future: Orchestrating collaborative spaces* (pp. 215–242). Rotterdam: Sense.

Slotta, J. D., & Najafi, H. (2012). Supporting collaborative knowledge construction with Web 2.0 technologies. In N. Lavigne (Ed.), *Emerging technologies for the classroom: A learning sciences perspective* (pp. 93–112). New York: Springer.

Slotta, J. D., Tissenbaum, M., & Lui, M. (2013). Orchestrating of complex inquiry: Three roles for learning analytics in a smart classroom infrastructure. In *Proceedings of the third international conference on learning analytics and knowledge* (pp. 270–274). Paris: ACM.

Sutherland, R., & Fischer, F. (2014). Future learning spaces: Design, collaboration, knowledge, assessment, teachers, technology and the radical past. *Technology, Pedagogy and Education, 23*(1), 1–5.

Tabak, I., Ben-Zvi, D., & Kali, Y. (2019). Introduction: Technology-enhanced learning communities on a continuum between the spontaneous and the designed (Chap. 2). In Y. Kali, A. Baram-Tsabari, & A. M. Schejter (Eds.), *Learning in a networked society: Spontaneous and designed technology enhanced learning communities*. Cham: Springer.

Temple, P. (2007). *Learning spaces for the 21st century: A review of the literature*. York, UK: Higher Education Academy.

Temple, P. (2008). Learning spaces in higher education: An under-researched topic. *London Review of Education, 6*(3), 229–241.

Weller, J. M. (2004). Simulation in undergraduate medical education: Bridging the gap between theory and practice. *Medical Education, 38*(1), 32–38.

Wild, C. J., & Pfannkuch, M. (1999). Statistical thinking in empirical enquiry. *International Statistics Review, 67*(3), 223–265.

Woodward, C. A., & Gliva-McConvey, G. (1995). The effect of simulating on standardized patients. *Academic Medicine, 70*(5), 418–420.

Zhang, J., Chen, M.-H., Tao, D., Sun, Y., Lee, J., & Judson, D. (2015). Fostering sustained knowledge building through metadiscourse aided by the Idea Thread Mapper. In N. Rummel, M. Kapur, M. Nathan, & S. Puntambekar (Eds.), *Exploring the material conditions of learning: The CSCL conference* (Vol. II). Gothenburg, Sweden: ISLS.

Ziv, A., Ben-David, S., & Ziv, M. (2005). Simulation based medical education: An opportunity to learn from errors. *Medical Teacher, 27*(3), 193–199.

Chapter 12
ICTs in Religious Communities: Communal and Domestic Integration of New Media Among Jewish Ultra-Orthodoxy in Israel

Nakhi Mishol-Shauli, Malka Shacham, and Oren Golan

Abstract In the past two decades, information and communication technologies (ICTs) have been deeply instilled into contemporary life. While domestication theory has focused on ICTs integration into modern families, its absorption into religious and bounded communities begs further scrutiny. While offering meaningful gains and opportunities, ICTs raise concerns by such communities for their potential rupture of cultural boundaries. Focusing on Israeli ultra-Orthodox Jewry, we inquire how grassroots socializing agents negotiate ICT usage within informal educational spheres for adults and children. Analyzing interviews and children's drawings, findings demonstrate that while ICTs are proscribed from formal ultra-Orthodox education and mass media, the home constitutes the epicenter of computer education, and web-journalism becomes a valued information outlet for adults. Thus, the study elucidates how traditionally inclined societies infuse new technologies, which subsequently leads to a negotiation process between long-established leadership and emergent socializing agents concerning these societies' opted level of insularity.

Keywords Domestication theory · Religion · Culture · Orthodox Judaism · Socialization · Informal education · Web journalism · Drawing-analysis

The integration of information and communication technologies (ICTs) into everyday life, including work, education, leisure, and overall personal management, has become a hallmark of modern societies since the 1990s. Considering this

---

N. Mishol-Shauli, M. Shacham, and O. Golan have contributed equally to this work.

N. Mishol-Shauli (✉) · O. Golan
University of Haifa, Faculty of Education, Haifa, Israel

M. Shacham
Department of Communication Studies, Ben-Gurion University of the Negev,
Beer Sheva, Israel
e-mail: shachamm@bgu.ac.il

© Springer Nature Switzerland AG 2019
Y. Kali et al. (eds.), *Learning In a Networked Society*, Computer-Supported
Collaborative Learning Series 17, https://doi.org/10.1007/978-3-030-14610-8_12

development, British scholars (Horst, 2012; Silverstone & Haddon, 1996) established the domestication approach to technologies, contending that technological integration processes within modern families and communities are not technology-deterministic but are largely affected by cultural and social factors. While these scholars explored modern-Western populations' legitimation of new media, further nuanced investigation of ICT integration among communities that manifest strong ideological, cultural, or religious objections to modern practice is required. Despite overall resistance, an apparent boost in Internet and new media use by members of such communities has been recorded and described by researchers representing various disciplines (Anderson, 2003; Busch, 2010; Horowitz, 2001; Lagerkvist, 2008, 2010). This study discusses the patterns and implications of ICTs' domestication and use in Israel's ultra-Orthodox (Haredi) community.

While ICT use has been banned at Haredi formal educational settings, it has been largely integrated into informal home and workplace settings. Considering the apprehension expressed by religious communities—especially enclaved and marginalized groups—regarding ICTs, as well as the opportunities they embody for these sectors, we question *how socializing agents in Haredi society negotiate ICT use within informal educational spheres.*

Haredi education has often been observed through its formal settings (Perry-Hazan, 2013; Spiegel, 2011; Stadler, 2009). By contrast, we contend that an exploration of the domestication processes affected by families and online journalists can shed light on the impact of spontaneous or semi-structured learning environments on religious and bounded communities. Tabak, Ben-Zvi, and Kali (2019) structure reciprocal relations as a continuum between spontaneous-ambient and designed learning. They contend that underlying interactions, knowledge constructions, social organizations, and power structures are preplanned in designed learning environments but occur spontaneously in those of the ambient variety. In the present study, we consider semi-structured learning to be nurtured by principles derived from both ends of the continuum and well observed through the legitimation of information and its permeation of bounded societies via ICT engagement.

We focus on two key fields of engagement with ICTs: (1) an emergent mass communication venue, namely, that of online journalism within the Haredi community, perceived as a type of informal education for adults that specializes in culture, norms, and identity (Dobbert, 1975; Eisenhart, 1995; McQuail, 2010; Polkinghorne, 1991; Scribner & Cole, 1973), and (2) everyday engagements with personal computers by family members, including children, within the Haredi household. While household socialization of children is a widespread educational practice, we believe that the religious underpinnings attributed to modern and technological artifacts have not been accorded sufficient attention in contemporary research.

As engagement with ICTs increases, parents and educators often raise concerns over chaotic consumption of technologies in modern societies, lamenting the abundance and ubiquity of new media technologies to which youngsters are exposed from an early age and noting that such developments may disrupt their socialization and erode their value system (Clark, 2013; Selwyn, 2016). Although much of this discourse may be attributed to overall moral panic regarding technology (Buckingham, 2006; Cohen, 2011; Ogburn, 1957), we suggest that Western-dominated scholarship in this field could benefit from the study of responses to new media among traditional groups, thereby acquiring an innovative viewpoint for reflection on new media integration in both modern and traditional societies.

Furthermore, as ICT literacy is often viewed as a pathway to social mobility (Hargittai, 2001), we suggest that understanding its integration among marginalized and religious communities can be conducive to bridging digital and economic divides. In the past decade, the Israeli Haredi population has displayed a tendency to grant some legitimation toward gainful employment and amend its overall conception thereof, explaining the integration of vocational training, including courses pertaining to hi-tech industries (especially among women) that promise relatively well-paid positions. Although technology remains a marginal source of employment among Haredim to date, there are some indications of increased interest in such occupations (Kahoonay, 2014; Lupu, 2005). Consequently, a greater understanding of both familial and broader ICT integration processes could shed light on these trends and highlight considerations regarding their adoption by educators, policymakers, and other stakeholders.

Literature Review

Israeli Ultra-Orthodoxy, New Media, and Modernity

This study explores ultra-Orthodox Judaism as an example of an insular community that has experienced continuous and complex negotiations over Internet use. It bears noting that "Orthodoxy" does not refer to a single cohesive unit but rather serves as a terminological umbrella for Jewish communities that aspire toward a traditional lifestyle (cf. Don-Yihya, 2005) governed by *Halakha* (Jewish religious law). All groups falling under this heading share many customs and beliefs, but divergent histories, migrations, and mores have resulted in subgroups with a fair share of unique practices and authority structures. Orthodoxy's chief sectors are Religious Zionists, devout *Sephardim*, Lithuanians (*Mitnagdim*), and *Hasidim*. Because of their traditional interpretation of Halakha and their leaders' staunch rejection of modern values (Stadler, 2009), the last three groups are often referred to as ultra-Orthodox (Haredi). These sectors further divide into subdenominational groups, each with its own rabbinic leadership, symbols, and mores.

Since the 1990s, Haredi leaders have been warning their flocks of potential "landmines along the information highway" (Herman, 1995). They portray the Internet as a gateway to sin (Campbell, 2010) that also entices devotees to violate communal norms. In their view, it is liable to spawn a breach of the religious-secular divide that will ultimately stamp out ultra-Orthodox piety. As such, they regard the web as antithetical to their basic ideals and goals, calling it "the seat of the scornful"

(Psalms 1:1) and declaring it to be devoid of religious value (El-Or, 1994). Free access to uncontrolled secular and licentious content is thus perceived as highly problematic (Tsarfaty & Blais, 2002). Consequently, Haredi authorities have invested considerable efforts in restricting the Internet to professional use only (Campbell & Golan, 2011; Cohen, 2012).

These remonstrations are not limited to secular platforms. In 2009, several prominent communal rabbis issued a ban against ultra-Orthodox websites that were then beginning to dominate the community's public discourse. This edict may be viewed as a rearguard action on the part of the Haredi elite to retain their ascendant status by delegitimizing emerging outlets of communal information.

It is worth noting that despite rabbinic objections to web activities, media tools aimed at eliminating morally objectionable material continued to flourish and Internet use persisted within the Haredi community. Filtering technologies gained popularity and became well accepted among ultra-Orthodox surfers, allaying the concerns of many devotees and thereby laying the foundations for an upswing in Haredi Internet use.

In 2012, a rabbinic injunction against smartphones was circulated among ultra-Orthodox *yeshivot* (Talmudic seminaries), bolstered by iPhone-smashing ceremonies and public edicts against using handheld devices to access Facebook, Twitter, and other sources of unfiltered content.[1] Concurrently, in May of that year, tens of thousands of Haredim rallied at New York's Citi Field stadium to protest Jewish use of the Internet, thus expressing a global objection to the medium and to its adverse effects.

Studies indicated that about 40% of Israeli Haredim attest to use of the Internet and 53% of Haredi households had personal computers at home, and this number has been steady for the last couple of years (Israel Central Bureau of Statistics (ICBS), 2012, 2016). Computer ownership, however, does not attest to the extent and character of its use or the rate of Internet integration (Hargittai & Hinnant, 2008). Indeed, according to a research focusing specifically on web use (Dror & Saar, 2012), only 24% of Haredim used the web every day, as compared with 75% of secular Israelis.

At the same time, a substantive boost in Internet and new media use was noted among Haredim, as more and more members of the community, men and women alike, seek to avail themselves of their vocational, practical, communal, and other benefits. These attempts are hampered, however, by a lack of the requisite social, cultural, and linguistic skills. About half the Haredi community consists of young people under 18. Haredi men study for an average of 14.2 years, but their schools are completely separate from the mainstream state educational system (and are consequently termed *unofficial*) and focus almost exclusively on religious teachings (Ichilov, 2009; Perry-Hazan, 2013). Only 10.6% of Haredim pass official high school matriculation examinations. Yet despite these impediments, they display a growing inclination toward modern practices, including use of digital media, a

---

[1] See http://www.jdn.co.il/news/46076

growing rate of participation in the labor force, and a rise in academic and vocational training. At present, 19% of the Haredi population obtains academic degrees (Malach, Choshen, & Cahaner, 2016). Furthermore, notwithstanding the Haredi ideal of a pious lifestyle centered on Torah study rather than on vocational commitment (cf. Friedman, 1991), the percentage of working Haredim is on the rise (men, 56%; women, 76%, according to The Knesset Research and Information Center—see Moshe, 2016).

Scholarly interest in the Haredi approach to the Internet has grown since the beginning of this millennium, especially with regard to the online habits of ultra-Orthodox communities (Caplan, 2001; Horowitz, 2001). In a way, the Internet offers a window into social interactions within the traditionally closed Haredi enclave culture (Tsarfaty & Blais, 2002) whose insularity is evident in the community's discourse and policy concerning the perils of modernity (Lev-On & Neriya-Ben Shahar, 2011). Taking such fears into account, ultra-Orthodox web surfers and designers must justify their use of the Internet (Barzilai-Nahon & Barzilai, 2005; Livio & Tenenboim-Weinblatt, 2007). Furthermore, rabbis are attempting to influence online norms by demanding that the plethora of information be filtered, the bastion of Halakha preserved, and their long-standing authority respected.

A handful of scholars have reemphasized the observation that most Haredim are interested in upholding traditional values yet may use the Internet to experiment with communal self-reflection. For example, forum discussions were viewed as a social niche that enables group members to work out personal problems, advance women's rights, and occasionally criticize the public conduct of rabbis (Baumel-Schwartz, 2009; Lev-On & Neriya-Ben Shahar, 2011).

Thus, in examining relations between ultra-Orthodox websites and the community, earlier scholarship primarily focused on Haredi perceptions of technology and Internet use. In comparison, later research accentuates questions of social control, sources of authority, and communal boundaries regarding ICT's integration processes and their agents.

Communal Integration of ICTs: The Case of Online Journalism

Over the past two decades, widespread use of the Internet has disrupted long-standing modes of knowledge sharing (Gillmor, 2006; Hargittai, 2001; Horst, Herr-Stephenson, & Robinson, 2010; Rafaeli & Sudweeks, 1997; Shirky, 2008). For example, the rise of new media journalism has shaken the foundations of traditional reporting not only on a global scale and in mainstream societies but locally and within religious-cum-insular communities as well (Benkler, 2012; Hargreaves, 2014; Zimmerman-Umble, 1996). The case at hand demonstrates a sharp increase in the number of Haredi news websites since 2005. Although not free of controversy, these websites provided the Haredi public with new modes of information sharing and may be viewed as informal manifestations of education.

In educational research, scholars often mention mass media as an example of informal education directed at a given community, although they tend to refrain from elaborating on the mechanisms involved (Bekerman, Burbules, & Silberman-Keller, 2006; Bhola, 1983; Hamadache, 1991; Livingstone, 2006). In this context, we draw on the anthropological legacy of cultural transmission and acquisition, highlighting the manner in which culture is acquired incidentally through daily practices and interactions, as contrasted with formal schooling (Dobbert, 1975; Eisenhart, 1995; Polkinghorne, 1991; Scribner & Cole, 1973). We also cite communication studies describing mass media as a crucial transmitter of shared cultural identities, practices, and norms (Carey, 2009; McQuail, 2010).[2] The dissemination of cultural ideals and the gradual changes taking place therein are promoted by fundamental types of socialization, such as formal schooling and the family.

The Haredi Family, Socialization, and ICTs

While formal schooling clearly impacts the socialization of children and youth, the family and home environment remain a primary source of education (Carter & McGoldrick, 1988; Minuchin, 2009). Carter and McGoldrick (2005) emphasize the lifespan of the family unit, stressing the cultural effects at each of its stages. They discuss how families define and tailor tasks to meet these stages, with each culture assigning differential weight to life transformations, intergenerational relationships, definitions of familial commitments, and parental and childcare expectations. Furthermore, they examine the norms and values of various cultures, adding that each nurtures forms of domestic stress. Consequently, they suggest that the pressure applied by cultural agents juxtaposes life transformation stress (in each of its phases), compounding day-to-day conflicts and hardship. Such emphasis on cultural effects is particularly relevant to the Haredi insular-religious community.

In his assessment of ICT use and the family, Hagen (2007) claims that many parents evaluate their parental authority according to their ability to control the quantity and quality of media content exposure. Media exposure rules implemented in a domestic setting may be indicative of moral judgments, ideological values, and the role of media in everyday family life, as parents attempt to assert their authority by controlling exposure.

In the past, fundamentalist clergy maintained a uniform public sphere through strict oversight of their community's discourse. The Jewish ultra-Orthodox daily printed press, like that of other bounded and fundamental communities, diverges considerably from the Western-liberal journalistic ethos in that it makes no pretense of objectivity, enjoys only limited autonomy, and accords precedence to supervision, including censorship, over immediacy (Amin, 2001; Brown, 2013; Deuze, 2005; Hafez, 2002; Lagerkvist, 2008; Pasti, 2005)—a situation well known to and

---

[2] For an analysis of journalism (and online self-expression) as an informal type of education, see Mishol-Shauli (2015).

even expected by Haredi readers (Neriya-Ben Shahar, 2012; Hayerushalmi, 1998; Michelson, 1990).

The characteristics of new media ICTs, namely, abundance, interactivity, mobility, and multimediality (Schejter & Tirosh, 2016), raise unique challenges concerning the ability to apply content control, thereby according such media an inherent openness unmatched by traditional media technologies. Moreover, computer use in earning one's livelihood has become ubiquitous, and working from home via the web makes it feasible for religious men, and especially women, to improve their income without compromising their modesty. These developments initially led the Haredi rabbinic leadership to ban computers and the Internet outright—an edict subsequently perceived as "a decree that the public cannot fulfill" (Horowitz, 2001). Haredim then sought ways of circumventing the rabbinic prohibition (Campbell & Golan, 2011; Cohen, 2012; Tsarfaty & Blais, 2002). Once partial use of technology becomes permitted, the community members and leadership must confront blurred boundary situations. Tensions arise among different interpretations and meanings, and interim solutions abound, some of them unique. Various studies focused on the trials and tribulations of Haredim as they face inclusion of web connectivity in computers and smartphones (Campbell, 2010 ; Rashi, 2012), encounter gender issues (Lev-On & Neriya-Ben Shahar, 2011; Stadler, 2009), and experience integration of the web in community life and its resulting adaptation to suit Haredi norms (Campbell & Golan, 2011; Golan, 2015; Tsarfaty & Blais, 2002).

Methodology

As we focus on the communal and domestic spheres to study negotiation of ICTs by socializing agents among Haredi society, we draw on two sets of methodological designs that were applied to the Haredi community. The first consists of an in-depth study of four families, with a focus on children's views of ICTs, entailing thorough acquaintance with the domestic environment, in-depth interviews with parents, and discussions with their children, who were asked to draw one picture showing their immediate family and the place the computer occupies in its space, as well as another portraying the family they dream of establishing in their adult lives and the place of computers therein. Drawings have a well-established legacy in psychology and art education but are relatively new and largely underused as a sociological tool (cf. Leonard, 2006). The basic premise is their status as a common form of expression for children. Furthermore, as Nieuwenhuys (1996) argues, they may prove more effective in bringing out the complexities of the children's experiences than approaches and research techniques customarily applied to adults (e.g., focus group discussions, questionnaires). Drawing may provide children with confidence and allow them some control over the research process. This, in turn, helps temper the ever-present adult-child power imbalance, thereby conforming with contemporary trends in the sociology of childhood that underscore the position of children as subjects rather than mere objects of research (Corsaro, 1997). As such, they may promote exploration of the children's *Weltanschauung*, particularly within bounded religious groups.

The second set of methodological tools examines online Haredi journalism, primarily by conducting 25 in-depth, semi-structured interviews with Haredim fulfilling various online press roles (i.e., editors, reporters, entrepreneurs, and photographers) at ten key Haredi news sites (out of 15 recognized news outlets). Participants were selected by the snowballing technique that serves as an effective research strategy in bounded communities (Lee, 1993; Stadler, 2009). Parallel snowballs were launched to account for the extensive heterogeneity of the relevant news sites (and the Haredi community at large). Other secondary information sources consisted of a public WhatsApp group published at the *Behadrei Haredim* website homepage between 2015 and 2016, various conferences and journalists' reports published in both the secular and Haredi press in recent years, and constant monitoring of the news sites themselves. Findings were analyzed by two researchers and disagreements resolved through dialogue to ensure high credibility (Corbin & Strauss, 2014; Olesen, Droes, Hatton, Chico, & Schatzman, 1994). Finally, key Haredi informants were consulted to clarify the meanings of certain problematic findings.

Findings

One particularly striking theme recurring among Haredi agents of socialization who confront ICTs was their common view of the web as a necessary evil or disruption. For example, the founder and senior editor of an online news outlet stated:

> The Haredi public suffered grave damage from the Internet: divorces, cheating couples, etc. I lament that for years, no one in our sector took up the gauntlet. Had someone done so on day one, we might have been able to route the public to a kosher, protected Internet, the type we are now aware of. The web is here to stay. There's no way back. No human force can stop this thing. What you can do is cope. You can provide tools to manage it. You can protect yourself. You can establish feasible rules.

The following project manager and mother of six assigns more neutrality to the web by equating it to another domestic appliance as a metaphor, demonstrating that she perceives the web as having uses, risks, and common norms that should be maintained:

> A computer is no different from a food processor: Even though it's a useful appliance that anyone can operate according to their own skills, in terms of safety, it is better for parents to use it (and not children). Also, you might get along without it, but it is easier to get certain tasks done with it. Finally, your guests don't have to see you use it.

Despite the prevailing negative attitude toward ICTs, particularly when impressionable youngsters are involved, some reluctant acceptance may be discerned within various spheres of Haredi society, particularly in the communal and domestic realms.

Community

Through its collective orientation, the community plays a pivotal role in individual life choices and largely dominates multiple life domains. Nevertheless, it is virtually impossible for most Haredim to follow the strictest interpretation of Halakha in every case. Despite multiple forms of social control, the individual is left with multiple fields of discretion to decide where and when to adopt a more permissive exegesis. For many, introducing ICTs into one's household is a private affair that is either concealed from or played down among neighbors and other community members. For example, one Haredi mother and journalist said:

Question: How did the community respond when you began using a computer at home?
Answer: I don't talk about it. I am careful to mention my job as little as possible and especially not to mention my web connection.

Similarly, a senior online reporter underscored his apprehension over revealing his Internet-related profession work to his children's school staff:

Even today... I hide my job. I mean that my young daughters, enrolled at a prestigious ultra-Orthodox school, know that dad works for a news website, but if they told that to their teacher, I'd be petrified.

Although not all parents respond similarly, many share fear of exposure. As noted above, the community's formal education system is viewed as a key agent of socialization and is highly regarded by its members and clergy. Highlighting its centrality, a young online editor of a Haredi news site describes ICT integration into schools as a major breach of the all-encompassing Haredi resistance to web use:

The ban against the Internet has been violated. I can tell you what its ultimate breaking point was: The obsolescence of fax machines, the last bastion of Haredi conservativeness. Our formal schools represent the ideal: They produce new Haredim and perpetuate the Haredi way of life. They must remain pure. Once they become compromised, it's all over.

Q: And they were compromised?
A: Yes, they were. You now need E-mail to work with state establishments. Just one crack in the wall and that's it, it's here.

A project manager and mother of six describes the joint efforts of community and parents to distance children from unwanted content:

I pretty much draw my own lines, but I allow my children no web access whatsoever. There is no way I can trust their discretion. That is why we installed a very strict content filter at home. Each and every movie, book, or song my children consume will be supervised and authorized. The school determines what is considered off limits, such as unauthorized cellular phones or portable music players. The children are allowed to subscribe only to the approved library [of our Hasidic group]. We only subscribe to one Hasidic weekly magazine. Our radio is not accessible to the children to prevent their inadvertent exposure to inappropriate content.

The project manager describes congruence and cooperation between the home and various communal establishments in protecting the young from forbidden information: parents and the sectarian/Hasidic school, library, and newspaper. Participants' remarks also confirm that wariness of new media has not allayed fears of old media dangers.

Communal supervision and occasional intervention are commonplace in Haredi society. From selecting schools and matrimony to minor lifestyle choices, Haredi members often seek guidance from the community and its institutions. Individuals rely on communal mores to guide their everyday lives and keep them on the right path, as described by a Haredi woman journalist:

> If I am ever able to remove the computer from my home, it will be thanks to the community's concern. Even though no one ever said anything to me directly, this is the overall atmosphere, for which I am thankful.

After confessing to having breached rabbinic counsel by admitting a computer to her home, this woman expresses gratitude nonetheless for the hovering presence of a pious community. By contrast, a project manager belonging to a different Haredi sect describes a more permissive atmosphere:

> **Q:** Did you sense any communal resentment after beginning to use the computer?
> **A:** We feared more than what actually happened. I guess that the limitations we set were enough for them. We feared that school rules might prohibit possession of a computer at home, but everything turned out fine.

The project manager's account reflects sub-denominational differences with regard to ICTs: While some groups demand that children have no access to computers, others allow some use, as long as it is filtered and supervised. Many Haredim use commercial ICT filtering services as a means of legitimizing their use of the Internet. In Israel, such services are highly developed and are often tailored to fit the local religious landscape (cf. Deutsch, 2009; Rashi, 2012; Rosenberg 2015; Rosenthal & Ribak, 2015). Such filters are considered mandatory in Haredi homes with web access and are also very common at workplaces and on personal smartphones. Accordingly, a senior reporter for an online newspaper reiterates previously noted anti-web sentiments but takes comfort in the partial solution afforded by filtering:

> I would not like to have my children exposed to the web. I wish they could grow up like I did, but you have to face reality. There is nothing we can do. It's [the web] already here. I believe that in 10 to 20 years, it will be in every home. For the time being, we use filters. There are various software companies, some more strict, some less so. If our public can adjust to that way of thinking, everything will be fine.

This journalist's position reflects a pragmatic stance toward ICTs. The proliferation of ICTs among the Haredi population is the key to his livelihood and affects his influence on the community.

We indicated above that journalism may be viewed as a type of informal education for adults on a communal level, affirming the community's boundaries by imparting its culture, norms, and identity. Haredi web journalism is in a precarious position, as it constitutes a new, secondary, and less supervised authority for the interpretation of reality, asserting said authority via ICTs that are themselves contested a priori. Most journalists in this medium are devout Haredim themselves, seeking equilibrium within their community by defining their niche as "guardians of the Haredi community in the web era"—a crucial role indeed. As previous citations demonstrate, these journalists strive to demonstrate their support of conservative Haredi views on modernity and pride themselves on customizing their websites to offer the mainstream Haredi crowd an opportunity to obtain online news without risking exposure to unsuitable content, as one such reporter states explicitly:

> The website exists as an alternative for the Haredi user. Haredim are using the web for news. That's a fact. If they didn't have our dedicated site, they would be browsing secular sites, potentially exposing themselves to negative influence.

Under these circumstances, tacit acquiescence has been obtained from the clergy, although official approval is not expected any time soon. A young female reporter describes the situation as follows:

> The rabbis reject the Internet in toto.
>
> **Q:** It's a sort of gray area, right?
> **A:** It's unclear. I'll tell you why… Every rabbi has a spokesman. They have really bought into the system; it has already turned into part of everyday politics. The public relations team, the functionaries, whoever is in their orbit, will call up our writer to say: 'Listen, the Rabbi is going to be here and there; photograph him, do [this or that] for him.'

While the Haredi communal sphere dominates multiple life domains, its overall orientation toward ICTs is ambiguous, manifesting conflicting orientations. On the one hand, it reflects overt repulsion by the Internet and its perceived evils, particularly with regard to younger generations, but on the other hand, it expresses an explicit demand for filtered use. Furthermore, various forms of communal legitimation have been identified, including filtering practices and tacit acceptance by relevant religious leaders. Finally, we note the rise of Haredi online journalists, who act as informal educators by instilling communal norms and fortifying community boundaries. The communal approach toward ICTs forms a key starting point for the Haredi public, but its ambiguity affords some degree of interpretive discretion that is manifest in another life sphere, as demonstrated below.

Domestic

As child rearing is a key means for transmitting the Haredi creed (cf. Heilman, 1992), it is hardly surprising that ICT use issues are of major concern to Haredi parents and other adults in the community. Discussions with parents, even those who professed ICT use for vocational and other purposes, often reflected concern over disruption of children's progress along the pathways toward becoming virtuous Haredi adults. Dismay regarding youngsters' exposure to the web and the excessive significance that children ascribe to computers was common to all participants. These sentiments were also echoed in parents' initial bewilderment over discussing computer use with children, fearing that the issues raised thereby might challenge their educational values.

Despite powerful apprehension regarding ICT use in the domestic sphere, personal computers with Internet access are integrated in Haredi households, necessitating the adoption of several strategies to balance tensions between Haredi parental concerns and modern inclinations. Such strategies are further explored in analysis of remarks by Haredi parents who were asked their opinions of web use at home, as well as in their children's drawings, reflecting the youngsters' perspective on domestic ICT use.

Domestic avoidance: limiting children's ICT access While ICT use is not uncommon in the ultra-Orthodox world, many Haredim avoid its inclusion in the household, while others commit to its limited use in shared spaces in which children are present. Age limits are imposed by prohibiting children's access to mobile phones and restricting web use to parents' workplaces or personal cellular devices.[3] Children's ICT use thus takes place primarily within sheltered and supervised household surroundings, if at all. The head of one leading online news outlet indicated that he has no computer at home but maintains several smartphones and three cutting-edge computers at his office. Although it does not entirely proscribe Internet use in everyday life, this strategy could be viewed as an extreme approach toward ICT use. Other participants proved more lax in practice. One tech-savvy editor discussed his integration of ICTs at home, emphasizing the stringent supervisory measures employed:

> Here [at the office], I have an open web. That's a journalist's job. This is the newsroom, so everything is open here. At home, none of us has open internet. When I'm home, I browse only via [filtering software].

A senior editor echoes the same approach, underscoring its popularity:

> **Q:** Is it still common to browse from work and from cellular devices and less so from home?
>
> **A:** Oh, it's common all right. Many of our (website) visitors browse only via smartphones, or from the office, not wanting web access at home, not wanting the kids to see the internet. But that's OK. I can understand that. We don't necessarily want our kids to browse the web for everything they do.

In his account, the editor sums up the two approaches: banning ICTs at home or allowing them in only under the strictest of supervision, i.e., applying various web filters that monitor and block access to undesired sites, images, and messages and adopting various additional restrictive strategies.

Setting parental boundaries: restraining domestic web use Haredi families that have introduced Internet access in their households are increasingly adopting grassroots practices to limit its use. Participants shared a set of temporal and spatial control strategies, reflecting their educational approach and their adherence to community ethics and moral codes. Computer use time for children was limited to about 40 minutes daily (with some additional time allowed on vacation days). Computers are usually situated in public domestic locations, i.e., in or near the living room, offering only rare opportunities for private use. Consequently, children consider Internet use a familial practice, as depicted in Fig. 12.1.

---

[3] Cellular phone use among Haredim has been explored in past studies (Campbell, 2010; Rashi, 2012), mostly underscoring the unique aspects of "kosher phones" that block Internet use. Notwithstanding their significance in the American and Israeli ultra-Orthodox communities, smartphone use is increasing among Haredim (often alongside that of kosher phones), although Internet and app use are screened stringently (cf. Golan, 2015).

Fig. 12.1 Computer in shared family setting (artist: girl, 13)

Fig. 12.2 Hierarchical approach toward household ICT use (artist: boy, 13)

This conception of the family as collective consumers of ICTs recurs in Fig. 12.2 which also reflects the family's hierarchical structure insofar as computer access is concerned:

While children may accept their lack of privacy as part of living in a large family (perhaps implied in the above portrayal of smiling participants), some parents have expressed their yearning for increased privacy during ICT use. One woman journalist was disappointed because the constant presence of children nearby limited her opportunities to browse various online information sources for professional purposes:

Q: How much privacy do you and other family members who use the computer have while working?

A: I would love to have more privacy, but to my discontent, the children do hover around and cannot avoid exposure.

This strategy leads parents to either limit or entirely prohibit their children's ICT use. The children's drawings further reflect how this strategy is applied in establishing parental control over Internet exposure while offering the opportunity for a positive collective experience at the same time. Although these conditions provide parents with a safe haven for supervision of their children's domestic sources of socialization, such efforts have to be balanced against parents' professional and personal knowledge needs. Furthermore, before allowing children to use the web, parents weigh the personal and educational advantages thereby entailed against communal and religious codes of conduct.

"Safe surfing": web literacy and parental intervention Many Haredi families have web-connected personal computers in their households with strict filtering services. Nevertheless, their children's encounters with the web often entail personal parental guidance as well. Parents not only position computers in the more public areas of the house but also vet content and personally supervise their children's computer use. Through this proactive strategy, adults' computer/Internet skills and overall outlooks frame a shared browsing experience with their children. Haredi society's more web-literate adults implement their specialized knowledge for educational reflection. A senior online news editor in his early 30s describes the need for parental involvement:

> Yes, there is web filtering, but still I supervise. I have a kid who knows computers. He enjoys playing and such, but I'm strict—I might even say very, very strict—because I know what's out there on the web.

The news editor underscores his own web competence as a reason for supervising his children's browsing experiences, claiming that he "knows what's out there" and sees himself as more careful (implying that less web-literate Haredi parents might not be as wary).

In a similar vein, a web journalist and new media entrepreneur who is highly skilled in software design reiterated the limitations of web filters, demanding that unaware parents be informed accordingly:

> **Q:** You claim that web filters have technical faults. What do you think Haredim should do about the web?
>
> **A:** My method is to cope. Get a good web connection and handle it. I know that filtering companies have fixed most of their bugs and are now offering fairly decent options. When consumers are aware of the deficiencies, however, they say: 'All right, I understand. I'll use the filter but I'll still supervise my kids' browsing because I know how easy it is to hack the system.' An informed consumer is thus a much smarter consumer.

Even when acknowledging filtering software as a valid option, this new media expert considers the importance of technical awareness in "protecting the young." By describing system limitations, he joins the previously cited project manager and young senior editor in a recurring theme reminiscent of the journalists' role as "guardians of Haredim in the Internet age," in that they use their web literacy and virtuosity to stress the importance of supervision beyond the levels mandated by community norms.

Discussion and Conclusions

Past scholarship has devoted attention to the study of marginalized groups and their a priori disadvantages in a modern technological age. In this context, researchers mostly underscored and developed the concept of *digital divide* to refer to uneven distribution of Internet access and asymmetric use thereof (Hargittai & Hinnant, 2008; Mesch & Talmud, 2010). By contrast, rather than addressing the "haves and have nots," Internet access, or even questions of skill differentials, this study focuses on a cultural impediment to ICTs' integration, namely, religious observance and maintenance of communal boundaries. Earlier studies did refer to voluntary avoidance of technology by various groups, such as the Amish (Zimmerman-Umble, 1996) or Haredim (Campbell, 2010; Campbell & Golan, 2011; Horowitz, 2001; Tsarfaty & Blais, 2002). The present study extends discussion of cultural barriers to ICT use by analyzing their integration through the prism of informal learning spheres. Following the legacy of informal education and the domestication of technologies (Bekerman, Burbules, & Silberman-Keller, 2006; Kahane, 1997; Mansell & Silverstone, 1996) and the ongoing study of technology-enhanced designed and spontaneous learning environments (Kali et al. 2015; Tabak et al., 2019), this study revealed the manner in which web journalists and parents struggle with questions of ICT integration and eventually find ways of incorporating these technologies within the community, as long as certain protective measures are taken.

Given the risks involved in the autonomy of individual use of ICTs (or networked individualism, see Rainie & Wellman, 2012), the ultra-Orthodox community has developed alternative agents of ICT integration. Moreover, in the communal sphere, our findings display an emergent balance between traditional lifestyles and a more modern habitus. We observe continuing glorification of the pious Haredi couple model, in which the husband is a full-time Torah scholar and his wife is employed in a semi-professional occupation, such as teaching (Friedman, 1991; Heilman, 1992; Zicherman, 2014), but we also uncovered markers indicating that alternative lifestyles appear to be gaining acceptance and legitimacy in the ultra-Orthodox community. These markers draw on other aspects of modernity, such as academic professionalization (for both genders) or the integration of modern modes of leisure (e.g., browsing Haredi news sites). We believe the adoption of these lifestyles may be facilitated by the integration of new media technologies.

This approach to an emergent Haredi habitus can be demonstrated in new media journalists' accounts of their target audiences. As noted earlier, many claimed that full-time Torah scholars are not their target audience, as such people are not even supposed to know that the web exists, "and that is how it should be." Evidently, acknowledging the benefits the web provides for many ultra-Orthodox users leads to the prevailing attitude of "if you can't beat it, customize it" (Friedman, 1991; Golan & Campbell, 2015; Sheleg, 2000; Zicherman, 2014). In this sense, Haredi web agents (such as online journalists) act as nonformal cultural transmitters that curtail knowledge and orient it toward tailored dissemination to a bounded and traditionally inclined public.

Fig. 12.3 Computer
absent in "future image of
family and computer"
drawing (artist: boy, 9)

In line with Haredi reservations toward ICTs, parents and educators exert efforts to marginalize ICT use in the domestic sphere. To illustrate, a child who draws a picture of his future without including a computer, even when asked to do so (i.e., Fig. 12.3), is considered an educational success by his parents.

As ICTs are almost entirely proscribed in the formal Haredi education system and other communal educational venues (e.g. library, youth centers), the home constitutes the epicenter of computer experiences for children. This bolsters the domestic sphere as a nonformal educational environment. This environment ordinarily relies on ambient learning but is transformed into a designed setting nonetheless through the lay efforts of parents rather than those of professional/institutional agencies (e.g., schools, MOOCs). In formal schooling establishments, the curriculum is prescribed and supervised by rabbinic authorities, whereas computer-based learning requires parental agency. Furthermore, findings suggest that under such circumstances, both men and women often gain prominence as informal computer literacy instructors despite traditional gendered division of educational labor among Haredi families. Future research could shed light on this relatively recent development in domestic education.

Concluding Policy Notes: Ultra-Orthodoxy and the Digital Gap

The contrast between low ICT use and the apparent shared desire of Haredim and Israeli authorities to reap the benefits of the web renders the Haredi digital divide a crucial problem for the Haredi community and the Israeli economy alike. We hope that understanding their choices and their reasons for use and domestication of such technologies can facilitate the bridging of this gap.

This study may suggest two possible lines of action for policymakers seeking to support assimilation of networked learning environments and helping Haredim overcome the digital gap they created between themselves and Israeli society without fearing for their culture's corruption. The first calls for acknowledging the impact of grassroots technology advocates from within the community, helping them gain their leadership's confirmation that ICTs can be used in ways that conform with Haredi core values according to their most widely accepted interpretations. The second could incorporate a voluntary tagging system (resembling *Kashrut* certification or, alternately, the American film rating system) that would enable users, by use of filtering software, to vet their opted content. This vetting system will allow users to personalize accessibility to public information in accord with their sensibilities. Hence, it would enable personal or parental discretion that could eventually permit use of a broader range of websites and still conform with religious users' values.

Nowadays, as some communities manifest formidable ideological, cultural, or religious objections to ICTs, they are pressed to adopt them due to economic and social circumstances and find pathways to domesticate these technologies. Our findings highlight a gradual breakdown of authority which well corresponds with the aforementioned inherent properties of ICT use. Following the suggested lines of action, policymakers' extended attention to bottom-up advocates, as well as top-down efforts of tagging websites, may enable concerned parties to assume informed viewing decisions. Elevating this awareness can be conducive to promoting the integration of apprehensive populations to modern practices. This includes involving fundamentalist variants in the Middle East and Europe in modern society, as well as fostering ICT integration for rural communities of developing countries. In this manner, these often marginalized communities can better hone their information literacy, thus enabling them to identify and acquire new sources of information to address present and future aspirations. Furthermore, not only does it pave the way to extended use of information outlets by these populations but can also foster civil society groups involved in education, media advocacy, and the such, all of which can be seen as conducive for a vibrant and democratic polity among reclusive groups.

Bibliography

Amin, H. (2001). Mass media in the Arab states between diversification and stagnation: An overview. In K. Hafez (Ed.), *Mass media, politics, and society in the Middle East* (pp. 23–41). New York: Hampton Press.

Anderson, J. W. (2003). New media, new publics: Reconfiguring the public sphere of Islam. *Social Research: An International Quarterly, 70*(3), 887–906.

Barzilai-Nahon, K., & Barzilai, G. (2005). Cultured technology: The internet and religious fundamentalism. *The Information Society, 21*(1), 25–40.

Baumel-Schwartz, J. T. (2009). Frum surfing: Orthodox Jewish women's internet forums as a historical and cultural phenomenon. *Journal of Jewish Identities, 2*(1), 1–30.

Bekerman, Z., Burbules, N. C., & Silberman-Keller, D. (2006). *Learning in places: The informal education reader*. New York: Peter Lang.

Benkler, Y. (2012). A free irresponsible press: Wikileaks and the battle over the soul of the networked Fourth Estate. *Harvard Civil Rights-Civil Liberties Law Review, 47*(1), 311–397.

Bhola, H. S. (1983). Non-formal education in perspective. *Prospects, 13*(1), 45–53.

Brown, L. M. (2013). *Breaking (Amish) News: Citizen Journalism in the Digital Age.* Wooster College independent study thesis.

Buckingham, D. (2006). Is there a digital generation? In D. Buckingham & R. Willett (Eds.), *Digital generations: Children, young people, and new media* (pp. 1–13). London: Lawrence Erlbaum.

Busch, L. (2010). To "come to a correct understanding of Buddhism": A case study on spiritualising technology, religious authority, and the boundaries of orthodoxy and identity in a Buddhist web forum. *New Media & Society, 13*(1), 58–74.

Campbell, H. (2010). *When religion meets new media.* New York: Routledge.

Campbell, H. A., & Golan, O. (2011). Creating digital enclaves: Negotiation of the internet among bounded religious communities. *Media, Culture & Society, 33*(5), 709–724.

Caplan, K. (2001). The media in Haredi society in Israel. *Kesher, 30,* 18–30. [Hebrew].

Carey, J. W. (2009). *Communication as culture: Essays on media and society.* London: Routledge.

Carter, B. E., & McGoldrick, M. E. (1988). *The changing family life cycle: A framework for family therapy.* New York: Gardner Press.

Carter, B. E., & McGoldrick, M. E. (2005). *The expanded family life cycle: Individual, family and social perspectives* (3rd ed.). Boston: Pearson.

Clark, L. S. (2013). *The parent app: Understanding families in the digital age.* Oxford: Oxford University Press.

Cohen, S. (2011). *Folk devils and moral panics.* London/New York: Routledge.

Cohen, Y. (2012). *God, Jews and the media: Religion and Israel's media.* London: Routledge.

Corbin, J., & Strauss, A. (2014). *Basics of qualitative research: Techniques and procedures for developing grounded theory.* London: Sage.

Corsaro, W. A. (1997). *The sociology of childhood.* Thousand Oaks, CA: Pine Forge Press.

Deutsch, N. (2009). The forbidden fork, the cell phone holocaust, and other Haredi encounters with technology. *Contemporary Jewry, 29*(1), 3–19.

Deuze, M. (2005). What is journalism? Professional identity and ideology of journalists reconsidered. *Journalism, 6*(4), 442–464.

Dobbert, M. L. (1975). Another route to a general theory of cultural transmission: A systems model. *Council on Anthropology and Education Quarterly, 6*(2), 22–26.

Don-Yihya, E. (2005). Orthodox Jewry in Israel and in North America. *Israel Studies, 10*(1), 157–187.

Dror, Y., & Saar, G. (2012). *Israelis in the digital age 2012.* Rishon LeZion, Israel: College of Management Academic Studies.

Eisenhart, M. (1995). The fax, the jazz player, and the self-story teller: How do people organize culture? *Anthropology & Education Quarterly, 26*(1), 3–26.

El-Or, T. (1994). *Educated and ignorant: Ultraorthodox Jewish women and their world.* Boulder, CO: Lynne Rienner Publishers.

Friedman, M. (1991). *The Haredi (ultra-orthodox) society: Sources, trends and processes.* Jerusalem: Jerusalem Institute for Israel Studies. http://haredisociety.org/uploads/files/46498206618101313-haredcom.pdf

Gillmor, D. (2006). *We the media.* Beijing: O'Reilly.

Golan, O. (2015). Legitimation of new media and community building among Jewish denominations in the US. In H. Campbell (Ed.), *Digital Judaism: Jewish negotiations with digital media and culture* (pp. 125–144). New York: Routledge.

Golan, O., & Campbell, H.A. (2015). Strategic management of religious websites: The case of Israel's orthodox communities. *Journal of Computer-Mediated Communication, 20*(4), 467–486.

Hagen, I. (2007). 'We can't just sit the whole day watching TV' Negotiations concerning media use among youngsters and their parents. *Young, 15*(4), 369–393.

Hafez, K. (2002). Journalism Ethics Revisited: A Comparison of Ethics Codes in Europe, North Africa, the Middle East, and Muslim Asia. *Political Communication, 19*(2), 225–250.

Hamadache, A. (1991). Non-formal education. *Prospects, 21*(1), 109–124.

Hargittai, E. (2001). Second-level digital divide: Mapping differences in people's online skills. *First Monday, 7*(4). http://ojs-prod-lib.cc.uic.edu/ojs/index.php/fm/article/view/942/864

Hargittai, E., & Hinnant, A. (2008). Digital inequality differences in young adults' use of the internet. *Communication Research, 35*(5), 602–621.

Hargreaves, I. (2014). *Journalism: A very short introduction*. Oxford: Oxford University Press.

Hayerushalmi, Y. L. (1998). Ultra-Orthodox Journalism: Information approved Kosher by Rabbinical Authorities. In Y. Landres (Ed.), *Yearbook of the Association of Tel-Aviv Journalists* 1998 (pp. 227–239) (Hebrew).

Heilman, S. C. (1992). *Defenders of the faith: Inside ultra-Orthodox Jewry*. Oakland, CA: University of California Press.

Herman, Y. (1995). Landmines along the information highway. *Jewish Observer, 2*, 21–27.

Horowitz, N. (2001). The Haredim and the internet. *Kivunum Hadashim, 3*, 7–30. [Hebrew].

Horst, H. A. (2012). New media technologies in everyday life. In H. A. Horst & D. Miller (Eds.), *Digital anthropology* (pp. 61–79). London/New York: Berg.

Horst, H. A., Herr-Stephenson, B., & Robinson, L. (2010). Media ecologies. In M. Ito et al. (Eds.), *Hanging out, messing around, and geeking out: Kids living and learning with new media* (pp. 32–41). Cambridge, MA: MIT Press.

Ichilov, O. (2009). *The retreat from public education: Global and Israeli perspectives*. New York: Springer.

Israel Central Bureau of Statistics. (2012). The 2010 Central Bureau of Statistic's Social Poll – Tables 32 to 37. 1477. Central Bureau of Statistics Israel. http://www.cbs.gov.il/webpub/pub/text_page.html?publ=6&CYear=2010&CMonth=1. Retrieved on October 10, 2017. [Hebrew].

Israel Central Bureau of Statistics. (2016). Annual data 2016 – diagrams – society and welfare. ISSN 0081-4679. Central Bureau of Statistics Israel. http://www.cbs.gov.il/reader/shnaton/templ_shnaton_diag_e.html?num_tab=07_05&CYear=2016 . Retrieved on October 10, 2017. [Hebrew].

Kali, Y., Tabak, I., Ben-Zvi, D., Kidron, A., Amzaleg, M., Baram-Tsabari, A., Barzilai, S., Brami, U., Duek, O., Elias, N., Kent, C., Laslo, E., Levy, K.S., Rafaeli, S., Tal, T., Weiss, P.L., Hoadley, C., and Kirschner, P. (2015). Technology-enhanced learning communities on a continuum between ambient to designed: What can we learn by synthesizing multiple research perspectives? In Linkwall, O., Hakkinen, P., Koschmenn, T., Tchounikine, P., & Ludvigsen, S. (Eds.). Exploring the material conditions of learning: Proceedings of the computer supported collaborative learning (CSCL) conference, Gothenburg 2015. 2, 615–622.

Kahane, R. (1997). *The origins of postmodern youth: Informal youth movements in a comparative perspective*. Berlin: Walter de Gruyter.

Kahoonay, S. (2014). *Integration of the Haredi sector in Israel's workforce—Status and implications*. Jerusalem: Knesset Research and Information Center. https://www.knesset.gov.il/mmm/data/pdf/m00898.pdf. [Hebrew].

Lagerkvist, J. (2008). Online journalism in China: Constrained by politics, spirited by public nationalism. In C. Paterson & D. Domingo (Eds.), *Making online news: The ethnography of new media production* (pp. 127–141). New York: Peter Lang.

Lagerkvist, J. (2010). *After the internet, before democracy: Competing norms in Chinese media and society*. Bern: Peter Lang.

Lee, R. M. (1993). *Doing research on sensitive topics*. Newbury Park, CA: Sage.

Leonard, M. (2006). Children's drawings as a methodological tool: Reflections on the eleven plus system in Northern Ireland. *Irish Journal of Sociology, 15*(2), 52–66.

Lev-On, A., & Neriya-Ben Shahar, R. (2011). A forum of their own: Views about the internet among ultra-Orthodox Jewish women who browse designated closed fora. *First Monday, 16*(4).

Livingstone, D. W. (2006). Informal learning: Conceptual distinctions and preliminary findings. *Counterpoints, 249*, 203–227.

Livio, O., & Tenenboim-Weinblatt, K. (2007). Discursive legitimation of a controversial technology: Ultra-Orthodox Jewish women in Israel and the internet. *The Communication Review, 10*(1), 29–56.

Lupu, J. (2005). *New directions in Haredi society: Vocational training and academic studies*. Floersheimer Institute for Policy Studies. http://fips.huji.ac.il/publications/new-directions-haredi-society-vocational-training-and-academic-studies

Malach, G., Choshen, M., & Cahaner, L. (2016). *Yearbook of ultra-Orthodox society in Israel*. Jerusalem: Israel Democracy Institute. https://www.idi.org.il/books/3872. [Hebrew].

McQuail, D. (2010). *McQuail's mass communication theory*. London: Sage.

Mesch, G., & Talmud, I. (2010). *Wired youth: The social world of adolescence in the information age*. London: Routledge.

Michelson, M. (1990). Ultra-orthodox journalism in Israel. Kesher, 8, 10–22 (Hebrew).

Minuchin, S. (2009). *Families and family therapy*. Cambridge, MA: Harvard University Press.

Mishol-Shauli, N. (2015). Fundamentalist Knowledge Brokers: New Media Journalists as Agents of Informal Education among the ultra-Orthodox Community in Israel (Master's Dissertation). Haifa: University of Haifa. (Hebrew).

Moshe, N. (2016). *Data on Haredi employment*. Jerusalem: The Knesset Research and Information Center. https://www.knesset.gov.il/mmm/data/pdf/m03737.pdf. [Hebrew].

Nieuwenhuys, O. (1996). Action research with street children: A role for street educators. *PLA Notes, 25*, 52–55.

Neriya-Ben Shahar, R. (2012). "Some outlooks are not our own, but if I happen to see one I'll look at it from time to time": Self-definition of Haredi (Ultra-Orthodox) women according to patterns of exposure to the Haredi press. In K. Caplan and N. Stadler (Eds.). *From survival to consolidation: Changes in Israeli Haredi society and its scholarly study* (pp. 137–161). Jerusalem: Van Leer Jerusalem Institute (Hebrew)

Ogburn, W. F. (1957). Cultural lag as theory. *Sociology and Social Research, 41*(3), 167–174.

Olesen, V., Droes, N., Hatton, D., Chico, N., & Schatzman, L. (1994). Analyzing together: Recollections of a team approach. In A. Bryman & R. G. Burgess (Eds.), *Analyzing qualitative data* (pp. 111–128). London: Routledge.

Pasti, S. (2005). Two generations of contemporary Russian journalists. *European Journal of Communication, 20*(1), 89–115.

Perry-Hazan, L. (2013). *Ultra-orthodox education in Israel: Law, culture and politics*. Jerusalem: Nevo and Magnes.

Polkinghorne, D. E. (1991). Narrative and self-concept. *Journal of Narrative and Life History, 1*(2), 135–153.

Rainie, L., & Wellman, B. (2012). *Networked: the new social operating system*. Cambridge, MA: MIT UP.

Rafaeli, S., & Sudweeks, F. (1997). Networked interactivity. *Journal of computer-mediated communication, 2*(4) https://doi.org/10.1111/j.1083-6101.1997.tb00201.x

Rashi, T. (2012). The kosher cell phone in ultra-Orthodox society. In H. A. Campbell (Ed.), *Digital religion: Understanding religious practice in new media worlds* (pp. 173–181). New York: Routledge.

Rosenthal, M., & Ribak, R. (2015). On pomegranates and etrogs: Internet filters as practices of media ambivalence among National Religious Jews in Israel. In H. A. Campbell (Ed.), *Digital Judaism: Jewish negotiations with digital media and culture* (pp. 145–160). New York: Routledge.

Rosenberg, H. (2015). Cellular Use in Israel 2014. In R. Mann and A. Lev-On (eds.) *Annual report: the media in Israel 2014: agendas, uses and trends* (Chapter 6). Ariel: Institute for the Study of New Media, Politics and Society.

Schejter, A., & Tirosh, N. (2016). Audio-visual regulation transition in Israel: A view from within. *International Journal of Digital Television, 7*(1), 39–63. https://doi.org/10.1386/jdtv.7.1.39_1

Scribner, S., & Cole, M. (1973). Cognitive consequences of formal and informal education. *Science, 182*(4112), 553–559.

Selwyn, N. (2016). *Is technology good for education?* Hoboken, NJ: John Wiley & Sons.

Sheleg, Y. (2000). *The new religious Jews: Recent developments among observant Jews in Israel*. Jerusalem: Keter. [Hebrew].

Shirky, C. (2008). Here comes everybody: The Power of organizing without Organizations. UK: Penguin

Silverstone, R., & Haddon, L. (1996). Design and the domestication of information and communication technologies: Technical change and everyday life. In R. Mansell & R. Silverstone (Eds.), *Communication by design: The politics of information and communication technologies* (pp. 44–74). Oxford: Oxford University Press.

Spiegel, E. (2011). *Talmud Torah is equivalent to all. The ultra-Orthodox (Haredi) educational system for boys in Jerusalem.* Jerusalem: Jerusalem Institute for Israel Studies. http://jerusaleminstitute.org.il/.upload/spiegel.pdf. [Hebrew].

Stadler, N. (2009). *Yeshiva fundamentalism: Piety, gender, and resistance in the ultra-Orthodox World.* New York: NYU Press.

Tabak, I., Ben-Zvi, D., & Kali, Y. (2019). Introduction: Technology-enhanced learning communities on a continuum between spontaneous and designed (Chap. 2). In Y. Kali, A. Baram-Tsabari, & A. M. Schejter (Eds.), *Learning in a networked society: Spontaneous and designed technology enhanced learning communities.* Cham: Springer.

Tsarfaty, O., & Blais, D. (2002). Haredi society and digital media. *Kesher, 32,* 47–55. [Hebrew].

Zicherman, H. (2014). *Black blue-white—A journey into Haredi society in Israel.* Tel Aviv: Yedioth Ahronoth Press and Chemed Books (Hebrew).

Zimmerman-Umble, D. (1996). *Holding the line.* Baltimore: Johns Hopkins University Press.

Part IV
Commentary and Future Directions

Chapter 13
Learning Inside and Between Networks: How Network Perspective Determines Research Topics and Methods

Ulrike Cress

Abstract This chapter provides a reflection about the relation between networks, learning, and society. What does it mean if we consequently consider learning under a network approach and if we are aware that not just people constitute networks, but also knowledge artifacts and other informational resources are parts of networks. The chapter shows that schools and universities are themselves networks. They organize learning but they, at the same time, co-exist (and sometimes compete) with many other informal learning networks. Schooling, informational environments, and society cannot be treated as separate entities. Schools and universities cannot be conceptualized as closed systems. They have to be related to each other. The chapter shows – with regard to each of the 12 preceding book chapters – how this network perspective opens the learning sciences for new research topics, asks for new design requirements, and requests to expand our research methods.

Keywords Network perspective · The World Wide Web · Knowledge artifacts · Informational resources · Formal and informal learning networks · Networked society · Social systems · Learning in a networked society

Living in a Networked Society

The 12 chapters of this book provide an impressive overview of research at LINKS—an acronym that describes the topic and program of The Israeli Centers of Research Excellence very concisely: Learning In a NetworKed Society. Even if the term *network* is mathematical in origin, focus on the constructs of *nodes* and *edges* is evident in a broader context as well. Each node can be activated. The presence and strength of edges between the nodes allow for activity to spread across the network and create patterns of activation. Nodes affect their neighbors and are affected by them, forming a lively and highly vibrant structure.

U. Cress (✉)
Leibniz-Institut für Wissensmedien, Tübingen, Germany
e-mail: u.cress@iwm-tuebingen.de

© Springer Nature Switzerland AG 2019
Y. Kali et al. (eds.), *Learning In a Networked Society*, Computer-Supported
Collaborative Learning Series 17, https://doi.org/10.1007/978-3-030-14610-8_13

Describing society as "networked" presents a highly fluid and democratic view of society. Each individual is a node and all nodes influence the network. The individuals are not autonomous, however; they are embedded within an existing structure of links and relations. It is not just the individuals that define the activity of the whole network but also the networks that influence the activity of its members.

Society, however, does not constitute a single network; rather, it represents a network of networks. Each individual may belong not only to one but to many networks, each invoking very different influences. The private network of one's family, professional network of colleagues, or the local community are all networks that exist parallel to one another. They comprise different people and have different structures as well as special norms and rules. As such, networks are not only structural and neutral components that offer some kind of communication channels. On the contrary—networks are *social* structures. Each network develops its special rules and norms that members are expected to follow.

In the end, it is the network that shapes the content and code of communication, either explicitly or implicitly. In this sense, networks are *social systems* (Luhmann, 1995). They operate according to specific rules and are self-referential and autopoietic (capable of reproducing and maintaining themselves). As social systems, they apply their own norms and influence their members' communication and behavior. Members need to conform to these norms to avoid conflicts. Social systems shape the behavior of their members. They are conservative in nature, as they seek to maintain their own procedures and regulations. Mostly, however, they also aim to impact more people and reach more members by applying outreach strategies.

The norms of different systems differ. Those we face in our families are very different from the ones encountered in our professional lives or in the political parties we join. All networks evoke different behavioral patterns among their members. That is, we are not simply stable individuals who behave consistently in different contexts. Rather, in different networks, we behave very differently and may even *think* differently. For example, people's behavior may differ radically when acting as members of their religious communities and in professional life, respectively. These multiple memberships are likely to provoke intraindividual conflicts because we do not perceive the networks in which we are embedded as neutral. We may identify more with some networks than with others, and any of the networks may become an integral part of ourselves. We may even cease to identify with some of them and attempt to leave them. Consequently, different networks have different values for us—they influence not only our behavior but also ourselves.

All in all, the network perspective is complex and highly dynamic, describing the heterogeneous forces that influence an individual. It is obvious that social networks are not just a matter of activation of nodes (individuals) realized through the strength of edges (relations between individuals). Rather, they are a complex combination of social influences, norms, and roles that require mutual fulfilment of expectations.

Networks in a Digital World

It is no coincidence then that the topic of networked society has become so compelling and prominent in the digital age. The World Wide Web (hereinafter "the Web") is a global network, perhaps the densest and largest network ever. It connects people all over the world and provides access to every conceivable kind of content. Unlike all previous communication channels, the Web now not only makes direct, one-to-one contact possible but also large-scale, group-to-group communication. Through the Web, everyone is linked to everyone. Distances between people are reduced to virtually one link and one click. Information flows immediately, with no perceptible time lag; messages can become viral and induce rapid, unexpected dynamics. Even strong personal relations can be supported by the Web.

When we consider the World Wide Web, it also becomes obvious that networks consist of much more than individuals. Objects are parts of networks as well. In his actor-network theory, Bruno Latour (1986) states that there is no structural difference between people and objects. Both can be agents in a network and both can exert influence on other agents. Objects (e.g., cultural artifacts, tools, books, or even abstract content) are not just neutral entities that can be used in any possible way. The opposite is the case: Each object has specific behavioral affordances, exerts influences on other actors, and points them to yet another set of objects or people. Not only an individual but also an object can attract one's attention and specify what other objects this person will explore next.

A newspaper article may influence a reader to be more or less open to the arguments of opposing groups, and a tweet may provoke other tweets. Seeing a hammer and nail will make us aware of all the pictures we could hang in our surroundings. Every single object we encounter can evoke influence and urge us to act. Whenever we surf the Web and search for information, we become part of a network of links, contents, and people. All are nodes in this network and impact us as agents. Every Google search is a journey through sources with different affordances and opportunities. The decision about which links to follow and which to overlook results not only from our individual needs but also from the affordances and attractions that the resources offer (Pirolli, 2007). They guide our browsing behavior, influence our emotions, and color our thinking and self-description. Being affected by such a network means changing one's position. It means learning!

Learning in a Networked Society

If we consider society as a network or even as a network of different networks—and if we also realize that people and objects in our networks can influence us as actors—we may ask: How does this network perspective change our view on learning? What does "learning" mean in a networked society?

The first and perhaps most important conclusion is to view educational systems as networks. Schools and universities are networks that organize learning. But at the same time, these formal learning environments coexist with numerous informal networks that are often more attractive than the formal ones. In these other (nonschool) networks, learning takes place informally and spontaneously. Every interpersonal communication or even Google search can be a type of a learning experience. Schools and formal learning environments are nothing but special cases of (designed) networks that compete with the learning taking place in many other networks to which people belong.

A second conclusion declares that formal education systems, such as schools or universities, cannot be conceptualized as closed systems, i.e., islands that shield learners from the influences of the other networks. One may no longer assume that learning primarily occurs in designed environments and that only then—as a second stage—are the results thereof transferred to other settings. If schools want to be effective, they need to bridge learning experiences within and outside of school.

In the learning sciences, there has already been a long and intensive debate about what constitutes learning. Educators are beginning to realize that "learning" needs to be considered from a broad perspective and described as much more than acquisition of knowledge. Learning occurs through cultural practices and through participation in knowledge communities. Lave and Wenger (1991), for example, describe how people learn in communities of practice and how they start as legitimate observers and over time become more and more central to the practice. They show how the growing experience changes the learners' role in the community as well as their self-conception. In time, people feel they are part of the community's inner circle and begin to be considered as experts.

Accordingly, Sfard (1998) posits that the "knowledge acquisition metaphor" for learning has to be replaced by the "participation metaphor," in which it is not abstract "knowledge" that is at the center of the learning sciences but rather "practices." Furthermore, Paavola and Hakkarainen (2005) added the "knowledge creation metaphor." Their concept of *trialogical learning* (Paavola & Hakkarainen, 2014) suggests that in addition to people and contents, artifacts are a critical construct in learning. Knowledge becomes manifested in jointly used artifacts through which interindividual knowledge can also develop.

All these current approaches in the learning sciences confirm what the network perspective renders salient: If knowledge, expertise, or practices are relevant in a network in any way, then people's participation in any of the networks in which they are involved influences their knowledge, expertise, and practices. Being part of a network induces learning processes. People (spontaneously) learn in all networks of which they are members, even if there are no clear learning procedures, teachers, or defined curriculum.

The network perspective thus raises a series of intriguing questions: How can we design learning spaces that seize the multiple opportunities that networked society offers? How can we reduce the problems that go along with this magnitude and complexity of structures and content? How can we design spaces that suit a democratic society? How can we ensure that people's daily experiences flow into the learning process they experience in designed learning environments? How should we deal with conflicts that arise when formal learning environments oppose what is learned in informal environments and vice versa?

The primary message of this book is that schooling and society can no longer be treated as separate entities but as related to one another. This brings new research topics into focus.

Learning in a Networked Society: Relevant Research Topics

The chapters of this book deal with topics that come into focus if we consider learning as a process that takes place within and between networks, applying to spontaneous and designed learning alike.

Perhaps the most obvious question is how people are influenced by the possibilities offered by the Web—the biggest network we have. The chapter by Baram-Tsabari and Schejter (2018) addresses these options, together with the barriers involved in using new media for learning. The authors ask if people can in fact make use of the unlimited channels, the abundance of content, and the growing interactivity, mobility, and multimediality of the Web. At first glance, the technical environment appears to provide enormous opportunities for finding information and exchanging it with others. From a societal perspective as well, the Web may offer major opportunities for participation and democratization. Empirical evidence, however, turns out to be rather alarming, indicating that the Web may well be what Baram-Tsabari and Schejter describe as a double-edged sword. People are overwhelmed by the abundance of information; they are unable to make adequate use of the variability of human capital behind the channels. The magnitude of channels, filters, and their algorithms does not necessarily widen people's horizons. In fact, we are becoming increasingly aware that they may even narrow human perspectives. People become trapped in echo chambers (Del Vicario et al., 2016) or filter bubbles (Pariser, 2011); they join groups polarized by opposing opinions. Divergent networks display little integration of different opinions, but rather opt for separation.

In considering the Web as a network, we also find much evidence that not only people but also objects are actors. A Google search, for example, is not merely use of a neutral searching tool; it influences its users as well. Research shows that weak information searchers mostly consider only the first or second search result and neglect others. Web links exert a similar effect: One affordance of hypertextuality is that people just click around, and their searching and browsing behavior often does not lead to an integrated mental representation of the content. People may get lost, especially those with little prior knowledge of the content or with low metacognitive skills. In brief, the Web might give everybody access to everything and might allow all people to make use of all the knowledge in the world, but in fact, it is only a minority of users who can really use it optimally.

Ostensibly, the Web might maximize freedom and self-determination for its users, but practically speaking, we are aware that it is full of affordances and forces that impact users negatively as well. Ultimately, it might not bring about democratic decision-making and deliberation but may instead exacerbate inequalities and the digital divide. To ensure that people make good use of the Web, we have to teach them to be competent information searchers, communicators, information providers, and information evaluators. These are formidable tasks for formal education to achieve in the digital age.

Kidron, Tirosh, Kali, and Schejter (2018) focus on these aims. The authors claim that contemporary media can provide an opportunity for democracy and education by supporting collaboration. Contemporary media can stimulate active participation, enable free movement of voices, and support equal and just expression of personal opinions and viewpoints. This is the special potential of social media. But to ensure the presence of these fundamentals of democracy, we require certain meta-level principles for the design of learning processes (Kali & Linn, 2008). These basic tenets generate situations of productive collaboration and collective meaning-making: Students should have access to content to become informed about a topic; they should experience the possibility of learning from each other and possess the tools required to render their thinking visible. These issues are fully in accordance with the trialogical approach to learning that is the basis of the knowledge creation metaphor (Paavola & Hakkarainen, 2005, 2014). Digital media can support each of these processes in many ways.

But networks provide much more than communication channels and accessible content. They are social systems, with different modes of operation, that even influence how their members feel, think, and behave. There are interesting situations in which people are members of different systems that have opposing views, living in two parallel but opposing worlds. The chapter by Shauli, Shacham, and Golan (2018) describes such a case: Ultra-orthodox Jewish communities that have a negative attitude toward digital technology and perceive the Web as antithetical to their basic ideals. They call it "the seat of the scornful" and declare it to be devoid of religious value. There are ultra-orthodox websites that warn against the inappropriate and nonreligious content available on the Web. Yet outside their own community, such people live in a world in which they are expected to use media in their professional lives, while their children confront media at school. Such situations not only engender a conflict between (religious and nonreligious) networks but also lead to interpersonal conflicts. How should one behave in situations in which the use of technology is expected, but religious norms do not allow it? Which rules do parents forgo when allowing/restricting use of media for their children? Can people link the different networks to which they belong? The chapter describes how people respond differently to this conflict. Some try to separate the two networks and accept that there are different rules for different parts of their lives, and others try to conform to religious norms at all times, while still others state that it is only a matter of time before positions come closer and the Jewish community changes its view.

In describing such conflicts, the chapter demonstrates vividly that media are essential parts of our networks but are used and valued very differentially in each.

Ultra-orthodox Jews are just one extreme example, but the processes the chapter describes are the same for all networks. Processes within one network do not stop at its border but influence other networks. When people belong to different networks, they may span boundaries. Friction may result from their dual membership and position between the networks, leading either to convergence or to further separation. Indeed, as members of networks, we develop and possibly change our attitudes and behavior. Hence, individuals and networks influence each other (Cress & Kimmerle, 2008, 2017).

Designing Learning for a Networked Society: Relevant Research Topics

Explaining development and learning processes in currently existing networks is one issue, and planning for learning is another. A key issue discussed in this book is classrooms of the future—"smart classrooms." This topic, addressed by Hod et al. (2018), should allow inquiry within the learning space, together with connection to the multiple knowledge communities outside it. The classroom of the future should link to networks outside school. Makerspaces may be seen as prototypes for that kind of linkage. They provide space for individual work and learning but also encourage informational social interaction and peer learning through providing shared working spaces. In these spaces, users can access, explore, and use craft materials and electronic components. These tools and materials may act as agents that attract learners' interest by linking them to other people and the tasks they are performing. They should allow for multiple uses and initiate collaboration. In a makerspace, different people work on different tasks but can see what others are doing. The shared room and tools serve as mediators for knowledge transfer and collaboration. While the Web is simply a virtual location for digital objects, makerspaces offer real and tangible artifacts and constitute real, physical spaces.

Learning spaces are changing, as are learning and teaching tools. The chapter by Har-Carmel, Olsher, Elkin-Koren, and Yerushalmy (2018) notes that the nature of textbooks is changing as well. They are becoming e-textbooks that are interactive and connected to other learning objects. They may be able to "observe" a learner's behavior and performance and adapt to it accordingly, providing instruction tailored to individual needs and performance levels. But they may also become dynamic. As open content (OER), they may be expanded, changed, reused, or remixed by other learners and teachers. Whereas the "old" textbooks were centralized and quality controlled, the new ones may represent the product of a collaborative enterprise. These new features have many consequences—legal issues regarding copyrights or privacy, as well as instructional matters concerning personalization of learning.

An interesting topic that could become part of future learning scenarios is *citizen science* (see chapter by Sagy et al., 2018). By bridging between schools and science, between novices and experts, it provides an outstanding example of spanning boundaries. Citizen science is a kind of democratic movement. It allows "normal citizens" (as scientific novices) to participate in (real) science. They can become involved in observations, in collecting or categorizing artifacts or in other scientific activities. There are citizen science projects in which people collect insects or flowers, report observations of wild pigs or foxes in a city, or categorize proteins in a game-like environment. Together with professionals, citizen scientists share a platform to which they contribute their data and render it accessible for further analyses. In the optimal case, novices can take over scientific activities and become part of the scientist network. They participate legitimately in the community of scientists and are allowed to deliver their "own" data, comment on others,' and interact with experts. By doing so, they demonstrate that they can make a valuable contribution to society while learning a lot about the specific topic and about science in general.

With all these possibilities available, citizen science appears to provide an opportunity with great potential to link citizens to the network of scientists, as they become interested in scientific topics and understand how scientists think and how science works. This can increase the grounding of science in society and lead to better understanding and acceptance of science. This is an idealized view, however. The authors note that unfortunately, empirical research shows that participation in citizen science projects does not guarantee that lay persons learn and acquire an adequate understanding of science or even of the specific content with which they are involved. Participation does not automatically lead to learning or a better understanding of scientific procedures. Furthermore, citizen science projects need to be designed meticulously in order to ensure that people learn the right things. A shared platform is not enough; people have to learn scientific thinking. Smart classrooms and future learning endeavors will have to find creative ways to use the benefits citizen science makes available to learners. We need to find appropriate bridges between the formal learning environments of classrooms within schools, the "real" knowledge communities outside schools, and the involved individuals' own informal networks.

Learning in a Networked Society: Adequate Research Methods

Considering the topics mentioned above, the book takes a very broad view of learning. Learning takes place in complex, networked scenarios, where physical and digital spaces, tools, and objects play as important roles as individuals and their networks. Analyzing learning under such a broad perspective requires a large methodological repertoire. Some of the chapters present interesting research methods that address this complexity well. The chapter by Kent, Rechavi, and Rafaeli (2018) shows that social network analysis provides a tool for analyzing learning processes in networks. Multiple network measures may be used for describing learning-relevant factors, and an individual's centrality can serve as a descriptor of one's expertise or reputation. The centrality of content (e.g., measured by links between pages) indicates the importance and relevance of shared content. We can identify people who span boundaries as well as objects: people or objects that are part of two networks and are thus essential in enabling networks to influence each other. They form the basis for change and development of networks. Innovation research has demonstrated that such boundary spanners are often the nucleus for innovation. Social network analysis provides measures that describe the networks, as well as measures that describe individuals within networks. Unlike "classical statistics," social network analysis explicitly acknowledges that learners are not independent from one another. On the contrary, there is a strong interdependence among members of a network. Network statistics take these interdependencies into account and try to model them. As such, network analysis appears to be the ideal tool for analyzing processes of learning in a linked society.

The chapter by Raban and Geifmann (2018) provides a further interesting perspective. Their self-referential approach considers LINKS to be a network consisting of people and research topics in which development and learning can be analyzed. Together, these sources provide LINKS with its sociointellectual capital. The authors analyze development and learning within the network by observing changes in relevant topics and in positions of LINKS PIs over time using artifacts as their empirical basis—all peer-reviewed publications of LINKS researchers, extracted from their Google Scholar profiles. Using topic modeling, the authors compared pre-LINKS research topics (2009–2013) with topics that emerged between 2014 and 2016. This led to interesting findings: LINKS originally evolved around three core topics: STEM Education, Content Exchange, and Gamification and Virtual Reality/Assistive Technology. The scientists contributed various perspectives on learning, including normative, behavioral, cognitive, practical, and social aspects. Tight face-to-face interactions among LINKS researchers enabled synergies that led the Center toward its predefined research agenda. Over time, three new topics emerged: learning communities, collaborative learning, and further expansion of STEM Education. Outcomes now deal with educational policy issues, the shape and meaning of physical spaces, and the promises and perils of networks and new media.

In my view, this is a prototypical study to describe learning in networks: It describes the specific contributions of people with certain defined backgrounds, the topics that the network originally considered, and how interaction among people changed topics and outcomes. It is this dynamic perspective that best demonstrates learning. Methods like topic modeling or network analysis can represent these complex dynamics visually.

Summary

The network perspective is useful for reflecting on learning and its design in the digital age. People live in networks and their learning and meaning-making take place in networks. This was also the case in the past, but with contemporary digital media, networks appear to be more ubiquitous, accessible, and influential. New media offer channels to access information as well as people. They facilitate participation in diverse collaborative activities in knowledge creation communities or other kinds of knowledge-related social contacts. The abundance of material and contacts present both opportunities and challenges for education and for democratic processes. We need to determine how to support the desired processes and how to adapt learning needs to address the double-edged sword of the vast informational environment (Buder & Hesse, 2017) in which we live today. Interdisciplinary research at LINKS provides valuable insights into these topics. LINKS itself is an example of a knowledge network, consisting of people and the artifacts they produce through collaborative work. In numerous chapters of this book, the authors bridge boundaries among different disciplines. Through their interaction and collaboration, the network develops continuously, expands its research, and addresses new challenges for learning in our rapidly changing world.

References

Baram-Tsabari, A., & Schejter, A. (2018). The double-edged sword of new media in supporting public engagement with science. In Y. Kali, A. Baram-Tsabari, & A. Schejter (Eds.), *Learning in a networked society (LINKS)*. New York: Springer.

Buder, J., & Hesse, F. W. (Eds.). (2017). *Informational environments: Effects of use, effective designs*. Cham, Switzerland: Springer International Publishing.

Cress, U., & Kimmerle, J. (2008). A systemic and cognitive view on collaborative knowledge building with Wikis. *International Journal of Computer-Supported Collaborative Learning, 3*, 105–122. https://doi.org/10.1007/s11412-007-9035-z

Cress, U., & Kimmerle, J. (2017). The interrelations of individual learning and collective knowledge construction: A cognitive-systemic framework. In S. Schwan & U. Cress (Eds.), *The psychology of digital learning* (pp. 123–145). Cham, Switzerland: Springer International Publishing.

Del Vicario, M., Bessi, A., Zollo, F., Petroni, F., Scala, A., Caldarelli, G., et al. (2016). The spreading of misinformation online. *Proceedings of the National Academy of Sciences, 113*, 554–559.

Har-Carmel, Y., Olsher, S., Elkin-Koren, N., & Yerushalmy, M. (2018). E-textbook: Challenges to pedagogy, law and policy. In Y. Kali, A. Baram-Tsabari, & A. Schejter (Eds.), *Learning in a networked society (LINKS)*. New York: Springer.

Hod, Y., Aridor, K., Ben-Zvi, D., Pion, C., Weiss, T., & Zuckerman, O. (2018). Future learning spaces: Exploring perspectives from LINKS research. In Y. Kali, A. Baram-Tsabari, & A. Schejter (Eds.), *Learning in a networked society (LINKS)*. New York: Springer.

Kali, Y., & Linn, M. C. (2008). Technology-enhanced support strategies for inquiry learning. In J. M. Spector, M. D. Merrill, J. van Merriënboer, & M. P. Driscoll (Eds.), *Handbook of research on educational communications and technology* (3rd ed., pp. 445–461). Mahwah, NJ: Lawrence Erlbaum Associates.

Kent, C., Rechavi, A., & Rafaeli, S. (2018). Networked learning analytics: A theoretically informed methodology for collaborative. In Y. Kali, A. Baram-Tsabari, & A. Schejter (Eds.), *Learning in a networked society (LINKS)*. New York: Springer.

Kidron, A., Tirosh, N., Kali, Y., & Schejter, A. (2018). Democracy, communication, and education in the 21st century. In Y. Kali, A. Baram-Tsabari, & A. Schejter (Eds.), *Learning in a networked society (LINKS)*. New York, NY: Springer.

Latour, B. (1986). Visualization and cognition: Thinking with eyes and hands. In H. Kuklick (Ed.), *Knowledge and society: Studies in the sociology of culture past and present* (Vol. 6, pp. 1–40). New York: JAI Press.

Lave, J., & Wenger, E. (1991). *Situated learning: Legitimate peripheral participation*. New York: Cambridge University Press.

Luhmann, N. (1995). *Social systems*. Stanford, CA: Stanford University Press.

Paavola, S., & Hakkarainen, K. (2005). The knowledge creation metaphor: An emergent epistemological approach to learning. *Science & Education, 14*, 535–557. https://doi.org/10.1007/s11191-004-5157-0

Paavola, S., & Hakkarainen, K. (2014). Trialogical approach for knowledge creation. In S. C. Tan, H. J. So, & J. Yeo (Eds.), *Knowledge creation in education* (Springer Education Innovation Book Series). Singapore: Springer.

Pariser, E. (2011). *The filter bubble: What the internet is hiding from you*. New York: Penguin Press.

Pirolli, P. (2007). *Information foraging theory: Adaptive interaction with information*. New York: Oxford University Press.

Raban, D., & Geifmann, D. (2018). Information and knowledge research @LINKS. In Y. Kali, A. Baram-Tsabari, & A. Schejter (Eds.), *Learning in a networked society (LINKS)*. New York: Springer.

Sagy, O., Angel, D., Atias, O., Abramsky, H., Baram-Tsabati, A., Ben-Zvi, D., et al. (2018). Citizen science: An opportunity for learning in a networked society. In Y. Kali, A. Baram-Tsabari, & A. Schejter (Eds.), *Learning in a networked society (LINKS)*. New York: Springer.

Sfard, A. (1998). On two metaphors for learning and the dangers of choosing just one. *Educational Researcher, 27*, 4–13.

Shauli, N. M., Shacham, M., & Golan, O. (2018). ICTs in religious communities: Communal and domestic integration of new media among Jewish ultra-orthodoxy in Israel. In Y. Kali, A. Baram-Tsabari, & A. Schejter (Eds.), *Learning in a networked society (LINKS)*. New York: Springer.

Index

CPSIA information can be obtained
at www.ICGtesting.com
Printed in the USA
LVHW081932090519
617267LV00001B/1/P

9 783030 146092